ATENCO LIVES!

PERFORMING LATIN AMERICAN AND CARIBBEAN IDENTITIES

Kathryn Bishop-Sanchez, University of Wisconsin, Madison
Series editor

This series is a forum for scholarship that recognizes the critical role of performance in social, cultural, and political life. Geographically focused on the Caribbean and Latin America (including Latinidad in the United States) but wide-ranging in thematic scope, the series highlights how understandings of desire, gender, sexuality, race, the postcolonial, human rights, and citizenship, among other issues, have been explored and continue to evolve. Books in the series will examine performances by a variety of actors with under-represented and marginalized peoples getting particular (though not exclusive) focus. Studies of spectators or audiences are equally welcome as those of actors—whether literally performers or others whose behaviors can be interpreted that way. In order to create a rich dialogue, the series will include a variety of disciplinary approaches and methods as well as studies of diverse media, genres, and time periods.

Performing Latin American and Caribbean Identities is designed to appeal to scholars and students of these geographic regions who recognize that through the lens of performance (or what may alternatively be described as spectacle, ceremony, or collective ritual, among other descriptors) we can better understand pressing societal issues.

ATENCO LIVES!

Filmmaking and Popular Struggle in Mexico

Livia K. Stone

VANDERBILT UNIVERSITY PRESS | NASHVILLE

© 2019 by Vanderbilt University Press
Nashville, Tennessee 37235
All rights reserved

First printing 2019

Library of Congress Cataloging-in-Publication Data on file

LC control number 2018013995
LC classification number HN120.A8 S76 2018
Dewey classification number 303.48/4097273—dc23
LC record available at *lccn.loc.gov/2018013995*

ISBN 978-0-8265-2223-8 (hardcover)
ISBN 978-0-8265-2224-5 (paperback)
ISBN 978-0-8265-2225-2 (e-book)

CONTENTS

ix Acknowledgments

1   Introduction

    ONE
27 Atenco and Machetes

    TWO
60 Cameras, Surveillance, and Ethical Practice

    THREE
91 Compañeros and Protagonismo

    FOUR
112 Breaking the Siege: Resistance and Autonomy

    FIVE
143 Distribution and Organization

167 Coda

173 Notes

183 References

193 Filmography

195 Index

FIGURES

- 31   1.1. The front pages of *La Jornada* in 2002 and *Vértigo* in 2006.
- 33   1.2. A widely distributed image of Atenco's central square on May 4, 2006.
- 49   1.3. Machetes being held in the air by protestors.
- 50   1.4. Poster announcing a political march in 2009 featuring an *ejidatario* with a machete.
- 54   1.5. *Ejidatario* with *cuetes* for a political demonstration.
- 61   2.1. Poster showing cameras used as weapons.
- 71   2.2. Still from *Zapatistas: Crónica de una rebelión*.
- 77   2.3. Still from *Atenco: ¡Tierra sí, aviones no! / Atenco: Land, Yes! Airplanes, No*
- 99   3.1. Graffiti in Atenco that brings together the Frente with the EZLN. The machete reads "Long live the peoples in rebellion. EZLN FPDT Long Live Atenco" (*Vivan los pueblos en rebeldia EZLN FPDT Atenco Vive*).
- 120 4.1. Still from *Romper el cerco / Breaking the Siege*.
- 154 5.1. Solidarity film screening.
- 159 5.2. Street vendor of documentary films at a political march.

ACKNOWLEDGMENTS

In 2009, I had the opportunity to chat with Sergio Beltrán of Universidad de la Tierra (University of the Earth/Land), Oaxaca, an educational collective strongly committed to social justice. I asked him, as I asked nearly everyone I was speaking with in those days, what he thought my responsibility was in representing Mexican social movements. He told me to remember always that this book was from the perspective of an outsider and a foreigner, and the book is necessarily enmeshed in a long history of colonial appropriation and looting of indigenous peoples. Not long afterward, I asked the same question of an activist who replied quite sharply, "Just remember that this book isn't about you." When asked the same question, most people in Atenco, almost without exception, told me to do my job and represent people and the situation as honestly and truthfully as I can. This book, as a physical object and a representation of Mexico and the Frente de Pueblos en Defensa de la Tierra, is as deeply imbricated in the ethical and political regimes that it describes as any film. One of the greatest struggles in writing it has been to triangulate its politics of representation and critical analysis among the same issues of *protagonismo* and solidarity that I describe filmmakers struggling with.

The first debt of gratitude that I owe is to the filmmakers and members of Frente who kindly and generously supported the research and taught me what they knew. I owe a special debt to the man I refer to as Humberto for always pushing me forward (sometimes literally) and arranging for me to live in Atenco. The woman I call Doña María was my landlady, mother, and closest friend while in Atenco. I cannot thank her and her family enough for hosting, advising, and caring for me. I also owe special gratitude to the man I refer to as Virgilio for spending so much time guiding and informing this work. The ideas presented here are more those of Humberto, Doña María, Virgilio, Mario Viveros Barragán, José Luis Mariño, Salvador Díaz, and Odette Castelao than they are my own. I often feel that to present them here as my own is an unforgivable act of protagonismo and appropriation. I am keenly aware that to list my name after a title with Atenco in it is to in some way benefit personally from the notoriety of the Frente. In the end, I put my name on this book not to claim it as my own, but to accept responsibility for where it may be lacking. I owe special gratitude to

Ignacio del Valle, for although he was held prisoner for the majority of the time during the active research for this book, his ideas and presence were no weaker for his physical absence.

The research for this book began as my graduate research at Washington University in St. Louis, and there are many people there whose ideas and suggestions pushed and influenced the project. I owe a deep debt of gratitude to the encouragement, ideas, and political example of my friend and colleague Bret Gustafson. The suggestions and advice of Rebecca Lester, Patrick Eisenlohr, Derek Pardue, Mary Ann Dzuback, Ignacio Sánchez Prado, Peter Benson, and Glenn Stone helped form the basis of this research from its earliest days. So did the advice, thoughts, and deep engagement of Katie Hejtmanek, Lisa Isenhart, Meghan Ference, Anubha Sood, Sean Gyshen Fennell, and Elyse Singer.

Funding for this research was provided by a dissertation grant from the Wenner-Gren Foundation and from the (no longer existing) Center for the Study of Ethics and Human Values in St. Louis. Grants from the Graduate School of Arts and Sciences at Washington University in St. Louis also funded early research. Grants supporting faculty research at Illinois State University funded return trips to Mexico in the last several years. Although they don't know it, funding for writing a significant portion of this book was provided by a Fulbright IIE grant held by my wife, Abigail C. Stone, to support her archaeological research in Mali. Although support for same-sex partners was not legal at the time, Fulbright's generosity and our own economy enabled a great number of these pages to be written at the Djenné-Djenno hotel café in Jenné, Mali, a place and time that provided more space, peace, clarity, tea, and lack of Internet than most have the privilege of while writing.

The book would not exist without the interest, engagement, and suggestions of Beth Kressel Itkin at Vanderbilt University Press and Kathryn Bishop-Sanchez. I am also deeply grateful for the ideas and challenges posed by a number of colleagues, named and anonymous, who have provided feedback on portions of this manuscript over the years, including versions of chapters presented at conferences. Jeff Juris, Maple Razsa, and Erica Cusi Wortham have all helped to push the project forward. Several colleagues at Colby College and Illinois State University also gave valuable feedback: Ryan Jones, Michael Dougherty, and Gina Hunter. I owe a special debt to Fred Smith and James Skibo and all my colleagues in the Department of Sociology and Anthropology at ISU for providing such a welcoming and supportive environment for teaching, scholarship, and service. Although you may not consider it so, your commitment to educating all people while living skillfully and healthily is a radical practice, and I thank you for your example. Research for this book truly began in the late 1990s with my friendship with Alejandro Ramos Amézquita and his family. Since I was a teenager, Ana María, Alejandro, Sandra, and Sergio have generously invited me into their homes to stay for extended periods of time. Ana María especially provided my home away from home and valuable motherly advice over the course of many years. Ana María, this project began as conversations over your kitchen table in Mexico City and is deeply indebted to your patience, support, and compassion. Thanks also to my family, Gary, Katy, and Jeremy Hinegardner, for supporting me and asking the most difficult questions about this research. My wife, Abigail C. Stone, also worked hard crafting this book, not just proofreading sentences, rearranging paragraphs, and challenging ideas, but also through her advice and support. Our son, Paul, has provided a depth of joy and the perspective needed in the last stages of writing. The greatest acknowledgement, of course, is that this book isn't about me, and it (probably) isn't about you either, even though you and I and everyone in this book are connected through a responsibility to create this world that we share.

INTRODUCTION

We took the clear and conscious decision that we ran a high risk. We decided that if the shit hits the fan [*si nos caiga la chingada*]—well, what can we do? We are doing something for the community. And this is more valuable. So you realize—you get a consciousness. A consciousness. I didn't even participate in the clean water assemblies [before]. I didn't participate in anything. I was simply another spectator. But, in the struggle itself, in the nine months of resistance, it gives you a consciousness.... When you realize, you are no longer the quiet, mute spectator that recorded video; you become in some way a protagonist of the film too.
—Eduardo Ríos

I first met Eduardo Ríos at a press conference in Mexico City announcing a new campaign called "Libertad y Justicia para Atenco" (Liberty and Justice for Atenco) in 2009.[1] The campaign was meant to free the remaining thirteen political prisoners who had been arrested and tortured along with two hundred others in the central Mexican town of San Salvador Atenco in 2006. The police action was largely seen to be a repression of a local social movement called the Frente de Pueblos en Defensa de la Tierra, or the People's Front in Defense of Land, which I will refer to hereafter as the "Frente."[2]

I had noticed during the press conference that Eduardo and another man were recording the proceedings with a small digital camcorder instead of the larger professional equipment of the commercial news outlets. When the event was over, I came up to Eduardo while he was packing up his camera equipment and asked if I could talk with him about how he saw the role of independent media in the new campaign. He leaned on a tripod casually as he spoke to me while his partner packed up and came in and out of the conversation. Eduardo explained to me that he was from the small farming community of Atenco on the outskirts of Mexico City and was arrested and tortured in 2006 along with the other members of the movement that the campaign was attempting to liberate. This was the first political event that he was openly participating in and recording since the police invasion. He explained to me, as the quote above demonstrates, that he became involved in the Frente and its struggle against neoliberal reform through making videos and had been significantly changed by the experience. "Every day you are discovering another Mexico," he told me, "when testimonies begin to arrive of people who have been dispossessed, maltreated, murdered in other parts of the country, or in the world. This surprises you and raises interest, and you get more and more involved." It was because of his continual work with the Frente as a filmmaker/videographer that he met activists from all over Mexico and the world who were working against the forces of neoliberal political and economic reform. By the end of our conversation, I realized that he was the primary producer of a documentary about the Frente that was frequently sold at political marches and that I had seen many times called *La tierra no se vende, se ama y se defiende* (Land is not for selling, it is for loving and defending, FPDT, 2002).

On the way home from the press conference, I stopped by the sidewalk stall of a young vendor I knew who used to sell Eduardo's films among other social and political documentaries. Rafael's stall was in downtown Mexico City near a very busy metro station, wedged between the curb and a stall selling men's socks and ties.[3] Most of the vendors on this side of the street sold plastic gadgets, like alarm clocks and toys, although there were a few stalls selling pirated commercial films. Rafael was selling used LPs, cassette tapes, and VHS cassettes. When I asked him why he chose to sell used LPs and tapes, Rafael told me that even though lots of people sell pirated and illegal materials, it is difficult because you have to pay the right people and the work is more dangerous. *Mafias*, he said, own the sidewalk and control who can set up stalls there. One has to pay them rent for setting up. He insinuated that those selling pirated goods are connected to large distribution networks connected to the mafias. By selling used media, he told me, he isn't breaking any laws, he isn't challenging the mafias, and he isn't selling goods (like plastic alarm clocks or neckties) that are made with exploitative labor in China and northern Mexico. "Besides," he added, "I like vinyl."

Rafael told me that he stopped selling political and social documentaries because of the police attention that they garnered. Even though he wasn't selling stolen or illegal goods, and the films he carried weren't copyrighted, the police came by every day to harass him and "confiscated" the films until he was forced to stop carrying them. He could have put up with the harassment, he told me, but the other vendors on the block didn't appreciate the attention their area was receiving from the police, and they threatened him, saying that if he didn't stop carrying the films they wouldn't let him set up there anymore. When asked why he wanted to sell social documentaries at all, he told me that it was "cultural diffusion" work (*difusión cultural*) connected to his activism. Selling films about the Frente was one part of his political participation that included many different kinds of activities, including helping to organize a social theory reading group and participating in the direct actions of a variety of social movements.

As part of his solidarity work, he went to the barricades in the town of Atenco in May 2006 that were set up to protect the community from the police invasion in which Eduardo Ríos was detained. When thousands of police entered the town in the early hours of the morning, he fought them. "We ran out of Molotov cocktails," he said. "We ran out of rocks; we ran out of everything. We ended up just throwing bottles of Coke at them." When it became clear that they would not be able to hold off the police, he ran. Somehow he climbed a building and tried to run across roofs, but there were helicopters overhead looking for people. "I jumped," he said and then blushed. "Well, I fell really—into someone's courtyard." Some people, he explained to me, tried to take shelter with people who turned them in to the police. "I was lucky," he said. The people in the house he fell into gave him a change of clothes and hid him instead of turning him in. At this point in the narrative, his face became contorted and pained, and his story trailed off.

The stories of Eduardo and Rafael reveal the multiple ways that social documentary film is incorporated into social movements in Mexico and throughout social movement networks in the twenty-first century. Both Eduardo and Rafael were using film production and circulation as one medium through which they were attempting to transform their own lives and the world. Eduardo's activism was defined by recording marches, political events, and even confrontational meetings with political officials as an activist in the Frente. Rafael's activism consisted of solidarity work and helping to lend a hand for a variety of social movements, as well as attempting to carve out a life for himself without depending on exploitative labor or being an exploited laborer himself. He saw the potential to combine these two political projects in the circulation of politically committed documentary films. This book examines the activism of people like Rafael and Eduardo who are attempting to use the production and circulation of film as a political practice and asks: What do these films *do* in the world? How do people use the production and circulation of film as political tools? How do they work (or not work) as a field of action and a medium of political organizing?

This book examines these questions in the context of the Frente of Atenco, one of the most recognized and contentious contemporary social movements in Mexico. The Frente is not generally well known in the United States, but in Mexico and in networks of anti-neoliberal activism (including US activism), it is immediately recognizable. Its successful prevention of the government's seizure of communal land in 2002 to make way for an international airport for

Mexico City, the Frente's first political struggle described in greater detail in the next chapter, was held up as a victory throughout transnational networks of anti-neoliberal social movements. In turn, the violent 2006 repression, which many believed to be a retaliation for the airport activism in 2002, was a crushing blow to anti-neoliberal movements in general, not just the Frente specifically. The Frente is a productive site to examine questions of how making and circulating films operate as a political tool in part because of the large number of films made about it (more than fifteen between 2001 and 2009), because its mainstream media presence and use of media was such an integral part of its activism, and because of its influence on anti-neoliberal activism throughout the world.

Mediating Activism

Generations of scholars have attempted to parse through the impact or consequences of various media on society and culture. Can political films radicalize people and awaken their consciousness? Do video games make teens more violent? Does pornography foment a culture of rape and the denigration of women? The overwhelming bulk of scholarship that attempts to understand the social, cultural, and political consequences of media concentrates on how media can change the way that people think about themselves and the world that they live in. As Manuel Castells has so succinctly stated, "the fundamental power struggle is the battle for the construction of meaning in the minds of the people" (Castells 2012, 5). This scholarship is incredibly valuable and is unquestionably true: the content of media has profound impacts on people's conceptions of themselves and the world around them. Indeed, the histories and messages of social movement media have had a profound impact on the thinking and consciousness of nearly everyone that this book describes. Numerous times in my interviews with activists, they have related to me experiences watching films or television that changed their view of how the world works and their place in it.

However, the mechanisms of what goes on "in the minds of the people" are notoriously difficult to pinpoint, even for fields such as psychology and neurobiology. Meanwhile, other very real visceral and social aspects of digital and visual media—how people use media in their daily lives to create, maintain, and transform relationships with other real people—are often either cast over or assumed to be an inherent property of the medium. However, the human relationships that are facilitated (mediated) through media are often their most impactful consequences. Eduardo's life and his conception of himself changed significantly as a result of the people that he met through making videos, even when the footage he was shooting never made it in to any finished work. Rafael used selling films as a way to tie his livelihood to his politics and attempt to purge his life of hierarchical relationships of exploitation, both activities that have little to do with the inherent properties of film.

We refer to film as a *medium* because it facilitates, or serves as a conduit for messages. However, the production and circulation of films also help *mediate* human relationships. The very human face-to-face interactions that come about through the production and circulation of films may ultimately have greater influence on the participants than the particular visual texts that facilitated them.

This conception of mediation is deeply influenced by the work of Terence Turner (1991, 1992, 1995) and Faye Ginsburg (1991, 1993, 1997; Ginsburg et al. 2002), who have shown how indigenous peoples have used the production and circulation of video and television in processes of what Ginsburg has called "collective self-production" (1997, 120). Turner describes how Kayapo videographers in Brazil used the production of videos to legitimate, and in some cases overturn, the political power of certain local actors (1991, 1992). These small-scale political upsets and reassertions of power did not happen because of what videographers captured on screen, but because of the micropolitics of who exactly would take possession of the video cameras Turner brought to the communities, who would learn how to edit, and where the videos would be stored. Similarly, Ginsburg describes how the stories and images of Aboriginal Australian television producers and filmmakers were important cultural activism on a national scale, but that the producers themselves emphasized the "activities of the production and reception of indigenous media" over the media texts because the "social relations built out of media practices are creating new networks of indigenous cooperation, locally, nationally, and internationally" (Ginsburg 1993, 575). In other words, the practices involved in the production and circulation of media texts were ultimately as important as, or more important than, the content.

Working with indigenous radio producers in Canada, Kathleen Buddle (2008) has argued that the "alternative economy of practice" of indigenous women's radio "calls into being new forms of subjectivity and action, and with them come new collective senses of belonging" (2008, 135). For Buddle, these new collective sense of belonging are directly related to the economies of practice. In other words, it matters that indigenous community radio operates very differently in its production and circulation practices than commercial radio. These production practices structure the quality of interaction of the people involved in the program toward being politically engaged, valuing one another's opinions, and downplaying hierarchies. The production of the show helps to characterize and define the new collective sense of belonging that it calls into being.

Using media to create new collective senses of belonging is the very project that Jeff Juris (2008) describes in his ethnography of the movements against corporate globalization. He demonstrates how activists used mediated political and social networks as instrumental tools to communicate with larger numbers of activists spread around the world, but also as a prefigurative utopian model of human interaction. He argues, "the self-generating network has thus become a powerful model for (re)organizing society based on horizontal collaboration, participatory democracy, and coordination through autonomy and diversity" (2008, 17). The electronic mailing lists and other digital technologies that Juris describes helped to mediate a particular ethical vision of human interaction, defined not just on an individual face-to-face basis, but also on a much larger social scale. They were interested in using media to help create a new networked society of nonhierarchical relationships and participatory democracy.

Rafael's vision of using media circulation to create a nonhierarchical, nonexploitative living for himself is very similar to the kind of prefigurative politics that Juris describes because Rafael is firmly embedded in the same networks of anti–corporate capitalist social movements. This broad network is also deeply intertwined with and inspired by a network of indigenous movements. La Otra Campaña, the social movement that Rafael was most involved with during the time that I knew him, was an outgrowth of Zapatismo in southern Mexico.[4] The Frente, the social movement Eduardo was a part of, has been closely allied with the Zapatista movements since its inception. Zapatismo, in turn, has been a substantial influence and inspiration for the global movements for social justice that Juris describes (see also Stephen 2002). The indigenous movements and groups that Turner and Ginsburg described in the 1990s are deeply intertwined in these transnational networks of anti-neoliberal and indigenous movements. In short, there are multiple real-world connections between the people described in this book and the people described and theorized in previous scholarship about social movements and media, even if on the surface they seem to exist in very different parts of the world.

There are also multiple overlapping connections between activists, scholars, and scholar/activists. Indigenous activists throughout Latin America have been influenced by scholars' efforts from the 1980s and 1990s to encourage indigenous peoples around the world to create media according to their own visual and organizational sensibilities (see Wortham 2013, Turner 1991). There is a direct line of influence from John Adair's (Worth and Adair 1972) project to see what kind of film Navajo people would make, through the state-sponsored indigenous video workshops throughout Mexico of the 1980s, to the alternative economies of practice that the Zapatista movement innovated in the 1990s, to the nonhierarchical, collaborative, participatory economies of practice of anti-neoliberal activists in the 2000s. The complex ways that indigenous and anti-corporate capitalist social movement networks intersect mean that what Buddle describes as indigenous alternative economies of practice are also closely connected to how people like Eduardo create film and how people like Rafael circulate it, even though they do not identify as indigenous themselves. What began with John Adair's project about cultural ways of *seeing* in the 1970s has transformed into a project about social, cultural, and political ways of *doing, organizing,* and *being,* not only among indigenous movements, but also among nonindigenous movements and professionals.

I will argue throughout this book that the "new collective senses of belonging" that Buddle describes (2008, 135) is one of the primary purposeful consequences of the production and circulation of political and social documentary film in Mexico. Many political film projects that begin as a pretext to practice being nonhierarchical, anticapitalist, and so on never have a final product (see Flores 2004, for example). Many of the final products that do get produced depart so dramatically from the conventions of commercial filmmaking as to be virtually unwatchable by all but the small network of people involved in their production. Still others are hardly watched but become gifts that help build relationships of solidarity between people. They then become valuable artifacts of a material culture of the Left, with their zine-like photocopied covers and Creative Commons licenses. They also might be screened in public places as a kind of occupation of space and political demonstration. As I argue in Chapter 5, a public film screening is as much an occupation and political performance of solidarity and strength as a rally, but with a very low barrier for participation. In all these cases, what the films are mediating has much more to do with the attempt to create nonhierarchical human relationships of solidarity and mutual support than they do the particular messages in the content of the films. They help do this not because of any intrinsic property of film or digital technology, but because activists purposefully use them in this way.

A large portion of research about social movements and social change is interested in whether or not movements have been successful. They often measure ideas of success by formal structural changes to policy or laws. Rafael, Eduardo, and the other people in this book care about these formal structural changes and use the production and circulation of films as one means to help bring them about, but they are also interested in other transformations that have very little to do with laws or policies. These less formal transformations have a much more complex and uncertain endpoint than formal legal changes, at the same time that they can be much more tangible for individual activists. Rafael's project, for example, of creating a living for himself out of selling social documentaries, has a much greater impact on his day-to-day lived experience than legal reform for communities in which he does not live, or the release of political prisoners that he does not know. However, the capacity to live an ethical, nonhierarchical, nonexploitative life is also much more elusive and complex than passing a law or releasing some prisoners. It is a complex, idealistic, perhaps even utopian goal. Furthermore, Rafael and others like him are keenly aware that creating this life for oneself is not only an individual struggle; it is also a large-scale social one. In attempting to create a particular kind of life for himself, Rafael was also attempting to create the social and political networks needed to support this kind of life for others. He was attempting to help create a culture of ethical, nonhierarchical, nonexploitative work. For his part, Eduardo is deeply and personally concerned with formal legal structures that might protect the communal lands of his town. However, he also has very little faith in these formal legal protections. Along with many people from the Left and the Right around the world, Eduardo does not believe that the state and its form of legality can be relied on.

One of the central slogans of another transnational social movement network that Rafael was involved with, the World Social Forum, is "Another World Is Possible." Through their video activism, Rafael and Eduardo were doing their small portion of attempting to create a new world that does not rely on oppression or exploitation. Working through the state to change laws might be one way to create this new world, but they are under no illusion that it is the only way, or even the most productive. This book describes how activists in Mexico are using the production and circulation of film as one tool to help create a new world, a new society, a new culture.

Generally the term "cultural production" is used to talk about the production of art, music, theater, dance, film, and other creative endeavors (Mahon 2000). It is a concept perhaps most associated with Pierre Bourdieu (1984, 1993). Bourdieu introduced the concept of a field of production in which works gain their meaning through their positioning in relation to other creative works. He also reinvented Aristotle's conception of *habitus* to mean a set of dispositions that are simultaneously the result of and a structuring force for an aesthetic or symbolic environment (1984, 170–72). Although he has a developed critique of how cultural production and aesthetic dispositions reproduce class hierarchies,

Bourdieu commented very little on how cultural production might be mobilized to disrupt class distinctions. In contrast to Aristotle's meaning, Bourdieu's version of the concept leaves very little room for purposeful cultivation.[5] His vision of cultural production is one in which producers are thoughtful about creating in relation to other producers and the meanings of other symbolic works but are not at all purposeful about the cultivation of habitus and self. For Bourdieu, these things happen to subjects rather than being created by subjects. Although he is intensely interested in material conditions and inequality, in Bourdieu's conception of cultural production, "culture" almost exclusively refers to texts (visual art, literature) and the fields of meaning the content of the texts engage with.

In the contemporary activist context, the production of culture takes on a more anthropological and purposeful meaning. Activism is an attempt to literally create new cultures; even if partial, hybrid, dislocated, or diffuse. The creative field comprises not only meanings and symbols, but also economies, political systems, and lives. The people that this book describes, including Rafael and Eduardo, are attempting to build new cultures in which corporate capitalism, neoliberalism, free market capitalism, and a host of other social, political, and economic forces that they see as damaging are devalued and a new set of ethics and values become norms. The content of the films that they are producing and circulating is important, but perhaps not as important as the daily practices that these activists innovate and cultivate in their attempts to build noncapitalist economies, nonhierarchical political associations, and different ethical senses of themselves as people.

These attempts to produce new cultures are not always successful. They may not even be mostly successful. Rafael, for example, was first thwarted in his attempts to sell social documentary films by the micropolitics of his street corner. He was later thwarted in his attempts to have a small business at all when the city planned a new public transportation stop on his street and police forcibly evacuated all the vendors on the block. Eduardo has experienced substantial transformation in his life as a result of his activism in the Frente, but he has also experienced significant violence. He, and others that this book describe, have also been criticized among their peers for not acting in completely ethical ways.

In short, this book does not attempt to refute claims that social and political media impacts people's minds and consciousnesses. Neither does it argue that the content of films does not matter. However, I do argue that changing minds is not all that films do, and maybe not even the most significant thing that they do. This book argues that the production and circulation of political and social documentary films in Mexico form a creative field of practice (not just a discursive field) in which people can purposefully cultivate certain ethically and politically committed senses of themselves, both as individuals and collectivities.

Self-Production and Ethical Practice

The lack, or even refusal, of identifiers is one of the key features of the new wave of leftist social movements that emerged all over the world at the beginning of the twenty-first century.[6] It represented a departure from what social movement scholars called the New Social Movements of the mid- to late twentieth century that were identity based (rather than "traditional" class-based movements of the early twentieth century).[7] These movements organized to promote the rights of people marginalized by their identities: Black, gay, female, indigenous, and so on. They reclaimed, redefined, and politicized the identities that were used to marginalize them and turned them in to strategic political tools to gain equality. They were interested in cultural change surrounding the meanings and values of categories as much as instrumental legal rights and protections (reconstructing Black to mean beautiful, building pride in being gay, reconstructing "woman" to mean strong and capable).

These identity-based movements still exist and are still important, but they are accompanied by and overlap significantly with a new range of social movements. This new wave of movements retains the focus on constructing and transforming cultural values and meaning, often even above instrumental political change, but does not attach their cultural focus to any particular identity. For example, as activists and cultural producers, Rafael and Eduardo have no identifier that they are attempting to celebrate, imbue with new meanings, or strengthen through their activities. Even Eduardo, who could very well claim to be indigenous if he chose, does not conceive of his media activism as a practice meant to produce an identity any more specific than being a good person, an effective activist, or just a more ethical human being. Activists like them are engaged in world-making and culture-making projects, rather than identity-making projects, even as they acknowledge the deep importance of identity and the intricacies of identity politics. The recent Black Lives Matter movement in the United States is an excellent example of this combination between acknowledging the importance of a range of identifications within a larger world-making project not confined to identity. In her "herstory" of #BlackLivesMatter, founder Alicia Garza asks the reader and larger movement to "lift up Black lives as an opportunity to connect struggles across race, class, gender, nationality, sexuality, and disability" (Garza 2016, 27).[8] She argues that

> when we are able to end the hyper-criminalization and -sexualization of Black people and end the poverty, control, and surveillance of Black people, every single person in this world has a better shot at getting and staying free. When Black people get free, everybody gets free. This is why we call on Black people and our allies to take up the call that Black lives matter.... We remain in active solidarity with all oppressed people who are fighting for their liberation and we know that our destinies are intertwined. (26)

This positioning acknowledges the importance of identity, while not defining itself as one particular identity. It recognizes that all Black people are also people with sexualities, genders, ages, nationalities, and so on that are no less a part of their humanity and no less a part of their Blackness. It identifies the state as the root of oppression and mass incarceration, Black poverty and genocide, heteropatriarchy, and the persecution of undocumented immigrants (among others) as aspects of state violence that disproportionately impacts Black people (*www.blacklivesmatter.com*). The movement is rooted in the oppression of Black people as Black people but refuses and transcends the single identifier.

In the United States, the #Occupy movement of 2011 is usually associated with a refusal of identity (see Mitchell, Harcourt, and Taussig 2013). Rather than an isolated movement innovated in the United States, however, the #Occupy movement was merely an outcropping of a series of movements spiraling out of Europe and Latin America (see Pickerill et al. 2016). Many of the features of the #Occupy movement that seemed strange to a US public were adopted from long traditions of organizing in Latin America. The tactical direct action portion of the #Occupy movement has roots in the Latin American tradition of *plantones* (camping out for long periods of time in public places in protest). The nonhierarchical, leaderless, consensus-based organizing model is also one that has deep roots in traditions of indigenous and peasant organizing throughout Latin America.[9] In part, this book is about recognizing and piecing together the processes through which tactics, ideologies, and self-making practices traveled from (or through) rural peasant communities in Mexico to hipster activists in places like New York City. In more ways than one (geographically, ideologically, tactically), Atenco is midway between peasant, indigenous activists in rural Mexico and more urban, middle-class activists in St. Louis, New York, Paris, and Buenos Aires.

As a series of networked social movements that is very critical of neoliberal economic and political reforms, these movements have also been particularly mindful of what many scholars and activists refer to as "neoliberal governmentality" (Sawyer 2004, Ong 2006, Escobar 2008, Lazar 2008).[10] These scholars argue that neoliberal economic and political reforms act as a Foucauldian technology of self-making that serves to create new political and economic subjects who are competitive, self-interested, profit seeking, and individualistic. David Harvey, for example, presents the idea that neoliberalism is "an ethic in itself, capable of acting as a guide to all human action and substituting for all previously held ethical beliefs" (2005, 3). These new subjectivities are formed as people respond to economic and political conditions based on neoliberal/free-market principles. Aihwa Ong defines the main elements of neoliberalism as a political philosophy as "(a) a claim that the market is better than the state at distributing public resources" and (b) a return to a "primitive form of individualism: an individualism which is 'competitive,' 'possessive,' and construed often in terms of the doctrine of 'consumer sovereignty'" (Ong 2006, 11). Ong adds that "neoliberal reasoning is based on both economic (efficiency) and ethical (self-responsibility) claims" (Ong 2006, 11). She argues that neoliberalism is a form of governmentality that profoundly reconstructs individual subjects (Ong 2006, 13).

The activists in this book are well aware of these critiques of neoliberalism, even large portions of the scholarship about neoliberalism, and are attempting to deny, resist, or exempt themselves from the economic and political forces working to construct them as competitive, self-interested, individualistic political and economic subjects. They name "neoliberalism" specifically as an enemy. Rafael, Eduardo, and the other filmmakers and activists who this book describes purposefully use the production and circulation of film as a creative field and an ethical practice in constructing themselves as the opposite of these characteristics: cooperative, selfless, and collectively minded.

Even as these activists are also largely fluent in Foucauldian ideas of governmentality and disciplinary regimes, the collective aspect of the social transformations they are attempting to bring about is a significant departure from Foucauldian thinking. Foucault (1977, 1988) focused his conceptions of docile bodies, discipline, and self-care on the individual. In contrast, the activists this book describes are primarily interested in what Ginsburg (1997) has called *collective* self-production. The "self" in question is not held within an individual body but is a collective, social body. The self in this context is a "we," not an "I." Individuals and attention to the individual self are important in the context of collective self-production, but the ultimate purpose is social change.

Ethics and governmentality may seem to be obscure concepts in what are very concrete political circumstances, but if we can take the most important global political tensions of the first decades of the twenty-first century to be Islamic radicalism (that conceives of Western Europe and the United States as a morally bankrupt system of infidels) from the Right and anti-neoliberal (or anti–corporate capitalist, anti–corporate globalization) movements from the Left, this ethical construction of humans as competitive, self-interested individuals has been the most important political issue at play. The economic and political frameworks of the global Left and Right are shifting in the Trump/Brexit era in which it seems that the strongest anti-neoliberal force is a nationalist/protectionist trend from the Right. However, the centrality of Donald Trump to these changes, a caricature of the competitive, self-interested, and individualistic ethic, has only served to amplify the importance of a personal ethic of being to the global economy and global politics. What has historically been the somewhat esoteric concern of anthropology—What does it mean to be human?—is precisely the issue on which global politics and the global economy has been hanging. This book describes a network of people who are asking a slightly different, more prescriptive question than anthropologists traditionally have: What do we *want it to mean* to be human?

The activists and filmmakers in this book are not always successful in their self-making projects, and in many ways this book is a description of how difficult a proposition this collective self-making, culture-producing project of transformation is. Often there are wildly differing ideas about what actions or behaviors are selfless and which are self-interested. Sometimes the qualitative goals of this self-making project seem entirely at odds with the unique technological capacities and requirements of filmmaking. (A documentary edited by consensus, for example, is almost assured never to be completed.) Although activists are intensively engaged in collective self-production, they often have no idea what the end result might look like, or even if there is an end result. Activism and cultural production, like human life in general, are a messy proposition.

Why Films?

If the production of individual and collective selves is a creative, artistic endeavor, it finds an easy home in the pursuit of other creative, artistic endeavors. Artistic practice is creation and innovation. Edited moving images with sound, whether we call the medium film, video, or television (the distinctions are rapidly falling away),[11] is one of the most popular contemporary artistic mediums.[12] The world in the twenty-first century is steeped in video. People all over the world consume tremendous quantities of television, film, and digital Internet videos. They also create remarkable quantities of video on a wide variety of platforms. From the briefest of Snapchat videos, to home movies, to full-length documentaries, video is one of the most popular and accessible media in the world today. While one might need a great deal of training to make a critically acclaimed, commercially successful feature-length documentary, creating a digital video has no such entry barrier. It is truly a popular medium, possibly the most popular medium in the world today.

The films that I describe in this book are often feature-length documentaries, and sometimes they are even made by filmmakers who have won very prestigious awards. However, none of the documentaries in this book has ever been entered into film festival competitions or attempted a commercial release in movie theaters. These are films that are shot extemporaneously on digital video (there are a few early local films that utilized VHS), edited on home computers using the programs FinalCut Pro or iMovie, and burned onto DVD. For some of the feature-length documentaries mentioned in this book, every copy in existence has been individually burned on someone's home computer. Without copyright restrictions, viewers are free to download films to their own computers and burn copies for their friends, or to sell them as Rafael does. Today, many of these films are available on YouTube and other video streaming sites. In 2008 and 2009, when the majority of the events described here occurred, YouTube had not yet gained the prominence that it has in 2018. Very few films were distributed online, in part because the necessary bandwidth was not yet commonplace in Mexico, even in Mexico City. Primarily, these films were distributed on DVD. Surprisingly, however (and as I show in the coda), the prominence of YouTube had not changed the preference for hard-copy videos very much well into 2016.

In part, the group of films described in this book are inspired by what has been referred to as Third Cinema, the political film of the Third World (see Gabriel 1982, Guneratne and Dissanayake, and Chakravarty 2003, for example). My dear friend Mario Viveros, a filmmaker whom I describe in Chapter 4, is fond of quoting the very influential French filmmaker Robert Bresson, as describing his own films as "not beautiful images, but necessary ones" (Viveros 2008). However, there are also some large gaps between the commercial films that are sometimes referred to as part of Third and Fourth Cinema and the Atenco films. The filmmaker Salvador Díaz (described in Chapter 3) refers to his work as *cine militante* (militant cinema) and overtly derides filmmakers who send their works to festivals and "go around looking for grants and things." Although sharing some commonalities with Third or Fourth Cinema, these films are more closely related to what has been called community media, radical media (Downing 1984), alternative media (Atton 2002), or citizens' media (Rodríguez 2001). They are much more closely related to the kind of indigenous media that Terence Turner (1992), Faye Ginsburg (1997), and Erica Cusi Wortham (2013) describe emerging from indigenous video workshops.

If the genre of this body of film is spoken of at all locally, it is referred to as *documental social* (social documentary). In part, this genre of film has arisen because of the particularities and strengths of the Mexican film and television industries. Mexico has one of the strongest commercial film and television industries in all of Latin America, but the industry is also heavily policed. Very few state critiques or representations of leftist politics are allowed on television or in commercial theaters. In another context, this might have been because of state censorship, but in the case of contemporary Mexico, it is simply because the commercial media are owned by very few players who tend politically to the right. It is not so much that the state controls the media as it is that the powerful capitalists who own Mexican media also have a very strong grip on the state. The combination of the politically repressive environment, a very strong culture of film and television production, and an even stronger history and culture of revolutionary politics has meant that alternative/community/indigenous/citizen media is incredibly strong in Mexico. As I discuss in Chapter 4, media is wielded as a significant weapon in this context, not only in wars over meaning, but also in actual physical combat. Visibility, surveillance, violence, and political pressure all intersect in complex ways in attempts to discipline and punish both a misbehaving state and unruly citizen activists.

In this context, the distribution or circulation of films is a very active, participatory process. Distributors are not commercial companies, but activists who burn individual copies of films on DVD. In order for a film to be widely circulated, it needs the participation of large numbers of people who burn copies for their friends, organize screenings, and maybe sell a few copies like Rafael did. Circulation practices, just as production practices, mean donating time and effort to a political and moral cause. For this reason, when describing the opportunities for ethical practice that films enable, I group circulation together with production. This book isn't only about filmmaking as an ethical practice; it is about all the ethical/political practices that films help to mediate.

Mexico and Anti-neoliberal Activism

Mexico in the first decade of the twenty-first century was a very critical time for democracy in Mexico and a crucial place for transnational networks of anti–corporate globalization social movements. This means that the events and activism in this book are critical, not only for understanding contemporary politics in Mexico, but also for understanding contemporary leftist social movements around the world. Atenco, and the Frente, are at the nexus of both national and international struggles over neoliberalism.

In the 1990s, Mexico became a hub for transnational networks of leftist social movements because of the immense popularity of the EZLN (the Ejercito Zapatista de Liberación Nacional or Zapatista Army for National Liberation) of the southern state of Chiapas and their savvy use of digital media. They rose up on January 1, 1994, the day that the North American Free Trade Agreement (NAFTA) went into effect, to protest neoliberal economic and political reforms. Although they took the city of San Cristóbal de las Casas by force, they immediately laid down their weapons (without surrendering them) to become a peaceful anti-neoliberal social movement. The EZLN and their use of media were an inspiration and a pervasive point of reference for the 1999 protests against the meetings of the World Trade Organization (WTO) (Coyer 2005). The EZLN and independent media became one of the most important points of articulation for transnational networks of social movements against neoliberalism and global corporate capitalism (Graeber 2009, Juris 2008, Lindholm and Zúquete 2010). They also cemented Zapatismo and the use of independent media as ubiquitous points of reference for anti-neoliberal movements.

Meanwhile, Mexican national politics seemed perched on the edge of something momentous. The next year, 2000, Mexico chose its very first truly democratically elected president. There was an incredibly expanded sense that Mexico was democratizing, but this same democratization was also creating crises of legitimation and control. For the last seventy years, almost the entire era since their 1910–1920 revolution, the hierarchies and networks of one party (the PRI, Partido Revolucionario Institucional, or Institutional Revolutionary Party) had been synonymous with how the Mexican state operated. Now, with a president not from the PRI, it seemed unclear how the various levels of government (local, state, and national) would work together if a different party ruled each level of government and party hierarchies no longer unified them. What would happen with the drug trafficking organizations that the PRI had made deals with now that it was losing its grip on the country? What new opportunities did it open for social movements that the PRI had made a habit of violently repressing?

The new government and the new anti-neoliberal social movement networks were both put to the test in 2001 when President Vicente Fox announced the construction of a new international airport on the outskirts of Mexico City. The old (and current) airport was very near the center of the city and so had limited abilities to expand to accommodate the commercial air traffic.[13] The very same day, the farmers whose land had just been expropriated in order to build the airport blocked traffic on the stretch of highway running alongside their communities and created a national news spectacle. Over the next nine months (from October 2001 until July 2002), the newly formed Frente (Frente de Pueblos en Defensa de la Tierra or the People's Front in Defense of Land) staged demonstrations, confronted police, blocked traffic, networked with other social movements from around the country, and tried to connect as best as they could with anti-neoliberal and anti–corporate globalization social movements from around the world (Alcayaga 2002, Camacho Guzmán 2008, Kuri Pineda 2010). As part of its organizing efforts, the Frente used various documentary films made about it as part of its organizing efforts. I discuss these films in detail in Chapter 2.

When they won and the president abrogated the expropriation decree, the Frente became a symbol for what was possible for anti-neoliberal and anti–corporate globalization movements seeking to stop unwanted development projects. Their win was unprecedented in Mexico. The filmmakers who made the films that the Frente used to organize produced more films about the Frente's success. Rather than disband, the Frente used their new political power to influence political changes locally in their communities. They also began traveling widely around Mexico and the world to talk about their experiences successfully organizing against unwanted development. Everywhere that they went, they took with them the documentary films made about them to gift, screen, and explain who they were and what they did.

By the end of Vicente Fox's six-year term (presidents are not allowed to be reelected), he was largely seen as a buffoon who had destabilized the country. However, the very popular mayor of Mexico City (Andrés Manuel Lopez Obrador, or AMLO) was running for president, and for the first time the left-leaning urban intelligentsia of the country was optimistic that one of their own could be president.

At the same time, there was a renewed effort at organizing Mexico's rural, indigenous, and working-class social movements (movements the campaign described as "from below and to the left") emanating from the Zapatista movement in Chiapas. La Otra Campaña traveled the country visiting and forming solidarity networks with other movements, led by the wildly popular, masked, pipe-smoking Subcomandante Insurgente Marcos, and trailed by international independent media producers. These producers documented his movements and meetings according to the methods and through networks that they were developing through the transnational movements against neoliberalism and corporate globalization. Activists from around the world were watching as the campaign neared Mexico City and met with activists from the Frente. Soon after La Otra Campaña traveled to Mexico City, prominent members of the Frente were arrested in a violent, nationally televised spectacle on May 3, 2006. Locals shut down the highway on the outskirts of the community in protest, and hundreds of the supporters of La Otra Campaña (including Rafael) who had been there just days before returned to help defend the barricades against police. Just as Rafael described, in the early hours of the morning on May 4, the police broke through the barricades and, in an incredible display of violence, arrested hundreds of people, many of them pulled from their houses. Busses of detainees, their sometimes unconscious and bleeding bodies stacked on top of one another, were severely beaten and sexually assaulted on their way to prison.[14]

Another flurry of documentaries were made about the police violence. As I discuss in more detail in Chapter 4, some of these documentaries traveled around the world throughout the networks of activist independent media producers and distributors of the global justice movements. They showed a very different perspective of the police violence, which was largely justified on commercial television as a necessary measure to curtail the violence that erupted from the illegal activities of dangerous radicals.

AMLO lost the elections to a man, Felipe Calderón, from the same party as Vicente Fox (the PAN, Partido de Acción Nacional, or National Action Party), who played on voters' fears of destabilization and violence as part of his campaign. Very much like the US elections in 2000 between George W. Bush and Al Gore, however, the results were incredibly close and hotly contested. AMLO's supporters camped out for months in the center of Mexico City protesting election irregularities and demanding a recount. As in any large political march or *plantón* (sit-in or occupation) in Mexico, political and social documentary films, including those about the Frente, circulated widely throughout the encampments as entertainment, education, and commodities to be sold to interested passersby.

Three years later, in 2009, long after AMLO's encampments had subsided, the Frente began organizing for the release of the thirteen prisoners still in jail from the police violence of 2006 (the opening vignette of this chapter). Again they turned to documentary films, the ones made about them in 2002 and 2006, in addition to a new crop of films, as tools to help. Soon after Mexico's Supreme Court ruled that police had grossly violated activists' human rights in 2006 (but could not identify anyone responsible), the remaining political prisoners were exonerated, and warrants for the arrest of other activists were rescinded, allowing them to come out of hiding.

The Frente again played a role in the 2012 presidential elections. After nearly six years of the brutal war against drug trafficking that Felipe Calderón had waged, apparently not curtailing traffickers' activities as much as enraging them to further violence and heated turf wars, it seemed that the most likely candidate for president was a man named Enrique Peña Nieto, from the PRI. The drug wars had made people almost nostalgic for the times of the PRI, when the government could make unified and stabilizing deals with drug traffickers because they controlled every level of government. Peña Nieto had been governor of the state of Mexico and one of the men responsible for calling for the police incursion (if not the excess of violence itself) against La Otra Campaña and the Frente. As part of the election, candidates participated in the very first presidential candidate debate ever staged in Mexico. It was held at an elite private university in Mexico City, La Universidad Iberoamericana (Ibero-American University). Many students protested Peña Nieto during the debate, many holding signs with references to Atenco. Afterward, Peña Nieto tried to delegitimize the concerns of the protestors by claiming that they were not actually students of the university, but were hired by his opposition. As a response, these 132 students posted their college IDs on Twitter and other social media platforms under the hashtag #YoSoy132 (I am [one of the] 132). The hashtag became the rallying point around the opposition to Peña Nieto's candidacy. Despite the movement's best efforts, however, Peña Nieto won the election and was the president of Mexico through 2018.

In short, Atenco has been a flashpoint, a rallying cry, and a challenge to Mexican politics and Mexico's political culture throughout the early decades of the twenty-first century. The most famous spokesperson of the Frente, Ignacio del Valle, is one of the most well-known and recognized activists in Mexico, perhaps eclipsed only by "The Sup," Subcomandante Insurgente Marcos (who now prefers to go by the name Galeano). The Frente, and the national conversation about Atenco, is firmly embedded into Mexico's recent political transformations. No conversation about Mexico's evolving democratic process would be meaningful without consideration of the impact that the Frente has had on that process. Furthermore, the films about Atenco, and the Frente's savvy use of these films, are part of what has made the name "Atenco" such an important part of Mexico's politics since 2001.

Atenco has also been a powerful symbol throughout transnational networks of social movements organizing against neoliberalism and unwanted development projects. Mexico is a hub for what one former president of Mexico (Ernesto Zedillo) called "revolutionary tourism" in an effort to criticize all the foreign visitors coming to Mexico to satisfy their curiosity and build solidarity with Zapatista networks. The inspirational place of Mexican social movements, the extensive network of Zapatista supporters, and the pervasive "revolutionary tourism" of Mexico mean that an examination of the Frente and their use of media is ideally placed in efforts to understand the role of media throughout these transnational networks.

Methods

My understanding of the transformative role of visual media has evolved slowly over the course of nearly a decade of continual dialogue and engagement with social documentary filmmakers and members of the Frente and allied social movements. In turn, my engagement with Mexican social documentary film was rooted in twenty years of frequent visits to Mexico and experiences with Mexican political cultures (since 1997), long before I became an anthropologist. The primary fieldwork was conducted during eighteen months from the end of May 2008 until November 2009. For six months of this period, I lived primarily in Mexico City, speaking with urban filmmakers. For six months, I resided in Atenco with a Frente activist. For a final six months, I traveled between Mexico City, Atenco, and Oaxaca de Juarez, a city in southern Mexico and another important site of social movement in Mexico.[15] These eighteen months were augmented with fieldwork carried out during the summers between 2006 and 2015.

During these trips, I spent as much time as possible at the geographic and temporal intersections of social movement and film-related activities that I saw as my primary field sites. These included film screenings, political marches, plantones, round-table discussions, panel presentations, and any other political events that I became aware of, however tangentially they seemed to be related to the Frente or media production. I was often surprised by the interpersonal and political connections between seemingly disparate political and media events. In between these events, I participated in the daily lives of members of social movements and filmmakers as much as possible. I attended *quinceañeras* (coming-of-age parties for teen women), funerals, religious celebrations, cultural events, dances, and fairs with the older, widowed friend I lived with in Atenco. I got up early to make tamales and *tlacoyos* (bean-filled handmade tortillas) for large celebrations with her and other women in Atenco, and I stayed out late at parties with filmmakers, poets, artists, and nationally known activists in Texcoco. In

Mexico City, I attended upscale parties in Colonia del Valle and Coyoacán with Mexico City's leftist elite, I exercised at the *fresa* (upscale) gym near my house in Villa Coapa, I attended religious meetings and meditation conferences at Casa Tibet in La Condessa with the Buddhist Mexican family that I lived with, and I spent countless hours traveling through the city on busses and in the metro. I also hung out with anarchists from Argentina, Brazil, France, Italy, and the United States who came to Mexico to meet Zapatistas, chatted often with pirate video vendors selling their wares on the sidewalk, and had long conversations about international revolutionary politics with shoeshine men.

During this time, I conducted and recorded fifty-eight in-depth, semistructured interviews with members of social movements, filmmakers, and distributors. Frequently, these categories of interview subjects overlapped significantly. I presented myself to interview subjects as an anthropologist interested in the role of media, especially film, in social movements. I asked each interviewee how they would like to be referred to in publication, and I have, for the most part, followed their preferences. I refer to public figures and most filmmakers using their full, professional names.

I did not follow the initial preferences of two men who I refer to as Virgilio and Humberto. Both expressed a preference, although not a vehement one, to be named fully in publications. I interviewed and interacted with these two men frequently, and so their perspectives and voices are continual references. They each seemed wary that pseudonyms would amount to an appropriation of their stories and felt that the veil of a pseudonym was a false one. Each man told me, "What else can they do to me? They [any authorities that may take retribution] already know everything." Although the decision was a difficult one, I decided to go against their wishes and refer to them here under pseudonyms. Their noncommittal attitudes and immediate embrace of their pseudonyms in the written work I presented to them made the decision easier. However, ultimately, I made the decision based on the fact that authorities might not know everything, and it seemed possible that some information presented here could be used against them in judicial processes. I did not want to be responsible for presenting any further incriminating evidence should there be any, even if these participants were willing to take the consequences.

My presentation as a young, unmarried white woman and a foreigner deeply impacted my interactions with people. As a white woman from the United States, I was keenly aware that people who look a lot like me often come to Mexico to drink and have sex with local men. It was often assumed, sometimes by people I have known for more than a decade and consider close friends, that I had come to Mexico to find a husband. Men who I interviewed often propositioned me, and I continually fought perceptions (among participants and others) that my interviews with men were dates. As a result, I sometimes interviewed married couples together. This may have affected the interviewees' presentation of information, but I believe these joint interviews were more, rather than less accurate. Early on in my fieldwork I learned to subtly triangulate information with other interviewees to counterbalance men who exaggerated facts greatly, presumably to impress me.

Most people were wary of me as a spy of some sort, working either for the Mexican or the US government. Because of this perception, I preferred to avoid delving into specifics about names, dates, and exact locations in interviews and tried to concentrate on qualitative questions about opinions, processes, and histories. From an analytical perspective, the lack of this kind of specific information (who did what, when, and where?) was sometimes frustrating, but I was constantly aware that this type of information is exactly the most useful data for intelligence agencies. I refrained from asking these questions not only to show that I was not interested in incriminating anyone, but also because revealing this kind of information put both my informants and myself in danger. Through this process, I have come to think that a lot of misinformation and misunderstanding can be hidden behind sometimes-inconsequential facts, while a great deal of truth can be found in stories that lack some specificity.

Lastly, unlike in many places in the world, people from all walks of life in Mexico know exactly what an anthropologist is and how they have often been agents of colonialism and cultural imperialism. I have more than once been subjected to extended pontifications about Robert Redfield and Oscar Lewis (some surprisingly complimentary) before carrying on with an interview. If not a spy, I was often seen as the worst kind of *protagonista* (egoist) (a concept that I delve into at length in Chapter 3): the North American who comes to Mexico to appropriate stories for the benefit of their own career. Much like Virgilio and Humberto's wariness of appropriation, this accusation of protagonismo is not unfounded. Much like the people represented in this book, I too struggle against self-interested individualism within the sometimes-constraining traditions of sociocultural anthropology and the realities of being a professional academic in the United States. My friends and informants helped me appreciate the deep, and possibly irreconcilable, contradiction of building an individual career and benefiting personally from representing injustice and the suffering of others. I have tried not to let these contradictions paralyze me as a researcher and anthropologist at the same time that I recognize that monographs like this volume are problematic.

In a modest attempt to mitigate the difficulties of this contradiction, and also to be completely truthful with people, I identified myself as deeply committed to social justice, and in Mexico to learn how to make better social movements in the United States. Following Hale (2009), I always asked in interviews what my responsibilities as a foreign researcher were to the Frente and associated social movements, and what I could do to help. Most people told me that there was nothing I could do but tell the truth. I have tried to live up to that promise.

Organization of the Book

The chapters that follow are arranged thematically and roughly historically. In Chapter 1, I give a more in-depth account of the first phase of the Frente's activism, its tactics, and its symbolic language. This chapter emphasizes the degree to which the airport struggle and the Frente are rooted in local activism from the 1970s through the 1990s and a series of precursor "Frentes." My discussion of the Frente's tactics, which are famous in Mexico and throughout anti-neoliberal social movement networks for being confrontational, focuses on the Frente's primary controversial symbol: the machete. This chapter attempts to account for the pragmatic and symbolic use of the machete as both a tool (a farm implement) and a weapon (useful for defending oneself). I argue that the Frente's use of machetes, and the urban discomfort with their use, is indicative of both the challenges of the Frente and their attraction for transnational, anti-neoliberal social movements.

Chapter 2 focuses on the activism of three of Atenco's filmmakers. Woven throughout each of the accounts of these three filmmakers are multiple and sometimes-conflicting vectors of surveillance, sometimes mobilized by filmmakers and sometimes mobilized against them. I show that in the case of the Frente, there has been no direct relationship between the physical capacity of digital surveillance technologies (cameras) to record daily lives and disciplinary apparatuses, either internal or external. I argue that we need not fetishize cameras as either sinister devices that allow the state to overreach its authority into people's lives, or saviors that will hold state agents (police, officials) accountable for their actions. Both are much more dependent on the political and social cultures and structures surrounding cameras than they are on the technological capabilities of cameras themselves. I argue that the much more direct consequences of activist filmmaking practice are disciplinary consequences for the activists themselves in which state oppression and ideas of ethicopolitical practice work in concert to encourage a set of virtues related to selflessness.

Chapter 3 delves deeper into the specific practice of policing ideas of protagonismo among activists in leftist social movements in Mexico. Protagonismo could be translated as "egoism" or "grandstanding." It signifies those who seek to benefit personally from their activism, exhibit personal political ambition, or seek our political leadership to benefit themselves. In short, "protagonismo" is the name given to ideas of competitive, self-interested individualism associated with neoliberal subjectivity. Although it is not quite used in this way locally, I present the idea of *compañerismo*, or being a good *compañero/a*, as a useful term to represent the set of virtues against which ideas of protagonismo are cast. I show that a contemporary sense of compañerismo (building from deeply rooted intertwining historical legacies) calls into being a collectivist sense of self that shares some characteristics with the politicized identities of the New Social Movements of the twentieth century, but does not coalesce around any one identity more specific than a moral sense of a shared humanity. I argue that ideas of compañerismo challenge some of the foundational assumptions behind classically liberal, as well as neoliberal, conceptions of citizenship and personhood.

Chapter 4 tells the story of the most widely circulated documentary about the Frente, *Romper el cerco* (Breaking the Siege, Canalseisdejulio and Promedios, 2006). I use the story of this film to demonstrate a distinction between two divergent approaches to film activism: strategies based around ideas of resistance, and strategies based around ideas of autonomy. These two strategies come together in complex and sometimes-contradictory ways in the production and distribution of *Romper el cerco* and suggest that transformations in activist practice are more nimble than changes to strategic activist language. I use the idea of activist filmmaking strategies of autonomy to challenge the idea that *autoconsumo* (self-consumption or "preaching to the choir") is to be criticized. I argue that shedding ideas of Marxian consciousness or Gramscian hegemony can allow us to see autoconsumo as helping to build autonomous languages and infrastructures that are very useful organizing tools. I suggest that the concept can be extended to easy criticisms of social media activism.

Chapter 5 focuses on film distribution as a set of political and economic practices in the Frente's campaign to release political prisoners. Using the example of a solidarity trip that the Frente made to the southern state of Oaxaca in 2009, I show how processes and networks that form offscreen are integral to how social documentaries operate as political and ethical tools. I argue that three key ways that the Frente used films—gifting, screening, and selling—are all important ethical and political practices that help to build transformative noncapitalist material economies.

The final coda brings the events and arguments of the previous chapters into a more contemporary moment in which YouTube has come to dominate the world of noncommercial film distribution, Donald Trump (a caricature of protagonismo) is president of the United States, anti-neoliberalism has become a rallying point for the political right in the United States and the UK, and the airport so famously triumphed over in 2002 is well on its way to being built in Atenco. These developments in large measure underscore the importance of movements like the Frente in realigning political axes along ethical lines and the importance of small-scale (but long-form) media as a crucial political tool for social movements struggling against corporate capitalism.

CHAPTER ONE

Atenco and Machetes

Traveling from Mexico City to the center of Atenco is a significant lesson in local political geography. My middle-class and academic friends in Mexico City spoke of Atenco as if it were in the middle of nowhere and took days to travel to, even though the journey from the center of Mexico City to the center of Atenco usually takes under an hour. The trip from the central bus station to Atenco regularly took less time than the voyage from where I was staying in the city to the central bus station. And yet one filmmaker, who by 2009 had made three influential films about Atenco and was deeply committed to solidarity with the Frente, told me that there would be no reason to spend much time in Atenco because there was really nothing there. In contrast, the first time I visited Atenco in 2008, the man I refer to here as Virgilio texted me that we should meet at the Casa Ejidal (the Ejido Commission Office) of Atenco as if it were an internationally recognized center for anti-neoliberal organizing.[1]

I met Virgilio, a middle-aged man who has dedicated a significant portion of his life to political organizing, at a film screening in Mexico City. After the film, the filmmakers introduced me to him, we exchanged numbers, and he promised to show me around Atenco. Virgilio's plan in inviting me was to take me on a ritualized tour that almost all journalists, academics, students, and other outside visitors received. The most widely circulated film about Atenco, *Romper el cerco / Breaking the Siege* (Canalseisdejulio and Promedios, 2006), begins with scenes taken from a similar tour given to an activist film crew. The famous Zapatista spokesperson Subcomandante Insurgente Marcos and his entourage were given the tour in 2006 amid a densely packed crowd of admirers. The tour was also given to a small group of bewildered American college students who visited under the instructions of a well-meaning teacher while I was living there in 2009. As it is how people from the Frente most frequently represent themselves and Atenco to outside visitors, it is an appropriate way to begin to describe the town, both from the perspective of the political imaginaries that the name "Atenco" connotes in Mexican media, and the physical place where people make their everyday lives.

The particularities of the history and place of Atenco are heavy with meaning, but there is an incredible diversity of these meanings. Atenco has continually been headline news since 2001, a central node of political organizing in Mexico, and a meeting place for anti-neoliberal activists from all over the world. In this sense, it is famous and important to national and global politics. In 2009, when I was living in Atenco, it was not at all unusual for there to be film crews there, famous public intellectuals, or even the occasional rock star. Even so, in every other way it is not very different from thousands of other small municipalities throughout Mexico. Aside from the Frente and the political waves that it was trying to make, my filmmaker friend was right in saying that in comparison to the places where Americans usually stay in Mexico—San Miguel de Allende, Oaxaca de Juarez, Cancun, even San Cristóbal de las Casas—Atenco was not very remarkable. In most ways, it is a small town like millions of others in Mexico.

The Atenco ejido is not very old. It was formed during the large agrarian reform policies of the 1920s along with all of Mexico's ejidos.[2] This land reform converted large properties of rich landowners into the communal property, ejidos, of locals throughout Mexico. A local Comisariado Ejidal made up of the peasant farmers (*ejidatarios*) who work it manage the ejidos of each community. Within the ejido system, each farmer has an individual plot, or parcel, that he farms (ejidatarios are nearly always men, although women can be *ejidatarias*) and that he can pass down to his children and grandchildren. However, ejidatarios can never sell a parcel. If he moves away, or ceases to farm, or if his children don't want to farm, he must give it back to the Ejido Commission, and they will give it to someone else. The Comisariado in Atenco also manages the other communal lands of the town: the public park, public swimming pools, and the land that isn't currently useful as farmland. The Atenco Comisariado also owns a few tractors for plowing and cultivating that they loan out to ejidatarios and a water truck to transport water from the central park to fields.

During the 1990s, less than seventy years after they were established, the ejido system was dismantled by President Salinas as a part of initiatives surrounding the North American Free Trade Agreement and the popularity of neoliberal economic reforms. Under the reforms, ejidatarios could vote to privatize their land so that each farmer could sell, develop, and otherwise do whatever he wanted with his parcel. Ejidos could remain, however, if locals wished it. Atenco's land, like many ejidos around the country, has so far remained communal, although a vote in the spring of 2015, if it is found to be legitimate (its status is currently being contested), would privatize Atenco's ejido so that individual families can sell their parcels to companies wishing to "develop" the land.

Part of the continual struggle of the Frente since 2001 has been over what Lynn Stephen has called the "cultural packaging of violence" that make "particular groups of people susceptible to violent abuses and [allow] them to be treated with less than human respect and dignity" (2002, 28–29). Under the developmental logic that identified Atenco as a potential site for a new international airport, the area was a blank slate, a "nothing" that could be built into "something" through the attentions of transnational corporations and relatively wealthy consumers of international air travel. Because the geographical area was undesirable—an anachronism and a reminder of Mexico's poverty and underdevelopment—the people who resided there were also seen to be unimportant and undesirable. Some residents of the Atenco area also saw themselves in this way and continue to see themselves in this way. Some would much prefer to replace their semirural, farming way of life with another version of themselves. To the people that came to make up the Frente, however, and who at one time could count on the support of the vast majority of its residents, this thinking was the same logic of colonialism that imagined all the Americas as a blank slate to be filled with European enterprises. To Virgilio and others of the Frente, Atenco is a place rich with meaning and history that would have been completely destroyed by the expropriation.

The struggle in Atenco is primarily a struggle over who gets to decide the meaning and worth of the complex relationship between people and land. Furthermore, this struggle over meaning is not a two-sided oppositional struggle with a local population on one side with a consistent, homogenous identity and a unified oppressive state completely at the service of transnational corporations on the other. As any other community in any other place in the world, there as many views about what Atenco is and what it should be as there are residents living there. An ejidataria and member of the Frente, who I refer to here as Ana María, told me in 2009, "each one of us that makes up the Frente de Pueblos en Defensa de la Tierra, each one of us is a story and a different story, a story with many nuances, with many emotions. . . . I believe that every point of view is distinct."

This nuance and diversity of experiences is especially important to emphasize in cases such as Atenco that are so heavily burdened with meaning. Much as place names such as Kent State, Columbine, or Ferguson, Missouri, are in the United States, "Atenco" has become a touchstone for national and international conversations about political, social, and cultural transformations. In Mexico, "Atenco" is synonymous with dramatic social movement: an incredible triumph over the state and neoliberal reform in 2002, and a devastating police repression in 2006. The meanings of "Atenco" that play out on the front pages of national newspapers and magazines are heavily polarized (see Figure 1.1).

For some, the name is a symbol for the possibility of organized social movements to triumph over the overwhelming political and economic forces of corporate capitalist globalization. This is why the name was stenciled in spray paint on the walls of social science buildings at the national public university in Mexico City well in to 2009. It is why they can mobilize political marches in the capital of tens of thousands of people. It is also why filmmakers and activists from all over the world have traveled to Atenco and invited activists from the Frente to their homes in Canada, South Africa, and Australia, and throughout Europe. The image on the left-hand side of Figure 1, from the left-leaning newspaper *La Jornada*, is a representation of this set of meanings that the name evokes.

This image was published on July 13, 2002, in the heat of the Frente's first political struggle. The federal government had expropriated all the land of Atenco, its ejido land as well as a good portion of the land on which people live, and the land of thirteen surrounding municipalities. The headline, from a tense moment in the confrontation with the state, reads "Atenco on guard." Although the subheadlines refer variously to the "project in Texcoco" (the larger neighboring town), "Ejidatarios from San Salvador," "campesinos," and "the population" as actors and subjects of various news stories throughout the paper, the name "Atenco" stands in for each of these various actors and places in the headline. Atenco is represented visually by an image that takes up the majority of the front page: the dramatic silhouette of a single anonymous young man standing in front of a bonfire (probably a burning car) on asphalt. He looks to the side rather than toward the camera, and his body language is not confrontational. He appears to be unarmed. It was headlines like this that popularized the idea of Atenco as a single political actor rather than a complexity of actors from a variety of political positions and local municipalities. As in this image, Atenco was, and is, often dramatically romanticized.

The second image in Figure 1.1, the front cover of the right-leaning political magazine *Vértigo* on May 7, 2006, evokes a critical version of this same history that is fearful of powerful social movements and conjures images of violent uneducated peasants who destroy and riot. It was published to describe the second incident Atenco is known for: an occasion four years later in which residents and police clashed over the arrest of several local political leaders. The image shows many young men crowded onto the hood of a car with more young men beside and crowded behind the car. All their faces are covered with cloth or shirts so that only their eyes are exposed. One man, perched high on the car, is

Figure 1.1. The front pages of *La Jornada* in 2002 and *Vértigo* in 2006.

shirtless and wearing a gas mask. Many of the men are making what seem to be aggressive gestures toward the camera, and the men highest in the picture nearly stand on the moving car with their arms in the air. Upon closer inspection, the viewer may note that the aggressive gestures they are making are peace signs. The headline, written in large letters across the bottom of the image reads, "They violate the rule of law: ATENCO AGAIN." In this case, the name "Atenco" stands in for a specific meaningful physical confrontation of uncontrolled, chaotic violence that the reader is assumed to be familiar with.

In neither headline does "Atenco" represent a geographical region where a diversity of people live and make their daily lives. The political significance of the name is so heavy and divisive that it was difficult for me, as a foreigner and an outsider, to say the name aloud to a stranger, even a bus driver, and admit that I was going there the first time to meet Virgilio. The same filmmaker who told me there was really no reason to spend much time in Atenco told me that the local officials removed the sign at the city limits that identified the place as Atenco because the name had such a heavy weight of meaning. Several people from Atenco claimed that the name Atenco was removed from highway maps (although I never saw evidence of that in 2008–2009). The sign on the highway when I arrived there for the first time in 2008, however, did indeed label the town as "San Salvador" instead of "San Salvador Atenco." Aside from erasing the indigenous name of the place by relying solely on its Catholic saint's name, this superficial erasure further divorced the abstract and emotionally and politically charged meanings of "Atenco" from the physical location of San Salvador Atenco, a place with a market on Mondays, a juice stand in front of the church, a large central park with swimming pools, street vendors, bicycle taxis, and unique local festivals and traditions.

The shorthand of "Atenco" in the popular public imagination also erases the fact that the specific place of San Salvador Atenco is merely the municipal center of a wider region of thirteen smaller villages that run along the Texcoco highway on the east side of Mexico City that were all impacted by the expropriation decree in 2001 and whose residents have formed a part of the Frente from the beginning. Virgilio, for example, was not from Atenco proper but would be traveling there from his village to meet me there.

As in most Mexican towns and cities, the center square of Atenco is built around a large open space with the town's church on one side and government buildings along another. In 2008, Atenco's plaza also had a tall, rusty water tower standing alongside the churchyard with a Laundromat and two cell phone stores behind it. The arches of the government building faced the church and the water tower. As I approached on foot to meet Virgilio, a policeman in black body armor was getting a soda out of the vending machine outside his office under the arches. It was difficult for me to cut through the heavily politically and emotionally charged images that I had seen repeatedly over the last few years in documentary films and experience this mundane small town scene as a real place rather than a scene from a movie. It was even more difficult to see a police officer calmly drinking a soda in this place that I associated entirely with the most brutal police violence I had ever seen on film.

Right next door to the policeman was a scene I knew well from countless documentaries and scenes of political violence: a set of concrete steps leading up to a stage with an enormous mural painted behind it on two sides.[3] The mural graphically illustrated the political imaginary that I mapped onto the place, a giant portrait of Zapata (a Mexican revolutionary war hero who fought for land reform) surrounded by symbols of the local struggle. Images of men riding horses, red bandanas, and machetes are all strong symbols of the Frente. A woman's face painted red and black references their ties to anarchist movements, and the image of a "viejo," a man with a beard wearing a white three-piece suit, references a tradition of local cultural festivals. I knew this mural from images of press conferences announcing the retention or release of "retained" government officials, demanding the release of prisoners, and one famous image of a half-naked man crouched on his hands and knees over a pool of blood, an abandoned combat boot by his head (see Figure 1.2). I was standing on that very spot.

Across the street from the steps was a tall sign that at one time had lit up from the inside. It had a marquee but now just said, "Cine Teatro Atenco" (Atenco Movie Theater). The sign indicated that the steps I recognized were leading into an auditorium that at one time was used as a movie theater, and as a meeting place for general assemblies of the ejidatarios or of the entire municipality. (The sign that reads "Auditorium Emiliano Zapata" is covered by the EZLN banner in Figure 1.2) This was the auditorium where Virgilio told me government officials were held in 2002 for days in a dramatic televised standoff with the state government. It was the place where the film *Atenco: Un crimen de estado* (Atenco: A crime of the state, Colectivo Klamvé, 2006) showed people taking refuge as they watched their neighbors and family members on a small television in 2006, chasing police off of the closed highway with rocks and machetes. The film *Romper*

Figure 1.2. A widely distributed image of Atenco's central square on May 4, 2006. Photo by Jesús Villaseca.

el cerco / Breaking the Siege (Canalseisdejulio and Promedios, 2006) shows this auditorium in the background of scenes of terrific violence, explaining that people taking refuge there were pulled out of it before being beaten and raped by police on their way to prison.

I hadn't realized that the police station was only a few yards from this spot, just out of frame to the right. This sudden realization challenged the way that I thought about the conflict between the Frente and police. They coexisted in this space peacefully for five years, the police being able to see from their windows who was coming in and out of the auditorium. After the repression, they had coexisted here for three more years without incident. It was a horrific reminder of the continual tensions that exist in Atenco, but also a reminder that the scenes of conflict I associated with the place represented a few horrific days surrounded by decades of close living and working conditions.

On the other side of the auditorium from the police station was the Casa Ejidal. It wasn't labeled but was easily recognizable. It was absolutely covered in the symbols of the Frente: spray-painted political slogans and stencils, posters advertising political events. Sheets with political slogans on them hung from the balcony of the second story. All the windows on the second floor were blocked out with posters demanding that political prisoners be let free. One stencil depicted two men with their mouths open, presumably yelling, with their fists raised in the air, one with a machete. The words "Viva Tierra y Libertad!" (Long live land and liberty!) were stenciled across the top and among the corn.[4] The machete, the most recognizable symbol of the Frente, was painted or stenciled everywhere. This artwork marked the building as something different from the buildings around it. The graffiti yelled, assertively, confidently, that this place was a center of agricultural pride and political fearlessness. The transitory nature of the posters, graffiti, and painted sheets gave it a sense that here was a place that was active, and in a constant process of being constructed and reimagined.

One stencil showed cornstalks wearing EZLN balaclavas, referencing the Frente's ties to the Zapatista movement in Chiapas, and the commonality of their identification with agriculture. Another stencil showed a face that I recognized as a political prisoner from Oaxaca who had recently been arrested. The style of the stencil was not local but recalled the distinctive street art of Oaxaca, suggesting that friends of this political prisoner had come here to stencil his face on this wall. These references to other social movements declared the political strength of the Frente, and the support they had from movements throughout Mexico.

Before I could think of what to do next, I heard Virgilio calling my name. He stood in the doorway of the Casa Ejidal, behind a narrow metal-framed glass door. He led me through the small vestibule and then up the stairs, the only place to go from the vestibule. The second floor was one large, open space. All along the left side were windows with balconies overlooking the plaza. Five or six mattresses were stacked in the far corner. Across from them on the inside wall, a few computers sat on a table. A young man was sitting at one of the computers reading a webpage. Along the same wall, opposite the balconies, was a table covered in boxes, posters, signs stapled to wooden planks, folded sheets painted with political slogans, and an enormous papier-mâché puppet. Above this table was a white board on which a large white piece of paper had been affixed with masking tape with the heading "Festival Cultural de Resistencia" (Cultural Festival of Resistance) with items listed below such as *lucha x presos politicos* (struggle for political prisoners) and *lucha x mujeres campesinas* (struggle for women peasant farmers). Next to the white board was a chalkboard with a few announcements on it listing dates and times. In the center of the room was a table around which half a dozen middle-aged men were sitting eating cookies and drinking orange Fanta. They all appeared to be in their fifties and sixties, with dark-brown skin and deep lines in their cheeks and under their eyes, wearing jeans, boots, and button-down flannel shirts or colorful woolen vests.

They were discussing the new announcement, given just an hour or more ago, that once again there were plans to buy up and develop the land of Atenco. There were plans for an ecotourism park and a series of hotels and upscale shopping malls, a tourist corridor. Virgilio showed me the contents of a legal-sized manila envelope sitting in front of him while one of his visitors poured me a Styrofoam cup of Fanta and offered me some cookies. The papers were photocopied from the originals, first copies of an official decree with its flourishing signature and rubber stamp and then photocopied maps of where they planned to develop.

One man announced quite formally and eloquently that they wouldn't sell. There are too many people who have died, who are in prison, who have been raped, for them to simply give up and sell right now. There was a moment of silence before another man spoke. He said that even if they offer one farmer one million pesos for his land (about US$100, 000), what would he do with it? First, he's going to buy a new car, which will be one hundred thousand pesos, then he'll work on either buying a new house or fixing up the one that he has, which could easily cost eight hundred thousand. If he doesn't, his family will want to go on vacation. They'll go to Cancun or to Acapulco, and the money will be gone in no time. And then he'll have no job, no land, and no money. He'll end up working in a hotel, or in a department store, or the ecological park as a poorly paid slave while the owners of what used to be his land are getting rich.

Virgilio pointed out that the parks that might be built there charge over one hundred pesos per person to get in, and there are thousands of people that come every day. The ecotourism park will be very, very lucrative, and the men will miss out on all of that if they just sell the land. He said that they have to develop it so that they become the business owners instead of selling it to others that will make the money. One of the neighbors had constructed a few greenhouses and was growing tomatoes and squash instead of corn and beans. He was making money at it. If they could get a few investors, they could also have a series of greenhouses and could set up shop around the new ecotourism park to sell vegetables. He had been talking with someone from a local university about organic farming methods, and he figured if they did it organically, they could make more money. Water was another important issue. They need water and the ecotourism park would take a lot of it.

Virgilio started to write out points on a blank sheet of paper. Their demands would be that they want to make a deal in which they will be the business owners in their own projects and will continue to have access to water. They decided that someone would go look for the president of the farmers' association and tell them that they weren't going to sell and that they had conditions. They would do it at noon tomorrow. He asked a young man who had come in if he had a camera to record. He replied that he did, an mp4 video camera, and there would be several people recording what they could the next day while they tried to strike a deal.

Virgilio announced that this time around, they had to have a new strategy. Before, when the authorities came to expropriate their land to build an international airport, they were made out to be the aggressive radicals because they went against a legal decree. This time, he said, we need to have an agreement with them from the very start. That way, when they go off of the agreement (which they will because the government always does) *they* will be the ones who are doing something illegal, and *they* are the ones who will have to radicalize to get what they want. The written agreement and the video of the meeting would be proof that the government officials were the radicals. "They don't even really want to make an ecological park," Virgilio went on. "It's just something they are saying now so that people will go along with it. Once it is their land, who knows what they will do with it."

As the meeting wound down a man named Omar appeared and announced that he was there to take me to the fields. Omar insisted that I sit in the front seat, and Virgilio climbed into the back seat with a man who looked like he might be in his nineties. Wedged between my seat and the gearshift was a well-worn and recently sharpened machete in a leather sheath. "That's so that you can take a picture of me on the hill with my machete raised in the air," Omar said. I stammered and said with embarrassment that I didn't have a good camera, just the one on my very inexpensive, decidedly un-smartphone. I pulled out my digital sound recorder. "This is my recorder," I said. Omar gave me a very disappointed look.

It took about twenty minutes to drive out to the place that they wanted to show me. Soon we were passing dozens of small parcels of land on both sides. The plots were easy to distinguish from each other because each was at a different stage of cultivation, or was planted with a different crop. Each long, narrow field (about 20m by 500m) was assigned to a different family. As we drove through the fields, Omar pointed out to me which parcels belonged to which families. "This one belongs to Nacho," he commented, meaning Ignacio del Valle, then serving a sentence of more than one hundred years in a maximum security prison for his activism.

The small size and long, narrow nature of the plots is an important aspect of the attempts to privatize the ejido, Virgilio explained to me. One of the tactics of the companies that were trying to buy up the land was to get local ejido commissions to dissolve so that the land ceased to be communal and each farmer owned his own parcel of land. Then the farmers would be permitted to sell. The tactic seems to be giving power to local farmers, but unfortunately, even if only some farmers sell, it means that everyone's land is useless for farming. You can't farm a long, narrow parcel of land between two condominium developments, Virgilio commented. The implication was that if some people sell, everyone will eventually be obligated to sell whether or not they would prefer to keep farming.

Past the fields, we parked the car at the bottom of a small, dusty hill. The older man stayed sitting in the car, and Omar, Virgilio, and I climbed the hill on foot. Omar brought his machete, perhaps hoping that I was lying about not having a camera. From the top of the hill, there was a complete 360-degree view of the terrain. The view was impressive. Virgilio let me look around for a few minutes before pointing out the important sights. Omar wandered off down the other side of the hill with his machete. First, he oriented my shoulders toward Mexico City to the southwest. I could make out the tops of tall buildings sticking out of a cloud of yellow-brown smog. Atenco was very close to it, but distant enough that the outline of the smog was visible. To the north was Teotihuacan, the site of the ancient city with the enormous pyramids of the sun and the moon, possibly the largest tourist attraction in that part of Mexico. To the south were more pyramids. Virgilio began to tell me the history of the region and of the Frente, a favored topic of his that I came to hear many times over the next few years.

He told me that when the Spanish came, most of these lands were under water. This was the site of the enormous Lago Texcoco, a great salt lake and the home of Nezahualcóyotl, the famous poet king. Other locals on different occasions told me that when Cortés came to the region, there were roads twenty horses wide all around the lake and canals that traveled straight to the heart of the ancient city of Tenochtitlan (now Mexico City). There were also canals that traveled all the way down to Xochimilco, the only neighboring area to still have canals and *chinampas* (floating farm plots) in the twenty-first century. In the fifteenth century there were elaborate structures that protected the fresh water of Tenochtitlan and Xochimilco from the salt water of Texcoco. Atenquenses (residents of Atenco) told me that a few years after Cortés conquered the zone in the fifteenth century, there were floods, and the Spanish didn't know how to deal with the water. Instead of calling on the local indigenous engineers, he started to drain the lakes, a process that has been continual ever since.

Virgilio pointed out to me a sharp dividing line that ran north and south. To the left of the line, there were green fields and brown dirt. To the right, the soil was red with large patches of white and no crops. Because the lake was brackish, when it dried up (or was dried up), the salt remained in the soil, and so it wasn't very good farmland. The people of the area fertilized and worked the land to the left over a few generations so that it was now good farmland. The land on the right was still salty, as evidenced by the large white patches. Both kinds of land belonged to the ejido of Atenco, even though the salty lands weren't divided up into farming parcels. Virgilio emphasized to me that even though the land was salty and not currently good for farming, it could be just as productive as the current parcels if it were worked the way that the current parcels were.

Virgilio also pointed out a round, black shape in the near distance to the right of the great pyramids, what people referred to locally as the *caracol* (the snail or shell) because of its shape. A significant local landmark, the caracol is one of the last physical remnants of a company called Sosa Texcoco, one of many semipublic enterprises that utilized the expertise of Spanish exiles coming to Mexico to escape Franco's persecution in the 1930s. It was an enormous evaporator that helped extract minerals such as sodium bicarbonate from the salty land. A large percentage of the people in the communities around Atenco were employed at Sosa Texcoco for decades, but according to Virgilio, when the Spanish man died, the formally subsidized enterprise became privatized as part of the increasingly popular neoliberal reforms. Workers went on strike against the new management and remained on strike for six years, from 1993 to 1999. There was a plantón that looked over the factory so that new workers couldn't be brought in. Sosa

Texcoco never reopened. Virgilio told me that the organizations that formed during these strikes throughout the 1990s built the foundation of what happened in Atenco in 2002.

Virgilio emphasized to me that what was accomplished with the airport was based in a long history of local activism. He has emphasized to me many times over the years that activists can't build something like the Frente de Pueblos en Defensa de la Tierra in a few months. Many of its members had years and years of formation in the communist party from the 1970s and 1980s. Virgilio said that he first began organizing with Ignacio del Valle and others in 1982 with a local struggle over taxes. "We won that battle," he told me in 2009. "I was nineteen years old." They were involved in student movements and organized a reading group for a long time that learned about history, politics, and social theory. They put this education to work in the 1990s in the Sosa Texcoco strike.

Months later, I stood on the same hill listening to a different member of the Frente talking about Atenco's history with a group of American college students. Someone asked why farmers in the neighboring ejido had voted to privatize their land and sell their parcels when Atenco hadn't. The ejidatario said that one of the reasons is that paradoxically, the people on the neighboring ejido had a closer relationship to the land. They had mostly never been a part of a wage economy before and so were anxious to stop farming and "modernize." In contrast, most of the people of the Atenco ejido had the experience of working at Sosa Texcoco and living through the strike. He said this experience made many people appreciate the land and how much it means. The strike made people realize that they couldn't depend on others for their livelihood.

Driving back from my ritual tour of the countryside with Omar and Virgilio, Virgilio told me that because growing corn, beans, or nopales (an edible cactus) in such a small plot is not very lucrative, in 2009 some ejidatarios had started to engage in more lucrative and more experimental operations. In addition to greenhouses, others were attempting to grow spirulina, an algae with medicinal properties that used to grow naturally in the lake and has come into fashion as an ingredient in green shakes, in shallow trenches. One family, in addition to the spirulina operation, had dug a pit to farm carp that they hoped to serve at a small café with spirulina products and local crafts. I asked Virgilio if anyone could live off of their plot entirely. "Oh, no," he replied, explaining that most people have other sources of income, mostly small businesses run out of their homes. Virgilio also did occasional seasonal work on offshore oil wells in the Gulf of Mexico. He had spent months at a time on oil rigs. He had also been a used car salesman for a few years. Although no one exclusively farmed, for most people farming was the only constant occupation that provided a backdrop to seasonal work or short-lived small businesses.

These new projects, coupled with the area's continually shifting relationship with industry and agriculture, reveal the complexity of the relationship between people and land in the Atenco region. For many residents, land represented economic stability, but according to Virgilio and others, a strong connection to land in some cases was abandoned and rediscovered through experiences with wage labor. Furthermore, even though there was a feeling that stability lay in agriculture and land ownership, ejidatarios struggled with making their plots economically profitable. There was intense local resistance to government plans to "develop" the area, even in the form of the proposed ecological park, and yet individual ejidatarios find a lot of excitement and possibility in projects experimenting with new crops and tourism. Atenco as a region was trying to build a new socially and economically stable place for itself out of any resources it could. For some people in the region this has meant abandoning agriculture, selling land to developers, and seeking a life somewhere else. For others, it has meant devoting their lives to fighting against corporate and government efforts to profit from their land. Most have a mixed strategy that includes compromises to ideals in some portions of their lives and firm commitment in others. Most people's strategies and commitments change throughout time. Although "Atenco" may be a popular shorthand that refers to a set of historical circumstances, the meanings, histories, motivations, strategies, and ideologies that make up what is referred to as "Atenco" are at least as numerous as the number of individuals whose lives have been personally impacted by what has occurred there.

While the group of American college students were listening to ejidatarios tell them about the Frente, a series of four or five large helicopters flew overhead in a dense line. "There goes Obama," one ejidatario said, explaining that the new president of the United States had been in Mexico City for the last few days and was probably in one of those helicopters either surveying the countryside or traveling to a different location to fly home. Our tour guides studied the helicopters intently trying to discern their origin and possible mission. Someone asked one of the college students for the pictures she had taken as they flew overhead. They speculated about whether President Obama or the Mexican military might be spying on them, making plans about a new use for Atenco's land, or simply using the fly-over to intimidate them.

Journalists are not the only ones to map fantastical political imaginaries onto the mundane details of everyday life in Atenco. The thought that President Obama might be interested in touring the place, or that the military would send half a dozen large military helicopters on a juvenile mission of intimidation, seems at once fantastically paranoid and entirely possible. It was paranoid to read such dramatic political meaning from a few helicopters, but entirely possible considering the scope of the battles over globalization, corporate capitalism, and international commerce that have played out in the recent history of Atenco.

The political struggles surrounding the place and the idea of Atenco are deeply entrenched in dramas of competing political and economic fantasies from a wide variety of perspectives: those of foreign scholars like me, filmmakers from Mexico City, transnational activists interested in global insurrection, politicians at the highest level of their national governments, businessmen interested in building a First World Mexico, and local farmers trying to build a life independent from what they see as the damaging, individualizing, profit-driven morality of corporate capitalism. Each of these perspectives is rooted in overlapping lived experiences of international politics and economic changes and has been articulated and dramatized through a wide variety of media.

Struggle for Dialogue over the Airport Expropriation: 2001–2002

One morning in early March 2009, when carnival celebrations were in full swing, I interviewed a man I refer to here as Humberto in my small room on the outskirts of Atenco. Although I recorded dozens of accounts describing the history of the airport struggle, Humberto's narrative was a particularly insightful window into the history of the Frente's politics and what became the Frente's primary symbol: the machete.

Humberto, like Virgilio, told me that on the day that the expropriation decree was officially announced, "we already had people" because of mobilizations against the government that had been happening at least since 1995. Several men told me that they had started political organizing when they were in middle school in the 1970s. Many of these same people found themselves organizing this most recent iteration of the Frente. Through the 1980s there were a series of different local movements referred to as the "Frente": the Frente Popular Región Texcoco (Popular Front of the Texcoco Region) in the 1980s; the Frente Democrático Nacional (Democratic National Front), which was formed to protest the 1988 election fraud; and the subsequent Frente Popular del Valle de México (Popular Front of the Valley of Mexico), which formed to prevent programs from taking the region's water to Mexico City. This series of Frentes, in addition to the experience of the Sosa Texcoco strike, meant that there was a great deal of familiarity with organizing locally, and so a pattern and a skeleton of an organized movement already existed when the expropriation decree was announced in October 2001.

Humberto told me that the new Frente began to form on the same day the decree was announced: "That is when we got harder [*nos ponemos mas duros*] and we closed the highway. That was October 22, 2001. We closed it about eight hours. And they send the riot police [*granaderos*]. They sent everything. And we were ready to fight with them because if the government expropriates us and no one from the government comes to explain to us why they are expropriating us—because they want to take our lands—no one comes, but they send the riot police? We were ready for anything."

The confrontation ended with talks with police in the middle of the night resulting in the police leaving peacefully and the ejidatarios unblocking the highway. Soon afterward, the Frente organized itself as a parallel structure to the Comisariado Ejidal, remaining separate, but following its organizational structure with representatives from each community. It formed commissions to work on separate projects involving the media, organizing meetings and political events, and following through on judicial actions. Commissions went to other parts of the country to speak with others who had had land expropriated for federal prisons and the present international airport in Mexico City. Humberto explained to me that while some ejidatarios had been paid for their land in previous cases of expropriation, most still had not been paid years or decades later. Even if the government did come through with their payments, Humberto told me, they were giving only seven pesos per square meter. At the time, that amounted to about fifty-three US cents per square meter, or a little over $2,000 per acre. As most of the ejidatarios "owned" less than a hectare, or a little over two acres, the average farmer would receive $4,000 to $5,000 for his land. "Imagine!" Humberto emphasized to me. "When they were going to sell to other countries at four thousand dollars a meter!" He quickly added, "And it wasn't so much that they pay us, but that the land is for everyone. It is our life. If we left the land, where would we live? Many people died in this time when—I mean the older folks—when they thought that they were going to take their land away, they died little by little."

President Fox, in a televised interview on November 3, 2001, described these compensations as "winning the lottery" (*les cayó la lotería*) for this population, who by anyone's standards were not wealthy people.[5] In his televised comments, Fox revealed a value for the land only in monetary terms. One day the land is nearly worthless, a "nothing," and the next it is worth money that the owners should be overjoyed to receive because they are so cash poor. Many people told me that Fox seemed to think they would be much happier to be baristas at a Starbucks in the new airport than be farmers. In contrast, in an interview in 2009, Virgilio explained to me,

> For us, the lake [of Texcoco] represents the roots of all of the pueblo of Mexico. In this lake, along what is today Mexico City . . . are the bases, the foundations [*cimientos*], of all our culture of our country. And it was our history too, our roots, our identity as a pueblo. So our community would lose all of this: our culture, traditions, customs, way of life, our diversity. . . . It is not just the fact of a territory, of a piece of land. No. It's a lot of things. There are our ancestors, there are our dead, our history. We can't leave it. It's not so easy for many to understand, but this is the worldview [*cosmovision*] that we have from our base, our land, our fatherland [*patria*], and everything that surrounds us. And this is what was defended.

In their comments, Humberto and Virgilio establish a moral value around the land that cannot be conceived of in terms of monetary value, even as Humberto admits that in the beginning many people joined the Frente not because they thought they could stop the expropriation, but because they thought they would probably never be reimbursed for it. Humberto speaks of the expropriation decree as "expropriating us," not merely expropriating the land. His simple turn of phrase is a very common way to refer to the expropriation in Atenco and reveal the high stakes that people believed were at play. Many people were truly willing to be killed in confrontations with the police or spend the rest of their lives in prison rather than "be expropriated."

Virgilio makes this connection explicit through merging his thoughts of a mystical connection to land with a patriotic concern for Mexican history and the importance of land in constituting the pueblo of Mexico. For Virgilio, the decree would mean the end of the pueblo of Atenco. In Spanish, the word "pueblo" refers both to the physical place of the town and to the people who live there. The linguistic connection between these two conceptions is a hallmark of Mexican politics that reveals the importance of the connection between land and people. It is impossible to refer to a place without implying the people, and vice versa. It evokes a romanticized idea of rural Mexico and the earthy, genuine, honest people who live there. Virgilio elaborates on this connection in the Atenco/Texcoco region, which is also tied to the greatly diminished lake of Texcoco and its role in the history and myths of pre-Hispanic Mexico.

The spiritual and mythical bond between people and the land is a cliché of Latin American anthropology that is so pervasive that it has worked its way into racial stereotypes and the exoticism of indigenous peoples. However, in part because it is a cliché, it is also open for appropriation and continues to be a very real force in people's lives and economic activities. As our guide pointed out in the Atenco tour for the American college students, many people in the area had become deeply imbricated in a wage labor economy, became disillusioned with its instability, and returned to the land as a source of stability and moral connection. A cynical perspective might interpret the invocation of this mystical connection by nonindigenous populations as a shallow or instrumental political strategy. A more nuanced view might hold that even in cases in which the sentiment may be strategically deployed, the lack of continuity with indigenous traditions hardly disqualifies people not identifying as indigenous from using the idea to articulate a deeply felt connection to land and history.

One of the Frente's top priorities was opening lines of dialogue with government officials in order to get information about the airport project and how their lives would be affected. They sought to open this dialogue through presenting themselves physically in public spaces where they knew public officials would be because, as they saw it at least, there was no level of government that was conferring with locals about the expropriation. "We went to the offices [of government officials] so that they would see us . . . and arrive at a clean agreement," Humberto told me.

> But we never came to a clean agreement. None of the offices we went to opened to us. If we went in, we went in by force. . . . No one received us. No one. We went to the House of Representatives, and not one representative came out. All the parties that there are, and when they come to do their elections—they even go around looking at people's houses. They go around knocking [on doors] so that one will receive them and support them in their elections at election time. But when we had a problem and we went looking for them, not one party received us. We entered by force.

The extent to which the Frente went in order to establish communication with the government illustrates the extent of the physical and symbolic barriers between the Frente and state and federal governments. He refers to "them" and "their people," drawing a distinction between "pueblo" and "government." In Humberto's story, this abstraction is manifested in very concrete ways through the physical inaccessibility of the Senate and House of Representatives buildings. The degree of the inaccessibility to government process is apparent even while physically in the buildings of government. "There in San Lazaro [the federal government buildings]," he told me, "we entered the Senate by force. We entered just to tell them that they were a bunch of Santa Annas [traitors], that they had sold the country. And we left soon after because it didn't matter because there was no one to talk to. Who received us? No one." Humberto mentions that the only contact they have with their government representatives is during an election ("their elections"). Attempts to communicate with elected officials were blocked at every turn. The only dialogue that the Frente is able to achieve is in situations in which the Frente gains physical control of space or people important to commerce or the government.

According to Humberto, instead of sending someone to speak with them as the Frente requested, the state sent granaderos, a local word that refers to riot police, also referred to as "public force" (*fuerza pública*). They are special forces that can exist on the local, state, or federal level who wear black plastic body armor and clear plastic face shields, and carry long, clear plastic body shields. They are officially not allowed to carry guns. Instead, they carry billy clubs and tear gas. The federal granaderos, the PFP (Policia Federal Preventativa, or Preventative Federal Police), which has since been disbanded, often appeared with tanks specially designed for crowd control that were topped with water cannons. Humberto interprets the granaderos as an unnecessary escalation of violence on the part of the state that often impeded their peaceful marches to Mexico City. On the day they went to the House of Representatives, for example, Humberto told me, "We had to break the [police] fence to enter [Mexico City]." The police knew the direction that the march was going to take, and they tried to stop them or send them through another path in to the city from Atenco. "But when we got to the reference point," Humberto told me, "the granaderos were already waiting for us and didn't let us go. That was the first battle that we had in Mexico [DF]. We got a beating [*trompiza*]." He held up his hand to show me his souvenir from the battle. "There's my broken finger." Continuing, he said, "They got four compañeros [comrades or mates]. We recuperated them too. That same night we got them back."

It was this habit of breaking through police barriers, marching into police stations to get activists out of jail, and breaking into the offices of public officials that built a name for Atenco as a contentious social movement. They even refused to pay for the use of the toll road connecting Atenco to Mexico City. As many members of the Frente saw it, the very high tolls placed on the nation's main highways were measures meant to prevent everyday people from traveling the country and assembling against the government. They were yet another barrier that kept campesinos out of the public life of the nation. When commissions of the Frente were traveling as a group, instead of paying tolls someone would simply get out of the Frente's van or bus, yell "Paso Atenco" (Atenco pass) at the tollbooth operator, and push open the breakaway mechanism on the electric arm preventing cars from going through the booth. Although I witnessed this maneuver a handful of times, only once, at a tollbooth very far from Atenco, did I see any resistance on the part of the tollbooth operators. The Paso Atenco was especially utilized on the toll highway that connected Atenco to Mexico City because, as many people were fond of reminding me, that used to be their communal land before it was expropriated for the highway anyway, and so they had every right not to pay.

The defining contentious tactic of the Frente, however, were "retentions."[6] It was ultimately this kind of direct action for which members of the Frente were arrested in 2006 (even though the particular individuals arrested were probably not those who had been involved in the retention). In 2009, Humberto described to me one of the early retentions of workers who had come to physically survey the land and begin construction of the airport. When the Bulgarian contractor arrived, Humberto told me that people went to where they were working and told them, "We don't want you to work here because these lands are ours. The government never came to talk with us. There is no negotiation and no permission for you to work here. Go away, and don't come back." Humberto told me that they gave the workers two weeks to remove themselves. When they didn't he said, "we detained their machinery and we detained their employees." They asked the workers to call their boss to come and get them. When the Bulgarian boss arrived, "we detained him, and we said, 'We already told you to leave and you didn't want to leave. So your workers go, but you stay.'" According to Humberto, they held the Bulgarian official for three days, "with no more than the condition that they show us the plan, because we didn't have the plan of the airport that they were going to do." However, he explained, the plan always seemed to be in transit, but it always conveniently seemed to get lost. In the end, "as they saw that we didn't let him go, the third day the plan finally arrived and we saw what the airport was. What the government—the state and federal governments—were taking had a twenty-five kilometer radius! And the airport was only going to be 10 percent of this land. The rest was going to be La Ciudad Futura [the City of the Future, the name for a multifaceted development plan for the region]."

In this case, the Frente gained access to the Bulgarian contractor through retaining his employees, and they gained access to the government plans for the region by retaining the contractor. It is important to note that this retention, and many others that the Frente was involved in, opened lines of constructive, peaceful dialogue with various levels of government and created positive outcomes for the Frente. Additionally, not unlike the nineteenth-century English peasants of E. P. Thompson (scholarship that many Atenco activists have studied), the retention gave them access to something that they considered a commonsense right: in this case, access to the development plan for their land.

In another incident in July 2002, after the struggle had escalated significantly over eight months, a few visible members of the Frente were arrested in a political march. As a response, members of the Frente went to regional government offices and retained a number of officials whom they housed in the municipal auditorium in the center of Atenco for several days, demanding that activists be released. People erected barricades at the entrances of Atenco as police and armed forces surrounded the municipality, threatening to enter and take back the government officials by force. According to personal communications by people who were there, including a sympathetic reporter who was on the scene at the time, this standoff very nearly ended in multiple deaths. According to several first-person accounts, a middle-aged woman positioned herself at a gas station at the edge of town and threatened—with a lighter in one hand and a gas nozzle in the other—to blow herself up along with the town in order to prevent armed forces from taking Atenco. According to some members of the Frente stationed at the municipal auditorium, some activists were also prepared to kill the retained officials. Fortunately the state released the prisoners, causing the Frente to release their retained officials, and the crisis was averted.

The tactics of Paso Atenco, retaining officials, and breaking into congressional buildings by force have little respect for "normal" government processes. However, from the perspective of many members of the Frente, Humberto included, these "normal" processes have been set up precisely to exclude people like campesinos from using them. It is the closed door, the lack of communication, the tollbooth, or the government official with whom one can ever get an appointment that are the invisible "normal" processes of injustice and structural violence that the Frente has been struggling against. Through very practical and immediate confrontations, the Frente has a history of breaking through these physical and metaphorical barriers. What they have usually gained are the things normally ensured to middle- and upper-class Mexicans, although often accessed through paying a toll, a fine, bail, or a bribe: a meeting with an official, access to the public works plan, travel on a major thoroughfare, immediate release from prison.

Este Machete Sí Corta Cuero (This Machete Does Cut Leather/Skin)

There is no better representation of the forceful rural pragmatism with which the Frente faced their plight than the symbol that the Frente chose for itself: the machete. Everywhere that the Frente went (starting in 2001, but continuing into my fieldwork in 2009) members brought with them a set of machetes. In 2009, these machetes were a set of six or eight (very dull) blades with orange plastic handles and political slogans written on them (see Figure 1.3). They were kept in the Casa Ejidal along with painted banners, and brought along to political events to be handed out to representatives of the Frente. People marched in political demonstrations with these machetes raised in the air and danced with machetes during political events. Even at roundtable discussions and panel presentations, there were moments where the few representatives of the Frente raised machetes into the air from behind conference tables and podiums. As Humberto told me, "For us, the machete is a symbol that has won our battles" (see Figure 1.4).

He explained to me that the very first time the granaderos came to Atenco was in 1995 for the Sosa Texcoco strike and he commented then to Ignacio del Valle that if they all carried machetes, the granaderos would think twice about being so violent. He reported that Nacho said no because machetes are *armas blancas*, sharp weapons. "And it's true," he told me. "It is an arma blanca. But also, for us, it is a work implement. The campesino that doesn't have a machete is not a campesino." My dear friend Doña María reiterated this same sentiment to me, adding mischievously, "The campesino has to bring his machete. They say when they go to the fields, if a snake comes and doesn't do anything to you, you let it go. But if it attacks, you give it the machete."

Although the iteration of the Frente involved in the Sosa Texcoco strike did not adopt the machete as a symbol and defensive weapon, years later, Humberto was traveling for work, and he came upon a protest of sugarcane workers demonstrating for a raise outside of government buildings in the center of town. "And the poor things were all sitting there," he told me, "and all these people were carrying their machete because they are sugar workers. . . . They were there demonstrating, there sitting nicely, not yelling or anything." Humberto laughed, at their charming naïveté. This was clearly a story that he had told many, many times before. He approached one of the demonstrators and asked if a commission of workers had been admitted to the government building to negotiate yet. The man said that the officials wouldn't see them. "'Well, let's yell at them,' I said. 'We're going to yell, and with these machetes that everyone has, well, we can make a goddamn revolution, sons of bitches [*puede hacer una pinche*

Figure 1.3. Machetes being held in the air by protestors. Photo by Eneas De Troya.

Figure 1.4. Poster announcing a political march in 2009 featuring an ejidatario with a machete. Photo by Livia K. Stone.

revolución, cabrones].'" Humberto laughed as he continued with his story. "And we begin to yell and everything, and when the government president realized, he came out shortly. . . . That same day the situation was solved. They gave them a raise. . . . And that was when I came back here [to Atenco] with the machete."

The story is less revealing as an accurate historical record of how the Frente began using the machete as a key symbol than it is an anecdote that envisions the power of the machete as a political weapon and tool.[7] In Humberto's story, the difference between the workers getting paid more for their sugarcane and prices staying the same lay in a slightly more confrontational demonstration style. The single factor standing between the sugarcane workers and their raise was the degree of threat that they represented to government officials. Sitting quietly in the square with banners did not move the officials to even talk with them, but yelling with machetes almost immediately gave them an audience and a resolution to their complaints. As with the retentions, it is important to point out that the resolution was a peaceful one that still came about through dialogue and a compromise between the officials and the workers. Raising their machetes in the air enabled a meeting; they were not held to the throat of an official while the movement extorted money from him.

Increasing the degree of confrontation was very effective for the sugarcane workers in the anecdote and has been very effective for the Frente on numerous occasions in accomplishing specific, concrete goals. The Frente found that direct confrontation with a degree of threat (not to be confused with actual, physical violence) simply worked. As Doña María so succinctly articulated in her sentiment about snakes, holding a machete doesn't mean that you go out killing snakes, only that you will be prepared if one tries to attack you. Another activist told me in an interview, "The struggle that we have carried in San Salvador Atenco is a peaceful struggle. Where we proudly raise up our machete because our machete is clean. We have not killed anyone. We do not fire guns. With this we won, with the force of our pueblo." This strategy of what might be called "armed nonviolence" has been very effective.

However, armed nonviolence often seems to make the Frente's urban sympathizers very uncomfortable, to say nothing of their detractors. I came to Atenco after spending six months in Mexico City working primarily with urban film producers who were sympathetic to the Frente. Most of the filmmakers that I talked to commented to me that a significant challenge for the Frente has been the commercial media's representation of them, and their use of machetes, as violent. Violence, of course, is a tactic that in the Mexican context as well as the US context is often seen to unequivocally cast a social movement in a negative light.

As a way of countering this trend in news coverage, these urban supporters vehemently denied that the machete was in any way a weapon. They insisted that this was a misunderstanding and emphasized to me that the machete was a farm tool, nothing more. Their view was that negative portrayal in the media constructed the idea of the machete as a weapon, but that this was simply not true.

Arriving in Atenco, I expected people from the Frente to assert the same sentiment, that machetes are farm tools and not weapons. However, most people in Atenco found it the perfect symbol exactly *because* it was a weapon *as well as* a tool for farming. Their frustration came in the news media's insistence that because they carried a farm tool/weapon, they were violent. Unlike their urban sympathizers, members of the Frente did not see a necessary connection between carrying weapons and being violent. They insisted that yes, the machete is a weapon; yes, it is very useful in police confrontations; yes, its power as a symbol lies in its suggestion of force. But, at the same time, we are a peaceful movement, and the machete is a peaceful symbol.

The discrepancy between the idea of machetes as tools and as weapons seems to emerge as a discrepancy between how activists of the Frente saw campesinos in general and how a much more privileged middle or upper class saw them. After all, the machete is, above all else, a marker of rural, unmechanized agriculture. Even though the Comisariado Ejidal owns tractors and water trucks for any of its members to use, the force that ejidatarios told me that they want to convey is the force of a rural, undeveloped, and powerless pueblo of campesinos fighting with the meager tools available to them. The Frente carry machetes to communicate to onlookers that they are simple farmers using the tools available to them as weapons to fight oppression. The machete is a local equivalent to the hammer and sickle—the tools of an industrial worker and a farmer, respectively—of the communist or workers' parties. The local traditional crops of corn, beans, and nopales are harvested with a machete, not a sickle (which is largely a European farm tool). The evocation is deliberate and meant to convey a sense of rural, campesino authenticity and the moral authority invested in the reasonable demands of honest workers and peasants.

In political marches they also use the fireworks usually associated with religious celebrations and the small cannons, loaded only with gunpowder, that are used in local reenactments of the battle of Cinco de Mayo. These too are artifacts of their rural, semi-indigenous traditions that also happen to be quite forceful and impressive. In the streets between high-rises in Mexico City, the explosions and subsequent reverberations from either the *cuetes* (large bottle rockets) or cannons can set off every car alarm on a city block. The cuetes at one time have also served as a kind of public address or warning system, different numbers of explosions in quick succession conveying distinct messages to activists (see Figure 1.5).

Although impressive, they argue, fireworks, toy cannons, and machetes have insurmountable disadvantages as weapons of brute force. The police have full body armor, billy clubs, plastic shields, tear gas guns, rubber bullets, tanks that shoot corrosive mixtures of water and acid at high pressures, helicopters, and, although they don't frequently use them, automatic weapons. Even unarmed officials that the Frente has confronted (both government workers and employees working for large multinational corporations) have the capacity to mobilize these forces through government channels. Against this kind of power and these weapons, machetes are merely a symbolic suggestion of force. They are little more effective than a rock picked up on the street. To Humberto and many others, the beauty of the machete as a weapon and as a tool is that it is really impossible to do much damage with it. If rules, regulations, timetables, secretaries, and meetings are effective weapons of bureaucrats because they are outside of the cultural milieu of campesinos, machetes are effective weapons because they are outside of the cultural milieu of bureaucrats.

The discrepancy between how members of the Frente see campesinos and a normative middle- or upper-class vision of campesinos, however, is that even this weak suggestion of force is too much power. A US audience might be more familiar with the use of pitchforks as a stereotypical dangerous weapon of rural mob justice. Pitchforks may seem dangerous and scary if you have never wielded one yourself. If, however, you work with a pitchfork every day to move hay or manure, it hardly seems like a weapon at all. The real threat that symbols like pitchforks and machetes evoke is the disruption of a social order that equates campesinos with powerlessness and disenfranchisement. It is the disruptive capacity of rurality in a public sphere where farm implements are not usually carried. This is a threat that is much more impactful than the idea of a cut across the arm. It is this symbolic disruptive capacity of machetes that makes them a threat much beyond their physical capacity to do any damage against bodies or property.

This symbolic disruption affects the political Left and Right equally, but in slightly different ways. The political Right, of course, can imply outright that campesinos are violent, anachronistic, irrational criminals who should be stopped at all costs before they destroy the progress that Mexico is making on the world stage. The elite political Left, however, also needs campesinos to be powerless in order to use their helplessness to justify its own political rule:

Figure 1.5. Ejidatario with cuetes for a political demonstration. Photo by Livia K. Stone.

social welfare programs, literacy campaigns, and so on. It is one thing to romanticize the idea of an old woman with a machete as a consumable symbol of rural authenticity. It is quite another for her to swear at you while waving her machete and demand that you leave her alone and pick up your trash on the way out.[8] If you are not accustomed to having your social superiority go unrecognized, you may feel that there has been some violence against you even though there was no harm done and her demands are quite reasonable.

If machetes are seen as tools exclusively, they are nonthreatening because they don't disrupt a social order in which campesinos are weak and backward. They ask nothing of the state or a political elite; they simply wait quietly until they are replaced with the seemingly superior technology of global corporate capitalism. Machetes used as weapons are quite threatening because they imply campesinos are not weak. A few slices through the air proves quite easily that this ancient technology is a match for at least the plastic shields and body armor of the granaderos, themselves symbols of a modern technological state. Members of the Frente can see machetes as both tools and weapons without contradiction because they don't conceive of themselves as weak and backward (and perhaps refuse to believe that many of their urban sympathizers see them that way). They also know that machetes are very useful, sometimes more useful than combines and guns. It is much easier to chop off a snake's head than shoot it in the head (this is not a metaphor), and combines are useless for harvesting some very useful crops like nopales. If you use a machete on a daily basis, you know that there is little difference between using the machete to clear a path to your field, using it to harvest your crop, using it to kill a chicken for dinner, and using it to kill the occasional snake. For an ejidatario there is no difference between weapons and tools.

Victory over the Expropriation Decree

By the time the expropriation decree was abrogated in July 2002, the vast majority of members of the Frente were engaged in some form of criminal prosecution. This meant that a significant percentage of the population of residents from Atenco and the surrounding communities were facing small criminal charges and had to appear in court on a regular basis. So many people were facing charges that the paperwork to process them overwhelmed regional bureaucratic offices, and the governor had to issue a blanket amnesty. However, the dual experiences of frequently engaging in face-to-face confrontations with police in political marches and having to navigate the complex and often obscure pathways of the

Mexican legal justice system permanently altered many people's opinions of the utility and efficacy of legal pathways, and the legitimacy of laws in general. This deep mistrust of government and legal pathways significantly altered how Atenco's political system functioned in years to come.

The success of the Frente was unprecedented among Mexican social movements. For the last decade, I have regularly asked people—ejidatarios, middle-class residents of Mexico City, colleagues at the national university, and activists from other social movements—why the Frente was successful. Urban Mexicans not associated with the Frente tended to tell me that in 2002, Mexico's very first democratically elected president was very fresh, had been in office for only a year, and maybe thought that Mexico could turn over a new leaf by accommodating the Frente. Others say that he was set up by a competing party, the PRI, to lose and start his six-year term with a humiliating loss.

A man I call Ramón, a relatively wealthy resident of Atenco with an advanced degree and a member of the Frente, told me how important he thought the Frente's two legal battles were. The first was attempting to get an *amparo*, a legal action that would have stopped the expropriation on the grounds that it violated the rights of the ejidatarios. The second was a case arguing that the expropriation decree violated the rights of the local government, or represented a "constitutional conflict" (*controversia constitutional*) of sovereignty between the federal and local governments.

> The federal government knew that it was losing the legal battle on two fronts: with the appeal [*aparo*], on which the right was on our side, and with the constitutional conflict. Alongside the force of the people doing the [social] movements . . . all this made the force. But definitely, the head of the spear are the movements. . . . It wasn't just one thing. It was various things that acted together. . . . Legally they were losing. . . . It seems there that the limited time that the court had to rule on the controversy was about to expire. This day, the court had to give a resolution. And there was every indication to show that this resolution was favorable to us, the inhabitants of Atenco. It would have been horrible for a local government to win a court case against the federal government. It would have been shameful. . . . And so the other recourse that federal government had, the honorable recourse that they had, was to take down the decree.

For Ramón, the Frente won through legal processes, but social movement pressure was necessary in order to assure the success of these legal pathways. In turn, the legal challenges facilitated official processes that could have the appearance of being independent from popular opposition through the movement.

In contrast to Ramón, the vast majority of people I spoke with in the Frente told me that the federal government abrogated the expropriation decree because of virtues such as honesty, solidarity, and dedication among the people of Atenco in their struggle. One woman, the wife of an activist who played little part in the Frente until her husband was incarcerated, told me that the Frente won because of its history organizing and the honesty and ideals of its organizers. Another woman told me, "First, as humans, as individuals, as a society, we were a brotherhood [*coyuntura de hermandad*]." She added, "We have very strong traditions here where we are accustomed to have solidarity." A third activist emphasized the "social fabric" (*tejido social*) through which "together we learned to walk . . . together. Very together." One man told me that they won because the people were firm in their decision and never rested: "The struggle was permanent. Day and night." He elaborated that there are many activists who, in the moment that they achieve dialogue with the government, "submit, or the government subjugates them with money and handouts and robs them of their intention. They rob them of their dignity." In Atenco, he explained to me, "many have been the example of [what] each Mexican should be: they are ready to give their liberty, their life, to risk everything for justice." Another man told me, "There was never a moment in which our people gave in. There was never a moment that the people buckled under the pressure of the government or the interests of the businesses that tried to corrupt our leaders [*dirigentes*]."

Such high-minded rhetoric is easily either passed over as meaningless by critical scholars or elevated and romanticized by those looking for what Mauricio Tenorio-Trillo (2012) has called the "Brown Atlantis" of Mexican authenticity. In either case, it is difficult to take seriously the idea of virtue as something that has real-world political consequences. One might be able to show how having lots of virtuous solidarity is helpful, but a comparative analysis of social movements, or even common sense, will easily show that social movements are not rewarded to the degree that their activists are virtuous. It is much easier to point toward the legal actions Ramón cites, or the intrigue among political parties. It seems much more likely that people revert to such idealistic speeches because they are what they think a foreign sympathizer like myself would want to hear, or because the events were too complex and incomprehensible to know for sure why the Frente won. Perhaps it doesn't even matter, or there is no answer to the question. As Ramón points out, there were numerous factors at play, including many that I haven't mentioned. Dialogue with the government opened up shortly after the very publicized death of an ejidatario who had been recently released from police custody, for example. Even so, there is no reason to discount such high-mindedness as meaningless, disingenuous, or invented for my benefit. I have recorded hundreds of hours of such speeches delivered in very public forums to crowds in which I was one of two or three foreigners. The emphasis on virtue was certainly not just for my benefit. I also have no doubt of speakers' depth of feeling. Several of the above quotes were delivered with such forceful emotion that both of us had tears in our eyes. I will argue in Chapter 3 that discussions of virtue, and particularly the virtues of solidarity, togetherness, and selflessness, are very important to understanding the Frente's struggles against powerful economic and political forces. It may be true that the state does not confer favors on the virtuous as a benevolent god, and yet, as I will argue, ideas of virtue and ethical practice are central to the Frente's views of and struggles against neoliberalism. They should be taken seriously.

Another important backdrop to the Frente's victory was its very public nature. The ejidatarios from Atenco were front-page national news for months. They traveled all over the country on solidarity visits and to ask for help from other social movement networks. They mobilized international global social justice supporters through their contacts with Zapatista activists in Chiapas. And there were a few feature-length independent documentaries produced about their struggle before the decree was abrogated that were actively circulated locally, nationally, and internationally among social movement networks. These documentaries were sold at political marches, handed on DVD to friends and contacts who copied and passed them on to their friends and contacts. They were also uploaded to burgeoning Internet video platforms.

Implicit in activist claims that the virtues of solidarity, dedication, and selflessness helped them strike down the expropriation decree is the fact that millions of people in Mexico City, throughout Mexico, and to a limited extent through transnational social movement networks, could *see* them being virtuous. Furthermore, government officials could see the Frente's political allies seeing them be virtuous. Machetes meant that this virtue was by no means unchallenged, even within their own supporters, but among the complex reasons that the Frente was successful lay their visibility, and the near excess of media production and circulation that enveloped and passed through the Frente. It is to the production and circulation of these videos that I turn in the next chapter.

Most of the people involved in the Frente, which in 2002 meant a significant portion of the local population in the Atenco area, went back to their normal lives after the expropriation decree was abrogated. They had won back their land, and there seemed to be no more reason to be involved in the movement. However, rather than disbanding and giving up the significant political influence that it had built, the Frente (made up of an ever-changing group of people who came in and out of serious activism) became an almost institutionalized local political force. The *mesa de diálogo*, or negotiation forum, opened between the state government and the Frente to settle the airport dispute effectively superseded the official municipal government as the premiere governing body of Atenco, leading one activist and scholar of the Frente to call it a parallel municipal power (Camacho-Gúzman 2008, 228–31). Local government found it very difficult to do anything that the Frente's activists disapproved of, and the Frente became a powerful intermediary for people in the surrounding area. When a real estate developer began building condominiums on what they felt was communal land in a neighboring community, for example, the Frente stepped in to broker a deal and prevent the development. (One activist from the neighboring town told me that they had planned on simply killing the developer before they met with Ignacio del Valle.) The Frente also continued to travel and support other social movements in other parts of the country. They were invited on solidarity trips to visit anti–corporate capitalist social movements in Australia, South Africa, and Canada, and throughout Europe. In addition to the two films already in existence, four more films about the Frente were made in this new era (2002–2006) celebrating its successes and serving as introductions to potential allies who had no knowledge of it previously. It is to the production and circulation practices of the three filmmakers of these six films that I now turn.

CHAPTER TWO

Cameras, Surveillance, and Ethical Practice

Video is like a new machete.... Video can be used as a weapon to defend oneself or as an instrument of construction or creation.
—Paco Vásquez, indigenous media coordinator (as quoted in Köhler 2004, 402, my translation)

In his exploration of how video is used in the Zapatista autonomous communities, Köhler (2004) quotes an indigenous media maker likening their use of machetes as both weapons and tools to their use of cameras in political conflict. "Video," he argues, "sometimes functions as a defensive weapon. The simple fact that indigenous people appear with cameras in situations of conflict have limited the actions of potential aggressors" (2004, my translation).[1] Much like their indigenous counterparts in Chiapas, the Frente has purposefully and successfully wielded cameras as well as machetes. While their urban allies found machetes problematic, but often wielded cameras with reckless abandon, most members of the Frente found machetes to be harmless and video cameras to be powerful and deeply problematic. Unlike machetes, cameras have a double edge. As in the case of the autonomous communities in Chiapas, the presence of cameras was productively unnerving to police and government officials, but rather than protecting activists, filmmakers often faced violence or intimidation by what Lynn Stephen has called Mexico's "sophisticated intelligence apparatus" (2002, 318). The images that filmmakers create can also be co-opted and weaponized against activists who appear in them. They can become intelligence working against activists as well as state officials.

The perceived power and importance of films to the movement, coupled with the delicacy of their possible use by authorities, also invited intense scrutiny from within the movement and among other politically committed filmmakers. Fellow filmmakers, professionally trained in film criticism, offered sometimes-brutal assessments of the quality and effectiveness of the works of their peers, cultivating lifelong animosities and rivalries between professionals who

Cameras, Surveillance, and Ethical Practice | 61

Figure 2.1. Poster showing cameras used as weapons. The poster advertises an activist festival of independent media in memory of Brad Will, an independent US journalist killed in Oaxaca in 2006.

otherwise have very similar political commitments. Fellow activists also endlessly and passionately debated tactics, strategy, and ideology in relation to the production and circulation of films.

In this chapter, I examine the activism of three Atenco filmmakers: Eduardo Ríos (a pseudonym), Salvador Díaz Sánchez, and Greg Berger.[2] Each of these filmmakers is the central figure of a small filmmaking team that produced two films each about the airport struggle. Their combined total of six films all came out in 2002. These three filmmakers represent the first phase of Frente activism over the airport struggle, and they also represent the concentric circles of activism around the Frente that formed during that early period: Ríos is a self-taught videographer and member of the Frente from Atenco who was directly affected by the expropriation decree; Díaz is an award-winning, professionally trained filmmaker and activist from the larger Atenco area; and Berger is a professionally trained filmmaker and activist from the United States. Each attempted to use filmmaking and film circulation as activist practices in solidarity with (or from within) the Frente. Each confronted significant censure from both their activist peers and the state for their activism, and each developed a unique vision of ethical filmmaking practice as a result. Woven throughout each of their accounts of their film activism are multiple and sometimes-conflicting vectors of surveillance, sometimes mobilized by filmmakers and sometimes mobilized against them. Enmeshed in their accounts are also multiple ways that they envision activist filmmaking to work as effective activism and as an ethical practice.

Of course, just because filmmakers say that their films work in a certain way doesn't mean that they do. One of the reasons that I moved to Atenco from Mexico City in 2009 was that I came to suspect that filmmakers had a distorted view of how important or influential their films were. Most scholarship on activist filmmaking is concentrated on celebrating the medium, its potential, and its effectiveness, measured in formal legal change. However, often there is very little evidence to demonstrate activist filmmaking as a very effective instrument of formal social change, at the same time that films do much more than just help win or lose instrumental battles with the state. Film production and circulation take a long time and have many other consequences that are equally important in the lives of the people involved.[3] Working together on a film can create lifetime friendships and political partnerships that long outlast the specific goals of a particular movement. Facing down a camera lens can scare a government official into opening a door even if the recording is never seen by anyone. Even if a film is seen by very few people, the experience of making and attempting to circulate a film might change the political commitments of its producers. These are also ways that cameras work as tools and weapons that emerge in the way that filmmakers discuss their production and circulation practices.

Foucauldian conceptions of surveillance and discipline, which emphasize how the specter of being watched curtails unethical behavior, are at the center of how activist filmmakers imagine cameras to work as political weapons (see Figure 2.1). However, these Foucauldian conceptions are ultimately inadequate to describe the multiple directions of surveillance and multiple ethical regimes that activist filmmakers are subject to and are attempting to create in their activism. Unlike Foucault's version of the state as using an all-seeing panopticon that forces the surveilled to self-police, the reality of camera surveillance for activists with the Frente is multidirectional. Cameras focus on both activists and state agents, often without regard to who is holding them. Footage recorded by an activist can be used against another activist as readily as footage recorded by a police officer. The context of activism also means that people on both sides of a camera (state agents on one and activists on the other) are often unwilling to allow themselves to be disciplined, giving rise to very complex and unpredictable relationships with surveillance attempts.

The surveillance that cameras represent has an uncertain relationship with any mechanism of disciplinary punishment when in the hands of either activists or state agents. In other words, the consequences of being surveilled are unclear and inconsistent. A casual observer might think that the surveillance of activists surely would have direct consequences, even death or imprisonment. This is certainly true in some circumstances.[4] However, in the case of the Frente, there is not much evidence to suggest that surveillance has had a direct relationship to individual disciplinary consequences. It is unclear if this is a purposeful state strategy to scare citizens away from even approaching becoming involved in the Frente, or simple incompetence. In either case, the effect has been a general atmosphere of fear and uncertainty that falls outside of the precise intelligence and discipline that accompanies Foucauldian techniques of surveillance. As in most parts of the world, the consequences of videos capturing state agents misbehaving are even more uncertain. Although consequences are possible through courts or simple public opinion, they are unreliable.

The uncertain consequences of surveillance don't mean that cameras are any less powerful, only that the power of cameras is unknown and unhinged from the real-world uses they are put to. This allows people's internalization and self-disciplinary techniques to wander significantly and vary wildly from person to person in efforts to avoid physical violence or personal consequences. People never know exactly what might work. This context of uncertainty makes clear that the political power of cameras is much more dependent on the political cultures of visibility and the presence of political structures that are prepared to deliver consequences than they are on the technological capabilities of cameras themselves to make something visible. Although perhaps obvious, this point is important to make in a world in which excitement over technology leads activists and scholars alike to fetishize technology.

One aspect of these cultural and social contexts of cameras in the Mexican case emerges as the much more significant technique of surveillance for activist filmmakers: processes of censure within activist communities about appropriate production and circulation practices. This social policing (unlike state policing) was swift, precise, and accurate and had meaningful consequences for how activist filmmakers developed their production and circulation activities as a form of ethical activist practice and how they transformed themselves into ethical activist filmmakers.

Finally, one might surmise that the subject-forming projects of the state and activists should work at cross-purposes, that fear of the state works to create subjects who are not willing to challenge its authority, and activists work to create subjects who are more capable of doing just that. Instead, it seems that these two forces work in concert to produce subjects who prize the same set of virtues surrounding selflessness. Rather than directly oppositional, selflessness seems virtuous to all parties, but as I argue in the next chapter, it is deeply subversive of liberal and neoliberal politics.

Eduardo Ríos: Filmmaking from within the Frente

I first met Ríos at the press conference that launched the Libertad y Justicia para Atenco campaign that called for the release of the Frente's political prisoners in 2009. I came up to him because he and another man were recording the proceedings with a small digital camcorder. After the press conference, as he was packing up his camera equipment, I asked if I could talk with him about how he saw the role of independent media in the new campaign. He leaned on a tripod casually as he spoke to me, in a remarkably open way considering it was our first time meeting, while his partner packed up and came in and out of the conversation.

I quickly realized that Ríos was from Atenco and had been recording the activities of the Frente since 2001. He was there at the news conference as part of the official communications commission of the new campaign whose responsibilities included creating multimedia communications on behalf of the Frente. He and his wife own a small video business in Atenco.[5] Their videos are compilations of events edited with music and graphics, with no commentary and only occasional titles to lead the viewer through the action. They are more video photo albums than documentaries, and people hire them as one might hire a wedding photographer—so that friends and family members can have a professionally produced video of an important event. They also record community festivals such as Carnival and sell the compilations to people who would like to remember the festivities. When Ríos sets up his stall, often projecting a recent video on a large screen at night, one can buy the video not only of this year's celebration, but often of the celebrations of years past.

At our initial conversation at the press conference, Ríos told me that when the movement began in 2001, he and his wife, then with small children, made a conscious decision to be a part of the movement. As they made their living making videos, they felt they could contribute to the movement:

> First, [I recorded] as an observer. It was to observe, to see, spend time with [*convivir*], and participate. I wasn't comfortable anywhere because I'm not an orator. I can chat for hours and hours, but I'm not a speaker with a microphone

or—even less if there are a lot of people. However, I did video. So in some commissions that were formed—[let's say] a commission has to be formed to go and protect the north point of the ejido, for example. So I went with my video camera to record. I began in a way, consciously or unconsciously, to support in what I knew how to do. Or what I try to do. That is to record with a totally amateur [*casera*] little video camera, because the resources don't allow [anything more professional]. However, we tried to give the activities that they do in the demonstrations the focus that we do in the fiestas. And in this way, little by little, I was collecting images.... And I was [part of] nine months of resistance with the Frente.

Although Ríos was not used to doing feature-length documentaries, he helped produce a film chronicling the airport struggle that was released in 2002 after the decree was abrogated called *La tierra no se vende, se ama y se defiende* (Land is not for selling, it is for loving and defending, Frente de Pueblos en Defensa de la Tierra, 2002). It is the only feature-length documentary to be signed as a production of the Frente itself. The film is a compilation of televised news reports spliced together in chronological order with footage taken of marches and demonstrations in the community. There is no voiceover narration other than the newscasters' narrations, although the action is often punctuated with written titles that supplement the (not always positive) narration of the newscasters. Much like a commemorative video of a party or event, the emphasis in the film is on a chronology and including a lot of material rather than providing a unique vision or analysis of events. There is no constructed climax or narrative arc to the film other than the simple chronology.

His primary audience, much like the primary audience of his videos of community events, was made up of the people of the Frente themselves. He told me "people wanted to see how they had participated in this successful struggle. And the people bought it." In other words, the emphasis in the film is not on providing analysis, articulating a unique vision of the Frente, or allowing the audience to see the events in a new way. Instead, people watched the video to see themselves, friends, and family members on screen, much how one would watch the videos of local festivities. It was an added thrill to see the reproduction of news broadcasts—"Look! There we are on the news!" Not many people recorded these broadcasts, and so to have them on DVD to rewatch and show was a special treat. I frequently asked people what their favorite Atenco films were, and people from the Atenco area almost without exception told me that they preferred *La tierra no se vende, se ama y se defiende*, although very rarely could someone tell me the title of the film. Mostly it was simply referred to as "the one from Atenco," the Frente's own film, or the film of Ríos and his wife.

Ríos also helped produce a unique multimedia CD with another local artist, Cayo Vicente. Cayo Vicente is a musician and poet who wrote numerous songs about the Frente during the airport struggle and was called on by the movement to perform at political events. He continued to perform political songs and poetry at plantones and political marches into 2009, and selling his CDs while he wasn't on stage. ¿Qué hicimos? ¡Vencimos! (2002) (What did we do? We triumphed!) is primarily a music CD that will work in a standard CD player, with alternating tracks of poetry and songs, all of which are about the Frente and the airport struggle or social movements in general. However, if put in a computer, there is the option to listen to the music while watching a compilation of still imagery and video that Ríos produced. It is something between a visual music video and home movies with a professionally produced soundtrack.[6]

The visual emphasis of ¿Qué hicimos? ¡Vencimos! is on illustrating the continuity between the local, cultural festivities of Atenco and the social movement. This is Ríos's own description of what he was trying to do visually in these pieces, and the visual connection is undeniable in the finished product. A consistent theme throughout is images of large numbers of people moving forward through the streets of Atenco dancing in parades and traditional costumes, fading into large numbers of people moving forward through the streets of Mexico City with banners and chanting slogans in political marches. The small cannons used as noisemakers to commemorate local celebrations meld with the same cannons used during protests in Mexico City. Images of men and women dancing in couples to folk music, advancing and retreating against one another flirtatiously, dissolve into images of protestors and police "dancing" together as they advance and retreat against one another menacingly. These images are an excellent companion to the soundtrack, in which Vicente sets political lyrics (sometimes entirely made up of common protest chants) to the tunes of local folk music. The effect is a portrayal of a unified community that deeply values its traditions and draws on them as a form of political practice. The traditions, treated uncritically as a naturalized part of community life, seem to teach the participants how to act to create change, even as the change is celebrated as a way of enriching the traditions.

Ríos told me that for him and his wife, filmmaking was a way to participate in the movement and contribute their particular skills in the struggle against the airport. Ríos also describes the process as deeply transformative for him.

We made the decision, my wife and I, to participate, because in the end, we were doing it with our family. Our children. Our future. Not us as people, but [as] the generations that would lose everything [if the land were expropriated]. So, we took the clear and conscious decision that we also ran a high risk. We decided that if the shit hits the fan [*si nos caiga la chingada*]—well, what can we do? We are doing something for the community. And this is more valuable. So you realize—you get a consciousness. A consciousness. I didn't even participate in the clean water assemblies [before]. I didn't participate in anything. I was simply another spectator. But, in the struggle [*lucha*] itself, in the nine months of resistance, it gives you a consciousness [*te llevaron una conciencia*], every day you are discovering another Mexico, when testimonies begin to arrive of people who have been dispossessed [*despojados*], maltreated, murdered in other parts of the country, or in the world. So this surprises you and raises interest, and you get more and more involved [*te vas clavando, clavando*]. When you realize, you are no longer the quiet, mute spectator that recorded video; you become in some way a protagonist of the film too, of course, from my point of work, which is to record video.

Ríos describes a process in which he made a conscious decision to participate in the Frente with full knowledge of the very high stakes of doing so. On the one hand was the potential loss of the community lands, and on the other the potential for incredible violence against him and his family because of their participation. In the process of participating, he describes an incredible transformation from passivity to action, from spectatorship to participation, from lack of consciousness to political consciousness.

One of the remarkable things about Ríos's description of his motivations for participating in the Frente is his emphasis on a particular ethics of activism. This high level of ethical commitment is a very important part of how activist filmmakers allied with the Frente discuss their production and circulation practices. Ríos was speaking more than seven years after he made a decision to participate in the Frente and in the context of only very recently taking up his camera for the Frente again after a few years of dormancy. His explanation of selflessness and lack of personal benefit from recording is very purposeful and has to be understood in terms of gossip and censure he faced from inside the Frente that questioned his motivations for recording so much of the Frente's activities with very few products. The implication of the rumors was that he could have been passing on his recordings to intelligence agencies or other government officials, or he might be selling the footage to officials or local factions who were against the goals of the Frente. Either action would mean that he was literally or figuratively "selling" the Frente to benefit himself. As a result, he is careful to frame his participation as a videographer and member of the Frente as a selfless act meant to benefit the entire community and even future generations of Atenquenses. He wanted me to know that he did not get involved in the Frente even to save land for himself and his own livelihood, but for his children, "the community," and future generations. He insists that they did not participate in the movement "as people," but merely as representatives of generations to come.

In our 2009 interview, the things that the communication commission were doing differently this time were at the forefront of his mind. He told me, "We try to synthesize the essence of the event and publish it immediately . . . and now not commit the error of 2001 and 2002 to keep everything." This "flow" of information was important so that people didn't think that they are hoarding footage for some nefarious purpose. The internal gossip and censure that he experienced from his fellow activists in the Frente resulted in changed production and circulation practices as he became involved in the next wave of Frente activism. He portrays his activism as setting a virtuous intention and then being transformed by his experiences participating in the Frente. His particular emphasis, which is widely shared, and that I discuss more fully in the next chapter, is the emphasis on selflessness and collectivity.

In part, this discursive emphasis on virtue, specifically the virtue of selflessness, is because filmmaking is a particularly fraught means of participating in a contentious anti–corporate capitalist social movement in Mexico. Even if one is caught on camera doing nothing more than walking in a march, histories and fears of social movement repression in Mexico (like many places) mean that innocence is no guarantee that one will be spared from police violence or intimidation. These suspicions or fears are heightened in the context of direct actions that may be prosecutable. A long and healthy tradition of commercial filmmaking in Mexico also means that it is possible that anyone with a camera will eventually make money selling the story of the movement, effectively appropriating and benefiting from the hard-won struggles of people who will see none of the monetary proceeds of the resulting film. Being behind the camera is as dangerous as being in front of it, as it is difficult to be an anonymous face in a crowd while holding a video camera to the eye, and anything that attracts the individual attention of police and state officials might identify activists as "leaders," or at least individuals of interest. This means that activist filmmakers, more than most rank-and-file members of a social movement, attract increased scrutiny from both their peers and their enemies.

Another significant error that Ríos felt he had committed was putting his name on ¿Qué hicimos? ¡Vencimos! He did not put his name on *La tierra no se vende, se ama y se defiende*. The only credits of the film were attributed to the Frente de Pueblos en Defensa de la Tierra, the thirteen affected communities of the expropriation decree, and the people who were killed in the struggle over the airport. In retrospect, Ríos felt that by putting his name on the multimedia CD, he made himself visible as an individual in the movement and opened himself up as a target for state violence.

Ríos's emphasis on selflessness recognizes and accepts the possibility of deep sacrifices and violence as a result of his participation in the Frente. The idea of "the shit hitting the fan" was not an idle supposition, but a real and painful consequence of his activism. During the repression in 2006 the police entered his home and pulled out everyone staying there, including his wife's elderly parents. He believes that he was being punished because of his involvement in the movement as a videographer, and it is clear from his story below that the police knew who he was and how he contributed to the movement.

> They went to the house and from there they took [everyone] out. . . . They take me, my father-in-law, my brother-in-law, my mother-in-law. And they tortured all of us. . . . An individual of the public force takes me [*me sujeta*] by the collar and says . . . "Now [Eduardo], you're not going to record." And I said, "No, I think that I'm not going to record now." And it begins to make him laugh. . . . [The officer] comes, and he says, "This is the one who records videos, boss. He records the videos." They interrogated me. And they stop the camera—because they were recording. They raise your face, and you have to answer what they ask. If you don't answer, they hit you. So I was saying that yes, I recorded videos. And, "Oh yeah?" They stopped the camera, "wait" and pom-pom, they hit me, and the next time they say, "Suffer. Suffer, so that you learn the camera well." [*Se pena, se pena, para que sabe bien de la camara*]. . . . We believe [they ransacked the house] more in the tone of looting than as a strategy of intelligence to see what I had. . . . They robbed money, jewelry, bracelets, half of the—things like that. Money. They took two cameras, one a still camera, computer memory, a hard drive.

Revealed in Ríos's narrative is the complexity of the power of visibility and the presence of the camera. The attacking police reversed the direction of the camera toward the filmmaker, joking that he wouldn't record that day and pointing a camera at his face as they questioned him. They were careful to turn off the camera while actually hitting him in an attempt to erase their physical violence and record only his submission. As Ríos describes them and his torture, the police felt that the camera was a weapon, one that they had felt was used against them in the past, and were relishing the opportunity to use against someone who had recorded them.

Much of the excited writing about the political potentials of grassroots media often seems to forget that cameras, like any other weapon, can be wielded by the state as well as activists. In the hands of the state, cameras are instruments of state surveillance. Iconic images from Chiapas in the 1990s show soldiers emerging from the tops of military tanks, not with firearms (although those were also in plentiful supply), but with video cameras, recording the faces of people in Zapatista communities. Lynn Stephen has described these convoys as "human machines" that "extend a very slow, deliberate, and intimidating gaze over the community" (2002, 200). Similarly, as illustrated in the epigraph of this chapter, indigenous videographers in Zapatista communities in the late 1990s famously used video cameras to record the incursion of military forces and to provide some safety from violent repression under the idea that if the military committed atrocities, they would be captured on camera to be distributed to international supporters. The result are images of a military convoy slowly rolling down a road pointing cameras at the indigenous videographers who are in turn pointing cameras back toward the tanks (see Figure 2.2).[7]

I witnessed the same mutual recording phenomenon in Frente political marches in 2008 and 2009 with cell phone cameras. It was during the brief period of time after cell phone cameras were becoming a standard feature and before smart phones. Activists opened flip phones and pointed them at police, and police did likewise from behind their plastic shields. I was on the receiving end of this surveillance once when I traveled to a political event on the official bus of the Frente. When rolling up to the tollbooth of a commercial highway, a few people came off the bus to implement "Paso Atenco" (as I describe in Chapter 1), but because this was a highway not often traveled by convoys of the Frente, they were not so easily let through the tollbooth without paying. The confrontation came to blows between the few police officers manning the tollbooth and the few people who came off the bus to push open the gate. Sitting near the back of the bus, I was only barely aware of what was going on when suddenly there was a rush of people—men and women, Atenco residents, and foreign activists—who rushed off the bus to overwhelm the few meager traffic police. Wanting to see what was going on, I leaned forward to peer out the bus window, only to look directly into the lens of a camera phone held by an official in a yellow polo shirt. The middle-aged woman who had been sleepily sitting in

Figure 2.2. Still from *Zapatistas: Crónica de una rebelión* (La Jornada and Canalseisdejulio 2003).

the aisle seat next to me the entire voyage suddenly leaned over me to hang out the window and yell abuse at the man taking photos that he had no right to take our picture. The confrontation was quickly over, with no apparent injuries on either side, and the woman next to me pulled her upper body back into the bus as it rolled through the tollbooth.

It is easy to imagine that the image of my face framed in the bus window (along with numerous other images that have undoubtedly been taken of me with the Frente) was forwarded to a supervisor who added it to intelligence files with mounting information about the activities of activists. Although it is incredibly intimidating to be recorded in this way, there is very little evidence in the Atenco case to show that the state effectively uses such images. It might seem to be wishful thinking for Ríos to mention that he felt the police were not going to use the footage that they took from his house against the Frente. However, his comment could also have been based on Ríos's years of experience witnessing how military and police intelligence played out in Atenco. He may have noticed, as I have noticed, that if police are in the habit of processing such images or video in some way, they are spectacularly bad at implementing any intelligence that they gather from them.

The forces that entered Atenco in 2006 certainly seemed to know who Ríos was. However, if they were after the most engaged or militant activists, they missed their mark with him. With relatively few exceptions, people from Atenco told me that in 2006 the police charged the wrong people for the wrong acts of civil disobedience and in general kept people in prison who had nothing to do with the Frente. Throughout the history of the Frente, excepting a few very visible activists who could be identified by any newspaper article about the movement, it seemed that those who faced the most severe police violence were actually not active members of the Frente at all. It is within the realm of possibility, of course, that this is a purposeful misapplication of justice on the part of the state, or that collective fictions circulate locally about police violence in order to claim innocence for those accused of crimes. However, it is unclear why either of these alternate explanations should be the case. Why would it be in the state's best interest to demonstrate how bad its intelligence is? And why would people circulate fictions about not participating in some acts of civil disobedience if they are equally free with admitting alternate acts that also might come with legal consequences? The much more simple explanation is that while the "strategy of intimidation" (Stephen 2002, 318) against some social movements in Mexico was still very much in place in the 2000s, in a context of legal impunity, the state simply didn't need very specific information in order to intimidate. In fact, it could be argued that consistently hurting people who were only very marginal to the movement could encourage people to stay as far away from the Frente as possible.

Based on multiple conversations I have had with Ríos over the years, his conception of state intelligence combines an idea that the state knows everything that goes on in Atenco with the idea that it doesn't really matter who does what because police violence isn't a precision disciplinary tool. For example, his clear preference is to remain anonymous in publications about the Frente, but he claims that using a pseudonym doesn't provide any protection for him because, as he has told me multiple times when I asked him about the ethics of including him in this book, "they already know everything." However, he also has a keen awareness that lack of participation in the Frente does not provide any security either. His in-laws, after all, were not members of the Frente and yet faced severe consequences for their mere presence in his house in 2006.

One of the main reasons that Ríos was singled out as a videographer became clearer to me when we discussed his torture again in 2014. By then, even though the Frente lived on and continued to fight against renewed plans for an international airport, Ríos and his wife were no longer politically active in the Frente. When I asked why, Ríos was vague and cited personal complications. He and his wife still sat with me and a few other people in his storefront in Atenco, however, and discussed how he saw the roles of their videos in the struggle. At one point, I asked him about his torture in 2006, and in his retelling, he said that the police wanted him to say on camera that he was recording video on the orders of Ignacio del Valle and was ordered to give all his footage to del Valle. He laughed uncomfortably at the absurdity of the accusation.

Anyone with even a passing acquaintance with the Frente would know that Ignacio del Valle did not give orders and would not be interested in surveillance tapes of police. Perhaps the police knew this and wanted to extract a false confession to make it easier to convict del Valle as an orchestrator and instigator of violence. Either way, the attempt to force an on-camera confession showed that they were not interested in factual or precise intelligence, but merely a blunt instrument of repressing the Frente in general and imprisoning the Frente's inspirational leaders and organizers. They simply didn't need surveillance images because the context of impunity obviated the need for precise allegations. When using such a blunt disciplinary instrument as repressive violence, the focus of that violence does not need to be accurate. It is quite possible, for example, that Ríos and his wife stopped participating in the Frente under a combination of continued state intimidation and family pressures not to put everyone in danger.

This same context of impunity has meant that the activist recordings of police violence and human rights abuses also have done very little toward disciplining police and political officials responsible for horrific violence. Images of abuses and testimonies of abuses were admitted to the Inter-American Commission on Human Rights (IACHR) and the Mexican Supreme Court cases having to do with human rights violations in 2006. Although the Mexican Supreme Court did officially rule in 2010 that human rights abuses had been committed, they also ruled that it was impossible to tell who was at fault because the individual police officers committing acts of violence had their faces covered. By 2015, the IACHR had issued a report classifying the case as "admissible" and conducting a hearing to assess the merits of the case before sending it on to the Inter-American Court. The Mexican state has made several overtures to the women bringing the case against it, but they have refused any friendly settlement, and the case is still pending judgment in 2018 (Díaz 2013, García Martínez 2016). In this way, the Atenco case contradicts the assumption that digital media and the ubiquity of recording technology has a natural relationship to providing accountability for state agents. Accountability in this case was thwarted by the very rudimentary technologies of facemasks, a code of silence, and labyrinthine legal processes.

Formal legal processes are not the only mechanisms of justice that matter, of course. There is also the de facto justice of the dominant popular narrative of events, or even simply a strong alternative narrative. Ríos's films have probably been crucial to building a collective local narrative in Atenco of what happened during the airport battle and beyond. And this narrative might ultimately be among the most important consequences of his films. However, the relationship between public opinion and specific works is incredibly messy and difficult to establish. Ríos's works are only one thread in an exceptionally complex matrix of personal experiences, oral histories, commercial news reports, alternate readings of commercial news reports, and the dozens of alternative media representations published about the same events. Although it seems obvious that widely viewed activist films have played some role in convicting the Mexican state of human rights abuses in the de facto court of public opinion, the role of these films in this process is ultimately unknowable.

A more clear consequence of Ríos's recordings is similar to the power of machetes that I described in the previous chapter. I argued that machetes are a powerful symbol because they invoke an idea of campesino authenticity holding their government accountable. I argue here that like machetes, cameras are also a powerful symbolic weapon because they invoke an idea of holding government accountable, even in circumstances in which there are no effective structures in place to enforce accountability. Police and government officials certainly feel this threat of surveillance and accountability in the moment that they have cameras pointed at them, even though they have every reason to believe that such images will have very few consequences. Video has no inherent political power because of its capacity to produce images and sound. The political power of cameras lies in how important people believe it to be, a power that is independent of its capacity to produce images. We should be wary of the technological fetishism that can overtake popular and scholarly discussions of technology and social change. In the end, the only one to suffer consequences was the man behind the camera and his family.

Greg Berger: International Solidarity

If activists and filmmakers can be seen to occupy widening concentric circles around Atenco, Greg Berger occupies the outermost ring. His connection to Atenco lies exclusively in the Frente's place in a transnational network of social movements organizing against unwanted development projects around the world. I first met Greg Berger in his home in 2007 and interviewed him about his personal journey through filmmaking. He came to Mexico many years ago as an adult, in part because he wanted to leave the United States and in part because he was drawn to Mexico as a place with an exciting political culture of social movements:

> I think that even though I had been vaguely [a] political activist all my life, . . . I think that when I came to Mexico [it] was the first time that I saw—that I got excited, not by resistance to a crappy system in which we live, but actually the most creative solutions and alternatives that I'd ever seen. So politically, I was very excited about staying down here. And the more I wanted to stay down here, the more I wanted to make films about what's going on.[8]

We didn't speak in-depth about his two films about Atenco, *Atenco: ¡Tierra sí, aviones no! / Atenco: Land, Yes! Airplanes, No!* and *Atenco: La rebelión de los machetes / Atenco: The Machete Rebellion*), until 2008, six years after they both came out. He was in Mexico City for the day, and we recorded the interview at night while sitting in his car, parked on a residential street outside a mutual friend's apartment. Berger is an energetic and animated speaker and sometimes hit his hands on the roof and against the windows of the car as we spoke to emphasize his points. The two Atenco films that he made with the assistance of a few other Mexican filmmakers were the first films that I saw about the airport struggle, in part because they are the most accessible films to a US audience in their audiovisual language and in their free online distribution method, and because they have very good English subtitles. However, I never met anyone in Atenco, other than Ignacio del Valle himself, who told me that they had seen Berger's films or remember them.

Remaining among an outer, transnational ring of activists and sympathizers was not Berger's aim when making these two films. When asked in 2008 about how he became involved with the Frente, Berger told me, "I certainly felt identified with the people of Atenco, and I believed in their struggle. And from the very outset the intent was to essentially embed ourselves with the people from Atenco." This production practice fit with how he conceived of the usefulness of filmmaking as a political project: "A lot of what successful community-based documentary does is provide a mirror for a community to see itself, not as they themselves would make a portrait of themselves, but perhaps through the eyes of others, and what others see in them highlights things that perhaps they themselves did not see in themselves. And therefore it is a useful and powerful mirror that then becomes reflected back at that community."

Even though the Frente and the people of Atenco themselves were a primary audience of the films, Berger's team made efforts to screen their films to other communities throughout Mexico and the United States in an attempt to inspire people to organize against unwanted development projects such as the airport. Berger explained to me the importance of the case of Atenco for this extended network of social movements:

> After Atenco there were all sorts of projects that were opposed, and all sorts of people around Mexico were emboldened by the Frente, which is part of the reason why they were repressed in 2006. But all sorts of local struggles throughout Mexico were emboldened by the Atenco victory. And we traveled all around Mexico showing ¡*Tierra sí, aviones no!* and *The Machete Rebellion* in different towns. . . . We used it as, you could say, an organizing tool, but also as a cheerleading device to convince people that you can organize and you can fight, and you can win.

In contrast with Ríos's activism, which was very focused on recording as activist practice, Berger's emphasis is on the final product, the film, as a powerful text. Although the cameras of Berger's film crew were often pointed at agents of the state in marches and events, the bulk of their original camerawork was recording the words, opinions, and stories of the everyday activists of the Frente. One of the hallmarks of Berger's films, in contrast to those of the other two film crews I discuss in this chapter, is that they are beautifully shot, contemplative interviews with residents of Atenco about the importance of their struggle and how they conceived of the issues at hand (see Figure 2.3). Berger and his colleagues were not as concerned with holding state officials accountable with their films as they were with the potential of their films to help organize other social movements. In our multiple discussions, Berger did not use language about the camera being a weapon to accomplish specific political gains, only the final products being a tool and "cheerleading device" for general social and political organizing. This literal as well as metaphorical gaze of the camera meant, in part, that the issue of surveillance, either attempting to surveil state agents or being surveilled by the state, was not as pronounced in the case of Berger's two films.

In terms of state censure for his activism, Berger was not even living in the same state as Atenco for the 2006 repression. More significant than his location was probably his lack of participation in the Frente. Although he made these films, he was never an active participant in the Frente's activism. As he is a foreigner, it is illegal for him to protest against the government.[9] If any of his activities are ever deemed protesting against the Mexican state, he could be deported and prevented from returning to Mexico for five years.

Figure 2.3. Still from *Atenco: ¡Tierra sí, aviones no! / Atenco: Land, Yes! Airplanes, No!* (Berger 2002a).

This law could be seen to make him particularly vulnerable to state censure. It certainly is very much on the minds of foreigners who have significant contact with Mexican social movements (myself included). It seems likely that the specter of deportation has made him cautious as to his production practices as well as the content of his films so that he will not have to face the kind of state censure that Ríos has. However, his US citizenship could also provide him a certain level of protection from violence, as friends and contacts told me that my US citizenship did. Perhaps he could be the victim of police violence or be deported, but if he were, it might also cause an international incident that would draw the direct attention of the US government and human rights agencies. The deportation of a US filmmaker, a professional journalist simply making a film about events in Mexico, might look very bad for the Mexican government's relationship to the freedom of press. On the other hand, at least one foreign filmmaker, the Chilean film student Valentina Palma Novoa, was arrested and deported in the repression in 2006 for being on the scene (Palma Novoa 2006). A government official also killed an independent journalist from the United States, Brad Will, in a confrontation in Oaxaca in 2006.[10] Neither case created an international incident. Perhaps also because of this provision, his Atenco documentaries, while clearly sympathetic to the Frente, do not make a specific call to action or make any specific denunciation of any level of Mexican government. They simply record the words and actions of members of the Frente. Most of his films since this time period are involved with Mexican politics but almost without exception are critical of the role of the US government, multinational corporations, and even international journalists in Mexican politics.

As successful as Berger's Atenco films might have been on a national and international level to inspire and help organize other social movements, things didn't go quite as he had envisioned on the local level in Atenco. In 2008 he told me about the unexpected barriers to his model of community-based documentary:

> The funny thing was that first we made *¡Tierra sí, aviones no!*, which only went up to December, so it was only the first two or three months of the struggle. And when we finished it, I still didn't really have a personal relationship with anybody from Atenco. The funny thing is that a very horrible thing happened to us, and that horrible thing actually set into motion a series of events which made my relationship with the people of Atenco much more personal. And it is a relationship that continues to this day. What happened was [the other filmmakers on the project] were able to convince someone . . . basically from the PRD to make *multicopias*, a whole bunch of copies [of the film]. So when they did that, unfortunately what they did was that they took the master, without our permission, [and] they inserted the PRD logo. . . . And they put the PRD logo all over the boxes. . . . And without our permission, they went ahead to Atenco with all of these boxes of tapes. And they started distributing them, and Nacho and América and Trini [Nacho's daughter and wife, respectively] and a whole bunch of other people basically seized them and said that they couldn't distribute them. And so when we got there, they were really pissed at us already and we were confused because we didn't know that this had happened. . . . And so we were kind of—I wouldn't say detained—but we were asked to come talk with them for a while. And on the one hand it was great because that was the first time that we really had a long heart-to-heart discussion with some of the main players in the Frente de Pueblos en Defensa de la Tierra.

Berger and his crewmates had a very difficult, serious conversation with people from the Frente because they were careless about how they distributed the film. The Frente had no relationship with Berger, and the film had no official status with the Frente at all. However, it was a film that communicated the messages of the Frente, and used images and interviews with local people who identified as part of the Frente. Most people, when seeing the film, would assume that the Frente collaborated with the PRD (Partido Revolucionario Democrático or the Democratic Revolutionary Party), a center-left political party, to make this film. That was a problem for a few reasons.

First, the PRD was not substantially supporting the Frente locally and were actually one of the political apparatuses calling for the airport. Putting their logo on the film would be taking credit for a popular position that they did not support. When asked why they would want to take credit for a position that they didn't take, Berger invoked a long-standing tradition of demonstrating political effectiveness through public works: "The PRD is filled with these operatives who advance in the political machinery by the kind of measurable works—kind of public works that they are able to achieve. Really for this schmuck who made all these copies of the film, it was just the same as paving a street. It was just one thing that he could stick a feather in his cap to try to get a higher rank—a higher position within the PRD framework." Second, according to Berger the problem with the PRD logo was not just a pragmatic political issue, but an ethical one having to do with political parties in general in Mexico: "It's the way that the parties operate. I mean they—the PRD—is all about appropriating social movements, and it always has been, right? It's about appropriating the authentic work that others do and trying to make it part of a corporate entity, essentially the PRD. That's what they do. [At the time] I just didn't know enough about the PRD." It was, in part, through the process of making and distributing his film that Berger became better acquainted with the intricacies of the PRD and local politics. What initially seemed devastating, however, turned into one of the best experiences of doing the film:

> It led to some good conversations with the people in Atenco, and personally it was the first time that this—"I mean, what the fuck are you doing here anyway? You're a gringo." And what it really did is that it started a much more intimate level of discussion with those guys and started a long road to friendship that continues now, and is particularly painful now because this person that I care about [Ignacio del Valle] is serving a life sentence in jail.

In other words, through making this film and, in particular, making a significant mistake, Berger came to hone his production and circulation practices and to become a more ethical activist filmmaker. Much like Ríos, he set out to make films about Atenco with politically virtuous although possibly naïve intentions, and he faced internal censure for his practices. Instead of causing a severing of his ties with the Frente, however, Berger's mistake only brought him closer to the movement and to a more intimate understanding of its struggles. Much like Ríos learned from a process of internal policing of his production and circulation practices, Berger also conceives of this process of internal censure as helping him become a less naïve, more effective, and more ethical activist filmmaker.

Although Ríos and Berger have two very distinct visions of the power of recorded images and sound as well as two distinct sets of production and circulation practices, both were held to a local ethical standard of activist practice in which personal gain (through personal career advancement, monetary gain, or even personal political power) was subordinated to ideas of a selfless commitment to collectivity. Furthermore, association with political parties, even on the seemingly superficial level of financing an otherwise sympathetic and helpful documentary, was considered a serious breach of this ethical standard. This is a topic that I will take up in more detail in the next chapter.

Salvador Díaz Sánchez and Odette Castelao: Militant Filmmaking

In the concentric circles of activism that have spiraled out of Atenco, Salvador Díaz and Odette Castelao of Producciones Klan Destino occupied a ring that is between the outer orbit of Greg Berger and the inner orbit of Eduardo Ríos. Díaz is from a small town in the Atenco area but has spent most of his adult life living in the nearby small city of Texcoco. Castelao, his domestic and filmmaking partner, is from Texcoco proper. Díaz teaches journalism classes at a local agricultural university (Universidad de Chapingo) and various classes at a local high school. In 2009 he was completing a PhD in rural development, arguing in his dissertation that the camera could be used as a research tool. During my time in Atenco I was frequently in their house while Díaz edited video or for numerous parties, two events that often overlapped. During the long hours at political events and marches with the Frente, I often found myself walking, chatting, and eating with Díaz, Castelao, and their fifteen-year-old daughter, Doro. José Alonso Martinez, a twenty-year-old former student of Díaz's who helped him record and edit video, was also frequently with them during this time period and was considered another member of the family. Although Díaz is the director and editor of his films, Castelao and Martinez recorded the vast majority of the footage in his films. Díaz described his political pedigree to me in 2008:

> I entered [film school] after studying [for] an undergraduate degree [*licenciatura*] in journalism and collective communication in the Department of Political and Social Sciences in the UNAM [National Autonomous University of Mexico]. While I was doing my thesis and supporting leftist

movements—unions, especially peasant [*campesino*] movements—I heard the announcement of the film school on the radio. So I went to register. Because my idea, half joking, half seriously, is to say, "I want to make the revolution, and film is a medium to make the revolution." I still think it.... The second year I did a film that is called *El edén bajo el fusil* [Eden under the gun].... In *El edén bajo el fusil*, I solidify many of my political aspirations because as a boy I wanted to be a guerrilla fighter [*guerrillero*]. I wanted to change the world with the rifle [*fusil*] and all of that. But I could never connect myself. I lived here in a pueblo, in Texcoco. I was a campesino, and I didn't have any contacts. But there in Guerrero, where the meaning of *El edén bajo el fusil* is, I find myself with diverse campesino movements: coco workers, coffee workers ... and especially the guerrilleros.

Although his boyhood dreams may have been to become a guerrilla, his career aspirations soon turned toward more mainstream political activities. Returning to Texcoco, he ran for political office several times in various left-of-center parties, including the PRD, and began to teach university and high school journalism courses. Between 1985 and 2001, Díaz was involved in the production of only two film projects. Díaz did not return to filmmaking in earnest until the availability of digital video and desktop editing software. He admitted that although he would have liked to make more films between the time that he graduated from the CUEC in the mid-1980s and his first purchase of an iMac computer in 2001, he simply didn't have the economic resources to make it feasible. In 2008, he prided himself on his productivity and the speed with which he could finish a film on his Mac.

When asked about his current or recent projects in 2008, Díaz listed a dizzying series of projects, some of which were produced in only a few days for very specific purposes, with titles such as *Las andanzas del sátrapa* (The adventures of the despot), *El divino llantar* (The divine weeping), *De luto visten los heroes* (Heroes dress for mourning), *Rojas estampas de la dulce montaña* (Red impressions of the sweet mountain), and *La vida en el alambre* (Life on the wire).[11] In July 2008, he boasted that he had made four films in the last six months. Some of these films were political in nature, and these he signed under the name Producciones Klan Destino, a pun meaning Clandestine Productions or Clan Destiny Productions and an allusion to a Manu Chao song about clandestine Mexican immigration to the United States. His more irreverent (or in his words, his "light" productions) he signs under the (intentionally misspelled) name Producciones Sal de Ubas (Alka-Seltzer Productions).

As can be seen by his titles, Díaz favors heavily poetic narrations, sometimes written in fantastically obscure literary Spanish. His usual process is to immerse himself in the topic, record as much as possible, and then sit down to write a script. Using his poetic narration as a guide, he pieces together the visuals of the film, articulating his ornate and philosophical verbal metaphors with local recorded imagery. Unlike that of Ríos, Díaz's process is deeply interpretive and analytical. Very much like Ríos, however, he has a deep appreciation for the history, culture, and nationalistic symbols of Mexico and the Atenco region. He delights in imagery of old campesino men and women, men drinking and singing, bullfighters, children, and agricultural landscapes.

Although he sees his work in classically Marxist terms of making a revolution through film by helping people develop revolutionary consciousness, he does not conceptualize the messages of his films as working through a logical appeal to ideas of justice or moral indignation. Instead, Díaz characterizes his work as resulting from a deeply emotional process that he hopes inspires emotions in his audience. "And I, obviously, when I am here [in my house] I am crying too when I am editing. With Atenco—[sighs heavily] the tears—the tears that—really—many, many. This is [political] commitment too. I was like this frequently [sniffing and wiping his cheeks and eyes], and the kids [who watched the film] were the same. It is this too. It is the possibility that your emotions flow into the documentary."

Díaz's purchase of an iMac and digital video camera in 2001 coincided with the expropriation decree in Atenco, and he began to record the movement from its earliest days. Castelao also began to record in 2001 and became a constant presence in the movement with her camera. Together, Díaz and Castelao combine the visions of activism of Ríos and Berger. Castelao, as the cameraperson recording confrontations between the Frente and state agents, conceives of her film activism much more in terms of the power of the camera, as does Ríos. Díaz, as the editor and director of their team, conceives of his activism much more in terms of the finished films, as does Berger.

Although nearly all the other filmmakers included in this research tend to see the adjectives "radical" and "militant" as pejorative, or at least detractors' attempts at deprecation, Díaz and Castelao see these adjectives as not only positive, but necessary. They are very proud to make radical militant films and strive to be ever more militant in their processes and political positions. In another interview in 2009, I asked Díaz what the characteristics that make a film militant are:

That you convert yourself into another member of the organization, even when it is circumstantial [*coyuntural*]. But that your commitment sympathizes with those of the organization. . . . So yes, taking sides [*tomar partido*]. But not the side of a political party. To take the side of an organization, for the people who fight, the people from below [*de abajo*]. . . . Everything that I want to do is build [*armar*] or try to wake up the consciousness of people. That's what it is. Someone who is not militant, they don't care [*le vale*]. They don't care if it reaches [the audience] or not. What they are interested in is making money [*sacar feria*], to do another one, and be applauded. . . . If I didn't believe in this, maybe I would dedicate myself to charging money [*sacar feria*] here and there. And go around looking for grants and things.

This passage reveals Díaz's conception of his filmmaking practice as positioned between two different kinds of actors: campesinos like Eduardo Ríos who are fighting for their own livelihoods, and professional filmmakers who are sympathetic, but who are also using their films to advance their careers.[12] As he is neither an insider nor an outsider, filmmaking allows Díaz to personally become "another member of the organization" and "take sides" in a partisan way as an activist in the Frente even though his family's land was not affected and he is no longer a campesino. Unlike a career filmmaker, however, and much like Ríos and Berger, Díaz claims that his target audience is made up of potential local activists, not outside consumers and film critics. If he were making the film for critical recognition or to be a commercial success, his efforts would ultimately be about his own career and less about the Frente and their struggles. He would effectively be using the movement to advance his own career as a filmmaker rather than using his unique skills to the benefit of the movement. In this way, he calls into question the political commitment and the utility of independent filmmakers who enter their films into film festival competitions and seek out grants to fund their projects. This kind of filmmaker, who presents work at festivals and seeks the recognition of other filmmakers, is not militant.

Instead, Díaz is incredibly proud that his films have been used as a "calling card" for the Frente. In an article he wrote for a university publication in 2006, giving a testimony of the production of his first Atenco film, Díaz wrote, "*La rebelión de los fulgores* served a very important didactic function; it served as promotion when the Frente motivated compañeros from other parts of the country; it was sold in many solidarity meetings, in encounters with other organizations, and soon I had to do a new edition of five hundred more copies [after the initial five hundred]. By the end of the movement twelve hundred copies had sold" (Díaz Sánchez 2006, 368, my translation).

Díaz does not consider selling some copies of the film to the Frente to be making money for himself because he sold them "almost at cost" (Díaz Sánchez 2006, 368), and the Frente turned around to sell them for slightly more. Díaz's vision of his finished films is very much like the realization of the community-based organizing model that Berger envisioned when he first began making films about Atenco. Díaz gave his film to the Frente to do what they liked with it, and the film became a valuable organizing tool for the Frente, publishing their view of the issues at hand and convincing people to get involved with the movement.

In contrast to Díaz's emphasis on the finished films, Castelao describes herself in those early years of the airport struggle as "the cameraperson of the movement." She remembers traveling everywhere with the Frente, sometimes beyond her comfort level. Castelao holds a university degree in chemistry, so using the camera was a new experience for her, but it was also a pleasant one. Unlike Díaz, Castelao told me that she doubts anyone changes their mind (or heart) because of a documentary, but she did describe the camera as a weapon that is very useful and necessary. She described a moment in which other activists brought her into the chambers of a judge who they had forced an audience with in order to record the interaction:

> They put me in the offices of the judges with the camera. If I hadn't have had a camera, they would have taken me out. But they [the judges] were mad; they said, "Don't record." And I recorded. Like it was a weapon. . . . I enter with a camera, it was to bother them, to show them that we weren't afraid of them, and that we are going to denounce, and that we are denouncing all their atrocities and unjust trespasses [*atropellos*]. . . . You asked me before if some people think that it changed their way of thinking and they joined the movement. No. But I forgot to tell you this: that it is a weapon. And yes they felt threatened by the denunciation of these documents. This is very important.

As they had in the presence of machetes, Castelao believed that the authorities felt threatened by the camera in an immediate situation because it showed the Frente didn't accept their authority and because of a belief that the camera could expose them. They may have even felt threatened by the resulting documentation of some of their behavior. However, Castelao does not mention anything about third parties, either international supporters or Mexican institutions using the images to convict or hold authorities accountable for their behavior. The only power in the camera, according to Castelao, comes down to the internal fears of authorities that the camera had the capacity to reveal the truth of their behavior.

Like Ríos, Díaz has come under some public scrutiny for his films, activism, and political commitments. Much like Berger, Díaz also ran into internal problems because of connections to the PRD. As he describes in the article cited above, *La rebelión de los fulgores* began as a project for a "radical faction" of the PRD who paid him a small sum to do a five-minute piece on Atenco for television. The resulting hour-long documentary was not exactly what they had in mind, but it still carried a credit at the end of the film that the PRD helped to support the project. Citing this credit, some members of the Frente initially rejected the film because of its association with a political party (Díaz Sánchez 2006, 366). And while Berger and his colleagues could perhaps claim naïveté when it came to the particularities of local politics, Díaz could not. He had even run for local office as a representative of the PRD. Even so, his relationship with the party was a complex one that had changed significantly over time as the party itself changed. According to his official account, when he arrived in Atenco to make *La rebelión de los fulgores*, someone asked him, "Are you still in the PRD?" He quotes himself as responding, "No, they're such *maricones* [wimps or faggots] that they don't go in for this kind of thing" (Díaz Sánchez 2006, 345). According to Díaz, although some people had their reservations about his work, his more complex relationship with the PRD ultimately did not prevent the Frente from using his film extensively. It probably helped that the mention of the PRD was hidden as a small line in the final credits of the film rather than a logo on every frame in the bottom corner, as was the product that Berger attempted to distribute initially in Atenco.

His relationship with the PRD wasn't the only issue with Díaz's activism. When asked their opinion of his films, some members of the Frente told me that his narration is overly poetic and interpretive, turning the collective performance of the movement into his individual creative expression. Others mentioned to me that it seemed suspicious to them that although Díaz had been at the scene of many violent incidents, police had never arrested or beaten him. The implication was that if he hasn't suffered physical consequences (as Ríos and his family have) then he must have been working for someone with power or informing on the movement.

All these accusations upset Díaz deeply, but he had a slightly different relationship to internal censure than did Berger and Ríos. He told me emphatically that his activism and ideals have not changed at all since he was a young man. However, he does justify his activist practice according to the same standards of activist practice that Berger and Ríos discuss as having helped them be more virtuous activists. He argues, for example, that his narrations are not meant to draw attention to his abilities and education, but to tug at the heartstrings of the viewer and celebrate the Frente. He believes that putting his name on films and running for office gives him a level of protection against violent police action because as a public figure the state has more to risk through punishing him. In short, he argues that he is visible as an individual because he is a professional, but he uses his profession entirely as a militant practice to promote the best interests of the movement. He does not sell his films, submit them to film festivals, attempt to distribute them commercially, or even seek to copyright them. He argues that he has always chosen a commitment to leftist social movements over personal recognition.

As evidence, he cited to me an occasion in October 2006 (after the May repression) when he was subpoenaed to appear in court and testify that he had made a specific documentary about the Frente. The documentary that they were interested in recorded specific acts of civil disobedience from four years previously, in 2002. According to Díaz, in this documentary was footage that could have incriminated some activists, but in order for the film to be admissible in court as evidence, the filmmaker had to appear and vouch for the documentary. If Díaz claimed the film as his own, it could be used as evidence and people might go to prison. Appearing with a lawyer and risking being held in contempt of court, he refused to vouch for the documentary. The case ended well in that Díaz was not held in contempt of court, and the documentary was not used as evidence. However, the case also had a chilling effect on him and his views of production. He felt that part of the reason he was called to testify was to show him that he was being monitored. He also learned that although he believed he was working with the Frente and in the Frente's best interests, his documentaries could have negative and unintended consequences. Although he continues to produce prolifically, he has not made a documentary about the Frente since.

Although people recounted to me many fond memories of Castelao's presence in Frente marches and political events well in to 2006, I never heard any censure of her recording practices, nor did she ever mention to me being the target of censure within the Frente. She was the target of intimidation by state agents, however. Much like Ríos, Castelao felt that authorities had singled her out because she had been seen recording. She had a warrant out for her arrest at the same time as Ignacio del Valle for her role in the movement, although in her case she spent only a few hours in jail. She turned herself in when a family member in local government told her that there was a warrant against her.

During her few hours in jail, an official tried to scare her into no longer recording through impressing on her how dangerous it was, but she was almost immediately released.

The difference in consequences for Ríos and for Díaz and Castelao, both as fairly active members of the Frente, is painfully class based. Díaz and Castelao are both middle-class professionals who live in the nearby small city of Texcoco, not in the more rural setting of Atenco. They have close ties to formal political parties and government officials. Castelao has close family members not only in the PRD, but also in the PRI. Díaz had been a local party member and candidate himself. Instead of blows to the head, they were disciplined with warrants, subpoenas, and court appearances that ultimately didn't result in jail time. (Ríos was not in jail for any significant period of time either.) Even so, Díaz and Castelao take it for granted that their actions are constantly monitored, and they must constantly regulate their actions and behavior so as not to be the object of violence.

Díaz and Castelao were also both as convinced as Ríos that the police were monitoring them. They believed in 2009 that their telephones were tapped and their activities monitored, in part as an intimidation tactic to curtail their continued activism. Castelao also believes that there was someone set to watch their house at all times in 2006. She said that they sometimes purposefully revealed themselves through shining a light from a field across from their house at night to intimidate them. She was scared enough during this time that she tried to keep away from windows and off of their roof patio for months. Although she tried not to allow the intimidation to curtail her activities, it seemed clear to me throughout our conversations that like many people who experienced the repression of 2006, she struggled significantly with fears of state violence. Castelao definitely changed her behavior as a result of state intimidation, but not her filmmaking practices.

Surveillance, Discipline, and Filmmaking

On the surface, the two distinct processes of policing filmmakers—the literal policing of the state, and the more figurative policing of community ethics among fellow activists—seem to follow a classically Foucauldian pattern. Through surveillance (or at least the suggestion of surveillance) and the threat of violence, the state disciplines its subjects to not speak out against it and counter its authority. Also the peers of activist filmmakers enforce community norms of behavior and selfhood through gossip and name-calling. Although operating on very different scales and for very different purposes, both are implicated in processes of creating and enforcing social norms.

However, the case of the Atenco filmmakers complicates this model in a few significant ways. First, there are multiple, and sometimes contradictory, vectors of surveillance, none of which have reliable mechanisms to produce consequences for transgressions. Rather, the effect, if not the structure of the Mexican state has been much more similar to how Foucault characterizes European penal practices prior to the eighteenth century: a "theater of terror" whose purpose is not to punish individual infractions, but to reassert the "unrestrained presence of the sovereign" (1977, 49).

Secondly, while Foucauldian surveillance is directed solely at subjects of the state, the surveillance I observed in Atenco is multidirectional. While the state attempts to discipline its citizens through surveillance, citizens (activist filmmakers) are attempting to discipline the state through surveillance. There is also a great deal of unintentional surveillance in that activists fear that footage meant to work for the movement will actually end up working against them.

Third, because the activists and the state are at odds, one might assume that the subject-forming projects that both are involved in would also work at cross-purposes. Instead, it seems that these two forces work in concert to produce subjects who strive for selflessness, horizontality, and anonymity. If the movement is leaderless, the state cannot identify individuals for punishment, and fellow activists cannot criticize them for being selfish.

Together, these complications cast into doubt any strict relationship between the power of cameras as a political weapon, either for the purposes of activists or the state. In other words, we need not fetishize cameras as either sinister devices that allow the state to overreach its authority into people's lives, or saviors that will hold state agents (police, officials) accountable for their actions. Both are much more dependent on the political and social cultures and structures surrounding cameras than they are on the technological capabilities of cameras themselves.

Ultimately, of course, Foucault's model suggests that the point of surveillance and the way that it is conceived as a disciplinary mechanism is that one internalizes the idea that one will be punished for misbehaving and might be surveilled at any moment and so always behaves. The nature or existence of the punishment quickly becomes irrelevant as subjects come to police their own actions. However, the context of activism changes the internalization of surveillance significantly. Activism is precisely the idea of challenging the political, social, and cultural norms against which people are supposed to be held. The whole point is to not allow oneself to internalize normalizing codes, but to challenge them. In this context, the actual physical consequences do matter because activists are consistently engaged in a process of weighing their activities meant to pose challenges against the possible risks of doing so. Simply allowing oneself to be disciplined and behaving oneself is not an option. However, because disciplinary punishment is so uncertain in the Mexican case, it is incredibly difficult for activists to predict the consequences of their activism and rationally weigh the possible consequences. The result is a fear of surveillance, but a fear that is detached from any sense that one's actions have consequences. Why not throw Molotov cocktails if one will probably not be prosecuted for it and might just as easily face physical violence for demonstrating peacefully?

In the case of citizen surveillance of the state, the possible consequences are equally unpredictable. It is unclear who holds the power to enforce disciplinary measures against the state. Is it the state itself, which can root out its own inconsistencies and injustices? Is it the body politic that votes out the criminal officials or demands that unjust laws be reformed? Is it international networks of leftist social movements that demand their own governments pressure the Mexican state? In any case, the government official in his office or the military policeman behind his barricade has no way of knowing for sure what the consequences might be when confronted with a delegation of machete- and camera-wielding activists. This isn't all bad for activist filmmakers. The uncertainty may work in the best interests of activist filmmakers, for example, if officials or police officers react to them above and beyond their real-world capacity to hold people accountable for their actions.

The 2015–2016 US cases of videos capturing police violence against African Americans is an excellent example of the uncertain relationship between surveillance and consequences. Of the cases of police officers caught on video killing unarmed black men that emerged (Eric Garner, Tamir Rice, Walter Lamar Scott, and Philando Castile, among others), most of these videos show very clearly what happened, and yet police officers have very rarely faced legal consequences for killing citizens. Even more rare are legal strategies that hold supervisors, training, law enforcement cultures, or other structural considerations at fault instead of the individual officers in frame. In other words, the power of the camera to make visible and the fact of surveillance is not in itself a politically powerful weapon. The videos are a very exciting change and may very well have played an important role in solidifying the Black Lives Matter movement, but they have had very few disciplinary consequences for police. There have to be social mechanisms in place that deliver consequences.

While the government's haphazard disciplining makes it hard for activist filmmakers to predict consequences from the state, fellow activists provide the much more direct and reliable source of consequences for particular activist filmmaking practices deemed unacceptable. In the cases of Ríos, Berger, and Díaz and Castelao, these pressures mostly surrounded ideas of selflessness: using films to aid the Frente without drawing attention to themselves, not benefiting personally from their film activism, or benefiting or not a particular political party. Rather than the movement or the state being disciplined by camera surveillance, it is the camera, with its single lens and individual cameraperson, that is disciplined into being a collective instrument.

It would seem to make sense for activist social pressures to be in opposition to the forces of state discipline that activists also faced. Oddly, however, the poor aim of state violence and legal action only served to enhance activist filmmakers' commitment to selflessness and collectivity in order to avoid state surveillance.[13] This commitment to selflessness and collectivity was quite varied, however: Salvador Díaz's conception of selflessly giving his films to the movement was quite different from Eduardo Rio's, whose conception differed from Greg Berger's. Their conceptions of how to avoid state censure through selflessness also varied. Although the community norms about virtuous activist filmmaking practice were at times inconsistent, they did follow a pattern of ethical activist practice that is roughly related to policing ideas of *protagonismo* (grandstanding or egoism) in leftist social movements in Mexico more generally. It is to a more in-depth examination of this concept and ethical activist practice that I now turn.

CHAPTER THREE

Compañeros and Protagonismo

In 2012, a decade after most of the events in the previous chapter, students at La Universidad Iberoamericana, a prominent private university in Mexico City, began a campaign called #YoSoy132 against the frontrunner in the national presidential election, Enrique Peña Nieto.[1] Shortly after Peña Nieto won the election, the movement went through a reorganizing and restrategizing period. During this time, only a few days after the election, the movement released the following e-mailed statement:

> The premature growth of the #YoSoy132 movement has given rise to attempts of protagonismo and actions that try to break its force; seeking to distort its principles through different actions, people, or groups. For this reason, we think it is important to denounce [this person], who has tried to position himself as a leader of the movement in the name of his [academic] department, contradicting all principles and seeking to satisfy personal interests. This person is also linked to acts of violence against some of the compañeros during previous democratic exercises. ... We categorically condemn the attempt to use the movement for private ends and any act of violence that any person or group commits in the name of the movement. (my translation)

The denouncement above censures an individual for simultaneously trying to position himself as a leader of the movement and using the movement to further his own personal career interests, both considered serious enough errors to prompt this statement charging him with protagonismo and disowning him from the movement. Accusations of protagonismo within Mexican anti-neoliberal social movements are a form of community policing that punish those who benefit personally from their activism, exhibit personal political ambition, or seek leadership. The implication is that activists with these characteristics are not desirable or virtuous and may be damaging to the movement or organization as a whole. As another activist told me in 2009, "For those who we notice are tempted [by protagonismo], we simply marginalize them from the movement."

In the previous chapter, I examined how Ríos, Berger, and Díaz and Castelao had all experienced social policing around their production and circulation practices. In this chapter, I examine the broader social context of policing protagonismo and the challenges that ideas of protagonismo pose to the liberal democratic template. I begin by establishing a vocabulary to talk about the meanings of protagonismo, including positing the term "compañerismo" as a useful concept to represent the positive antithesis of protagonismo. I then discuss several overlapping genealogies of the contemporary iteration of compañerismo: twentieth-century indigenous movements (especially Zapatismo), the indigenous *cargo* system of political leadership, liberation theology, gendered ideas of *caciques* and *caudillos* (authoritarian political bosses), and traditions of corporatist citizenship regimes. These historical legacies combine in the contemporary political environment to create compañerismo as a useful and potentially successful political strategy.

I argue that compañerismo (or anti-protagonismo) poses significant challenges not only to neoliberal politics, but to the foundations of liberal democratic citizenship. Instead of seeking individual freedoms and rights, the anti-protagonismo ethical framework calls people to embed themselves ever more deeply into interdependent human relationships and to purge those relationships of all hierarchies and oppression. This framework poses significant moral and ethical challenges to the practices of liberal democratic citizenship, with its focus on individual rights and freedoms. In contrast to many visions for social transformation, the critique of protagonismo does not have a particular political order in mind. Instead, it seeks to transform politics from the inside out, based in building a prefigurative ethical practice of activism, rather than from large formal or structural political changes.

The way the word "protagonismo" is used in Mexico reveals how people experience and consciously police one another's commitment and behavior surrounding ideas of collectivity, horizontality, and equality on the one hand and egoism, individualism, and hierarchy on the other. Protagonismo in Mexico is also nearly always referred to as a force or a tendency rather than described as an innate characteristic of a person. An organization or individual struggles with protagonismo; it is very rare that one would call someone a protagonista. Note in the #YoSoy132 statement above, for example, that the person singled out is not accused of being a protagonista, but being a person who is endangering the movement by falling into the temptations of protagonismo. Protagonismo is not a foreign threat that needs to be guarded against; it is an internal tendency that people should struggle with, both in the sense of coming from within a social movement as well as coming from within the individual. When I asked Ignacio del Valle in 2012 about the issue of protagonismo in general, he immediately used himself as an example, explaining to me, "Protagonismo is an attitude. In my case—I'm going to use myself as an example because they have also said that I am very protagonistic. Sometimes you have to speak. You have to put yourself in front. . . . But if there are more compañeros there and I am also there, I let another compañero speak. Why? Because one does [sometimes] fall into this protagonistic attitude." In this quote, and in the #YoSoy132 e-mail above, the issue of protagonismo is cast as almost as a disease among a group of compañeros.

Activist filmmaking is particularly burdened when it comes to issues of protagonismo. In 2014, when I asked Eduardo Ríos about the issue of protagonismo, he told me, "The simple fact that, for example, you are the cameraperson of your organization—there is a certain protagonismo there. There is a certain protagonismo because in some way—you go to the march, and they know that you have the camera, that you are the eyes of the organization. And they take you and put you in a special place so that you can record, to protect you. You become, in some way, a protagonist." Ríos describes his own relationship to protagonismo, and that of the Communications Commission of the Frente as a learning and transformational process through which the commission learned to practice what he calls "community journalism" (*periodismo comunitario*) and come to editorial decisions through consensus. In the same interview, he elaborated on the negative consequences of protagonismo, not only for the organization that one belongs to, but also for oneself as a person. "If protagonismo overtakes you, absorbs you, far from benefiting the organization, you slow it down, you dirty it, or you cloud it, no? Or you contradict it. . . . I think that protagonismo is limiting. You are limiting yourself. At first maybe you feel great that they applaud you, that they visit you. But it is a mistaken practice [*trabajo equivocado*]. You are no longer doing it in the name of the organization; you are using the organization to promote yourself."

Ríos went through a significant transformational process through his involvement in the Frente, a transformation that was in part developed through ideas of protagonismo as a negative and undesirable characteristic. In my initial interview with him in 2007, he told me, "When you acquire a consciousness— participation is also giving you an incredible degree of consciousness. You surprise yourself. You begin to leave behind egoism and personal protagonisms. And everything goes as a function of the collective and for the collective."

Ríos's words are almost identical to many of the testimonies that Marina Sitrin (2006) has compiled from activists involved in Argentina's neighborhood assembly and unemployed worker movements of 2001. Alberto, a member of an unemployed workers' movement told her,

> We need a transformation that isn't solely about economics, but one which also includes our consciousnesses. It's about being better in our work and health, but also creating another way of living. This is an experience that we construct on the basis of the collective and collectives, *in which individualism no longer figures among our values*, and similarly with the egoism, which is a part of this perverse society. Our relationship to the environment, the relationships among compañeros and compañeras and their children, these all need to be worked on; these relationship are integral. . . . *Our principal struggle is centered around this: the generation of new subjectivities, new relationships*, ones that have to do with the new transformations. (Sitrin 2006, 145; emphasis added)

In this quote, Alberto denounces egoism and individualism as moral perversities that people need to move beyond in order to generate new subjectivities and new ways of living. The quote is remarkably similar to sentiments that Ignacio del Valle expressed to me in 2012:

> The enemy is there: [It is] the voracity of this neoliberal system, this predatory system, that doesn't have respect for the human condition. . . . We see how human beings deteriorate like any other substance. The human condition is devalued, and we don't want this because our parents and our grandparents taught us that we have to help [one another], and *what we do, we have to do in a shared way. This supposed modernity makes us very individualistic. It makes us egotistical; more [egotistical] than human beings are in their natural condition.* (emphasis added)

Rather than claiming that more collectively minded subjectivities are a newly emerging concern of social movements, del Valle's metaphor implies that "living in a shared way" is a universal, basic characteristic of what it means to be human that is eroded through neoliberalism. In other portions of this same interview, he uses the concepts of modernity, big business (*gran capital*), and neoliberalism interchangeably to refer to this same damaging eroding force.

Although the ideas surrounding egoism are quite similar in the Mexican and Argentinian contexts, the vocabulary is distinct. Sitrin presents the word "protagonism" in the Argentinian context to have the very positive connotation of people "deciding for themselves, breaking from a past of political party brokerage and silence" (2006, vii). She sees the concept as one of the primary principles of horizontalism, stating that it "refers to a new collective sense of being where, through direct democracy, new individuals and collectives are being born" (2006, vii). This definition diverges sharply from Shannon Speed's definition of the word "protagonismo" in the context of Zapatista indigenous communities in southern Mexico: "asserting [one's] own agenda, wielding power over others, and flaunting the community's norms and collective will" (2008, 129). However, the difference in definitions in Mexico and Argentina is clearly a difference in terminology, not a contradiction in the ideas behind protagonismo. In both the Mexican and the Argentinian cases, people are experiencing and striving for an increased sense of collectivity.

Locally, there isn't a word that activists use to refer to the desirable condition or ethic against which ideas of protagonismo are cast. Sitrin uses the word "horizontalidad" in the Argentinian context, but I have never heard "horizontalidad" or "horizontalism" used locally in central Mexico. However, it is a banal fact of Latin American social movements that activists, union organizers, and even party members refer to one another as "compañero" or "compañera." Because the word refers to activists (people who are in danger of falling into the trap of protagonismo) I find the idea of compañerismo, or the state or ethic of being a compañero/a, to be an excellent way to refer to the positive ethic attached to the ideas of selflessness, collectivity, and consciousness that Ríos, del Valle, and many others describe as the virtuous state of being against which protagonismo is the foil. Literally meaning "one who accompanies," "compañero/a" has the sense of horizontality and shared experience that Sitrin describes as horizontalism. If someone is introduced to others in a movement as uno/a compañero/a, it is understood that the person is part of leftist social movements broadly conceived.

In short, one is or becomes a compañero/a through participation in leftist social movements or organizations and runs the risk of being tempted by or falling into protagonismo. However, I do not wish to reify the idea of being a compañero/a or compañerismo. One of the reasons that I find these words to be useful is that they are used locally in a completely unselfconscious way and have incredibly porous boundaries. As I argued in the previous chapter, there is very little agreement about what might constitute acting selflessly and beyond reproach. The road to becoming and being a compañero/a without falling into the trap of protagonismo is fraught with difficulties and paradoxes. One might not even know that one has fallen, and there might be a lot of disagreement about whether one has fallen or not. Compañerismo is not an "ism" in the sense that it is a purposeful ideology; it is simply a quality of being an ethical activist.

What being "ethical" means, of course, is relative and complex. For example, Salvador Díaz might see making films about Atenco as giving himself and his talents selflessly and at great personal risk for the betterment of the Frente and all of the world, but someone else might point to his practice of putting his own name prominently in the credits of his films as proof that he is using the notoriety of the Frente to advance his own fame and political influence. They might see that he is using the popularity of the Frente to sell his films and name rather than using his name and talents to support the Frente. Instead of being successfully "policed," Díaz and others may reject this interpretation of his actions.

Before turning to the possible effectiveness and implications of compañerismo and protagonismo, I first turn to their antecedents. This ethical regime is not a new or emerging idea but is a contemporary iteration that owes its existence to a plethora of ethical and political genealogies.

Genealogies of Compañerismo and Protagonismo

The contemporary manifestation of protagonismo and compañerismo in the Mexican Left arises at the intersection of several broad social, political, and cultural forces including twentieth-century indigenous movements (especially Zapatismo), liberation theology, gender expectations, clientelist politics, and even criticism of neoliberal subjectivities in contemporary scholarship. Each of these intertwining historical legacies has contributed to a contemporary sense of compañerismo that calls into being a collectivist sense of self that shares some characteristics with the politicized identities of the New Social Movements of the twentieth century, but does not coalesce around any one identity more specific than a moral sense of a shared humanity.

Ideas of selflessness and collectivity cast in opposition to individualism and egoism have long been attached to indigeneity in anthropological and historical scholarship of Mexico. Eric Wolf wrote, for example, "the mestizo would come to be the very antithesis of the Indian. . . . Where the Indian saw power as an attribute of office and redistributed it with care lest it attach itself to persons, the mestizo would value power as an attribute of the self, as personal energy that could subjugate and subject people" (Wolf 1959, 238–39).[2] One of the classic focuses of Mesoamerican anthropological research of the 1950s and 1960s was the indigenous *cargo* (burden) model of public service. In his description of Guatemalan indigenous political structures, for example, Manning Nash (1958) described the system of cargos as an economic leveling mechanism. Eric Wolf (1959) sees the cargo systems of Mesoamerica as a political concept in which, "a man cannot seek political office for its own sake, nor can he bend political power to his individual end. . . . It is the office that governs men, not its occupant. In this democracy of the poor, there is no way to monopolize power" (Wolf 1959, 218). The cargo idea of public service is one in which holding important public office (either religious or political) does not benefit the individual in office, but actually involves a significant burden (cargo) of time, money, and energy. Indeed, part of the prestige of the cargos is the selflessness with which one serves.

Scholars of Mexican political history have also helped define ideas of *caciquismo* (local authoritarian political bosses) and *caudillismo* (also political bosses, but the word connotes something closer to a warlord) that are also deeply intertwined with ideas of protagonismo. Caciques and caudillos are self-made, often exaggeratedly masculine men who wield power by the force of their cunning, bravado, and willingness to use violence. Alan Knight has argued, "there are probably few political actors who are as self-interestedly rational as the cacique and his close followers" (Knight and Pansters 2005, 8). They are actors who, far from being self-sacrificing, are more than willing to ruin others for their own political advancement. The idea of protagonismo is deeply influenced by the characteristics of caciquismo that in the contemporary context is seen to be a significant impediment to democracy. Policing protagonismo is policing the antidemocratic authoritarianism of caciquismo and caudillismo.

The polar opposite of the cacique is the *abnegada*, another very gendered Mexican archetype. Literally meaning something close to "she who renounces/negates the self," this term is defined by Olcott as being the embodiment of "selfless[ness], martyrdom, self-sacrifice, an erasure of self and the negation of one's outward existence" (2005, 15–16). Infused with a particularly Catholic Latin American sensibility, "abnegada" describes a code of appropriate conduct for women in many places around the world. The abnegada lives only for her children and her husband and thinks nothing of herself, much like a good compañero/a thinks nothing of him/herself and only of the collective. This gendered archetype and model of ethical behavior is also clearly embedded in a Catholic sensibility that prizes martyrdom and holds as one of its dearest symbols images of the long-suffering Virgin Mary.

Most of the midcentury scholarship that provided the foundations for thinking about these Mesoamerican archetypes of cargos, caciques, caudillos, and abnegadas unfortunately reified and homogenized these ideas as essentially indigenous. They were frequently described with significant racist connotations of noble savagery. Whereas contemporary scholarship and activism should be careful not to reify or romanticize these archetypes and the political ideologies attached to them, neither can we deny that the political and gendered ideas surrounding them have played a significant role in local conceptions of political organization and political morality.

Ideas of the cargo system, caudillos, caciques, and even abnegadas, because they have played such a prominent role in the anthropology of Mesoamerican peoples, have also come to influence how contemporary activists think about themselves, indigeneity, and indigenous political forms. As I mentioned in the Introduction, the classic midcentury ethnographies of Mexico are much more widely read and known in Mexico than they are in the United States. They have entered the realm of popular knowledge that actively constructs ideas of indigeneity. The conscious cultivation of an ethic of compañerismo and the social policing of protagonismo is not occurring separately from historic and contemporary scholarly theoretical debates over Mesoamerican indigeneity. Activists are very aware that competitive individualism is a part of neoliberal moral economies and that they are policing neoliberal tendencies when they police protagonismo.

The Frente is not an indigenous movement. However, its sense of moral struggle against forces of neoliberalism and self-interested individualism is strongly influenced by the political frameworks of indigenous movements. The most important of these movements in the case of Mexico is Zapatismo. The EZLN became internationally famous through its armed takeover of San Cristóbal de las Casas, on the same day the North American Free Trade Agreement (NAFTA) went into effect in 1994. The EZLN almost immediately laid down their guns to form a peaceful (though still armed) movement explicitly against neoliberalism and a globalization driven by transnational capital. Many Atenco activists certainly feel what Khasnabish (2008) has called the "resonance" of Zapatismo. However, it would be a mistake to see the Frente as a derivation or an iteration of Zapatismo. Instead, these two movements have influenced each other. Some people from Atenco who would later form the Frente went to Chiapas as early as 1994. There has been an exchange between the two legacies of political organizing for more than twenty years. Zapatismo has influenced Frente activists, but it is also true that Frente activists have influenced and helped to form contemporary Zapatismo (see Figure 3.1).

In communiqués, speeches, and the *encuentros* (encounters) that the EZLN has become famous for, speakers often address issues of individualism, egoism, and neoliberalism by name. The famous masked, pipe-smoking spokesperson of the EZLN, Subcomandante Insurgente Marcos, for example, has commented very publically and explicitly about the individualizing impact of neoliberal governmentality. In a dramatic demonstration of his rejection of individualism, he

Figure 3.1. Graffiti in Atenco that brings together the Frente with the EZLN. The machete reads "Long live the peoples in rebellion. EZLN FPDT Long Live Atenco" (*Vivan los pueblos en rebeldia EZLN FPDT Atenco Vive*). Photo by Livia K. Stone.

released a statement in 2014 announcing the "death" of Marcos; or rather the retirement of Marcos as an idea that had outlived its use (Galeano 2014). In this statement, a masked person easily identified as "The Sup" Marcos, denied that Marcos was ever an individual, just a "hologram" or a "colorful ruse" collectively created by the autonomous indigenous communities in order to better relate and communicate with a world that insists on the importance of individuals. He explained that as the hologram of a person, Marcos was a character who was played by many different people as one step in order "to find those who would see us, not from above or below, but face to face, who would see us with the gaze of a compañero." Throughout the communiqué, the speaker (identifying as Subcomandante Insurgente Marcos at the beginning of the speech and Subcomandante Insurgente Galeano at the end) criticizes the "cult of individualism" that devalues the collective and that has a difficult time understanding Zapatismo.[3]

As a concept, the communiqué implies, the individual itself is a ruse, a hologram that neoliberalism has reified to impose its vision for society. Marcos/

Galeano recognized that his central role as a visible and charismatic leader was contrary to the spirit of equality and collectivity that Zapatismo values, and so he retired the character, perhaps in part because he realized (or others told him) that Marcos was too much of a protagonist. He used the occasion to challenge his supporters to consider the concept of individuality itself as a social and political construction that may be used as a contingent tactic, but that is not ultimately helpful.

The scholarship and activism surrounding liberation theology has also strongly influenced Zapatismo and ideas of compañerismo in Atenco. The set of virtues that I am referring to here as compañerismo are nearly identical to what Paul Farmer has popularized as "accompaniment" in his scholarship and medical work through his organization Partners in Health, translated as Compañeros en Salud in Chiapas. Farmer is Catholic and has been deeply influenced by liberation theology (see Griffin and Block 2013). The mission statement of Partners in Health ("preferential option for the poor") is taken from Father Gustavo Gutiérrez and colleagues' seminal book *A Theology of Liberation* (2014 [1973]) in which he elaborates, "St. Paul asserts not only that Christ liberates us; he also tells us that he did it in order that we might be free. Free for what? Free to love. . . . The freedom to which we are called presupposes the going out of oneself, *the breaking down of our selfishness and of all the structures that support our selfishness*; the foundation of this freedom is openness to others" (Gutiérrez et al. 2014 [1973], 24; emphasis added). Gutiérrez and colleagues further argue that "all struggle against exploitation and alienation, in a history which is fundamentally one, is an attempt to vanquish selfishness, the negation of love" (2014 [1973], 103). Under Gutiérrez's conceptualization, selfishness and a turning inward toward the individual is a sin that is at the root of all social inequality. Liberation comes through loving God and other human beings, or more precisely, loving God *through* loving and having solidarity and social ties with other human beings (Gutiérrez et al. 2014 [1973], 115).

This was an idea also emphasized to me by some religious members of the Frente. One woman, who compared Ignacio del Valle's arrest to the persecution of Jesus, told me, "I've arrived at the conclusion that this is a struggle of good against bad. We don't want the bad. [We want] peace to reign, love to reign, everyone to be well. This is my vision in addition to knowing that God created the world so that we would feed ourselves, and not to exploit one another and get more and more and more money. . . . In the Bible, it says that God is on the side of justice." According to the Catholic morality of liberation theology, itself deeply inflected with indigenous as well as Marxist sensibilities, competitive, self-interested individualism is a sin. As a sin, it is a force that is as seductive as it is damaging. It entraps humans and leads them astray, away from the more virtuous state of humanity based in mutual interdependence, equality, and selflessness.

These various religious, gendered, and political genealogies of compañerismo also intersect with traditions of clientelism and corporatist citizenship regimes in Latin American politics, in which various levels of government dealt primarily with large voting blocs such as unions and peasant organizations instead of individual citizen voters. According to these political models, politicians appeal to large voting blocks of compañeros who are obligated through their organizations to vote together. Party leaders and union organizers may use their voting blocks for personal benefit through promising that their voters will vote for this candidate or another (or attend this political rally or that one) in exchange for personal gifts, political posts for themselves or their families, and so on. The politicians they are voting for are largely seen as patrons to be appealed to rather than representatives of their voters. In other words, although party members and leaders may refer to one another as compañeros and follow an ethic of solidarity, their "equality" is embedded in deeply problematic systems of patronage.

In her examination of indigenous citizenship in Latin America, Yashar (2005) argues that corporatist citizenship regimes inadvertently protected local autonomies prior to the twentieth century. Local communities were largely allowed to operate how they wished, with the voting block structures acting as mediators between citizens and the state. When these corporatist structures were eroded with the neoliberal policy shifts of the 1980s and 1990s, indigenous movements arose throughout Latin America to challenge these changes and protect previously uncontested local autonomies. Under this narrative of Mexican political history, indigenous challenges to neoliberal citizenship regimes arose out of the conditions under which they were controlled under previous regimes of political oppression rather than pre-Hispanic indigenous social, political, and cultural forms. In this light, resistance to this individualization also seems remarkably undemocratic and backward.

However, it is also unquestionably true that the political tradition of corporatist citizenship regimes arose out of long histories of institutions attempting to communicate with and in some way integrate themselves into the lives of diverse indigenous peoples throughout Latin America. These institutions negotiated their practices and conceptual frameworks as a result of working with indigenous peoples. If political structures survived and became influential—if they were effective—it is because of resonance with local conceptions and practices. Catholic saints were fit in and merged with indigenous gods, and likewise colonial political forms of control were fit in and merged with indigenous political forms. Rather than corporatist citizenship regimes acting from above to completely dictate the terms of political ethics in Atenco, it is much more accurate to say that continuing high-stakes battles over political regimes since before the Spanish conquest resulted in the negotiation of corporatist citizenship regimes.

Ideas of caudillismo, clientelism, liberation theology, Zapatismo, and many other influences have contributed to the Frente's sense of compañerismo and protagonismo, which is itself complex and multifaceted. It would be a mistake to reduce this complex ethical struggle to any one of these historical legacies. Political and cultural genealogies are complex. There is no beginning, and influences tend to cross one another, circle back, and have unintended consequences. Simple genealogies that pretend to point to one predecessor erase the interrelated histories of all these legacies. Identifying or arguing for a single source also tends to erase the importance of indigenous peoples in creating institutions and traditions because their contributions to ideas of liberation theology or corporatist political organizations (among others) have historically been subordinated to European influences.

Compañerismo as a Pragmatic Strategy

These historical legacies that have helped to shape ideas of what Holston (2008) has called "substantive citizenships" of compañerismo come together in the contemporary context of social and political power in which it is mobilized as a pragmatic and strategic choice. The contemporary ethical dedication to selfless collectivity in the Frente is partially created by the coercive threat of violence from the state that punishes visible leaders of a movement.[4] The basic concern of the Frente is to make a better life for themselves and others, and to stay alive and unharmed while trying to do so. Part of this project is to stay out of reach of the state physically. Compañerismo helps them do that.

For example, Ríos, the videographer from Atenco described in the previous chapter, felt that police tortured him as a direct result of his making himself visible as an individual with an important role in the movement. While he has changed his political practice to avoid censure for protagonismo within the Frente, a much stronger motivator for him is avoiding the literal and violent policing of the Mexican state. Ríos's avoidance of protagonismo and cultivation of selfless collectivity helps him gain respect among other members of the Frente as a virtuous activist while it simultaneously makes him less identifiable to the state as a desirable target for violence.

As a result of political violence against the most visible activists, the topic of leadership within the Frente is a difficult one. Some members of the Frente have no hesitation about saying that the Frente has leaders. Others make subtle distinctions between ideas of inspirational leaders, *dirigentes* (directors), *cabezas* (heads), and *líders* (leaders). Still others adamantly insist that the Frente has no leaders or dirigentes at all. The inconsistency and uncertainty on the topic of leaders is a conversation that is steeped in the delicate issue of protagonismo and state violence. One issue at stake is accepting the state logic of political protest in which if people are demonstrating in the street, it must be because a political agitator or charismatic leader stirred them up.[5] If this is true, then whatever people are protesting is not the fault of the state but is the result of one person attempting to grab power for him- or herself, which is an act of protagonismo that delegitimizes the movement. As a result, the state seems constantly looking for leaders who cause popular uprisings and popular movements. The implication is that the Frente is not a popular movement with broad support, but a hierarchical personality cult of a few individuals that would simply dissolve if the agitators were removed.

There are a few reasons that cultivation of an ethic of compañerismo might be effective. The first is that activists who remain selfless are also likely to be individually less visible and collectively more virtuous. If the activists of the Frente are seen to be acting selflessly, then the Frente has a greater chance of being seen as being innocent and authentic in the uncertain gaze of public opinion. To the degree that they can be constructed as dangerous criminals, or a small band of dangerous radicals, the state can justify violence, even illegal violence, against the movement.

Second, if they have specific leaders, they are much more easily co-opted or punished by the state. The Mexican state very successfully used the co-optation of social movement leaders to neutralize movements in the 1960s and 1970s (Anderson and Cockroft 1966, Davis 1976). To the degree that there simply aren't leaders to co-opt, a movement is much more difficult to neutralize in this way.

Third, the code of compañerismo seems harmless, even conformist. Its emergence can partially be attributed to its resonance with widely held systems of morality that judge who is a good person. It is difficult to imagine a political system in the world today in which the idea of selflessly giving oneself over to the collective benefit would not be seen as a virtuous commitment. It is the near universality of this claim, even if it emerges specifically from indigenous political forms, that allows the Frente to politicize the idea of human beings as relational.

As are the most effective social movement slogans ("women's rights are human rights," "Black Lives Matter"), it is simultaneously a banal truism and a radical articulation. This is what makes compañerismo subversive.

From another perspective, however, compañerismo can be seen as a self-defeating process that ensures the movement never produces individuals that can incorporate the goals of the movement into a mainstream political platform. Compañerismo without protagonismo means that the state can rest easy knowing that its own political authority is in no danger of being taken over by a stronger power because compañerismo does not seek power. Social movements under an ethical regime of compañerismo are resistant to cooptation because of the lack of leaders, but they also pose very little real risk to political power because they do not seek to take over. They may even be self-defeating, as activists spend a great deal of effort policing each other.

One member of the Frente told me a joke that he meant to illustrate what he described to me as the self-defeating nature of Mexican anti-neoliberal activism. In the joke, there is a crab fisherman who is traveling around the world learning about different fishing techniques. In every region of the world, fishermen place their crabs in a basket with a lid because the crabs learn how to get out of the basket in regionally specific ways. (US crabs launch one crab over who helps the others escape. Asian crabs cooperatively use their bodies to build a ladder so that they can all escape.) The man notices that unlike all the others, the Mexican fisherman doesn't use a lid on his basket. When asked why, the Mexican fisherman replies that the crabs never escape because "when one crab tries to get out of the basket, the rest pull him back down." The joke illustrates how policing protagonismo might be seen to serve the oppressive interests of the state: activists are so busy pulling each other back for the sake of horizontality that no one ever makes it out of their basket of oppression. They are effectively oppressing one another without the state having to intervene.

The joke echoes the implicit critique of compañerismo that locates its origins in traditions of clientelist and corporatist oppression: horizontality serves only to ensure that large groups of undifferentiated people can be effectively controlled. Local autonomies created by corporatist political organizations organize themselves to pick up their trash and to install electricity and water and largely pose very little threat to the political power of the state.[6] Likewise, compañerismo as a form of substantive citizenship can ensure that these social movements never gain much power.

The dim view of compañerismo implied in the joke is possible, but it is also quite cynical. It assumes that political leaders and state officials (the fishermen) are outside the reach of egalitarian ethical regimes. It assumes that there will always be fishermen who exist to oppress those who wish to be egalitarian. The less cynical perspective, and the view I would wish to advance, holds that those in power are well within reach of more egalitarian and less oppressive political structures. Part of the work of social movements is to build these ethical political structures (new political cultures) in order to subject oppressive leaders to them. Before turning to how the production and circulation of films are imbricated in the creation of these new ethical regimes, I wish to first examine how compañerismo as an ethical regime poses significant challenges to ideas of liberal democratic citizenship.

Citizenship, Power, and Neoliberalism

There is a tension, perhaps even an irreconcilable tension, between the moral foundations of what I am calling compañerismo and traditional conceptions of citizenship in a liberal democracy, even as the two also share some characteristics. This is not simply a tension that is playing out in Mexico, or even Latin America, but is a more widespread turn throughout transnational networks of anti-neoliberal social movements that are trying to innovate a means to do what John Holloway (taking inspiration from Zapatismo) has called "change the world without taking power" (2002). In short, these activists argue that the liberal democratic template is steeped in oppression, and so they are seeking a way to transform political cultures without being oppressive themselves. Because of the incompatibilities between ideas of compañerismo and the political practices allowed under liberal conceptions of citizenship, activists have little choice but to find other political arenas, such as filmmaking, to develop and practice the ethic of being the kind of political subject that they wish they were. Before returning to the larger implications of this challenge, however, I'd like to first turn toward what this ethical discrepancy between liberal/neoliberal citizenship and compañerismo looks like for the Frente locally.

In his narrative of the history of the Frente that I presented in Chapter 1, Humberto mentions how distasteful it is that politicians "go around knocking on doors" before elections to promote themselves. Self-promotion, the hallmark of any political campaign, is necessarily protagonismo. According to a perspective critical of protagonismo, even voting on substantive issues is a spurious activity. In a general assembly in 2014, for example, the majority of ejidatarios in Atenco voted to privatize individual parcels of land so that individual farmers can sell them, effectively dismantling the local ejido system. The issue is currently in a contested legal status because of Frente allegations that the voting was manipulated in various ways to result in an outcome of privatization.[7] In the eyes of the Frente's activism, however, any outcome shows the antidemocratic nature of voting: if the vote were manipulated, the process of voting was used to legitimate a decision contrary to the opinions of the majority. If the vote were legitimate, it would mean that each ejidatario voting in his/her own individual best interest rendered the communal lands useless for farming for everyone else. According to activists who are against this privatization, if only a small percentage of people sell their parcels to the corporations offering increasingly large amounts of money for them, then everyone's parcels become useless. "What good is my parcel," Virgilio asked me, "if I have a hotel on either side?" Through even bringing the matter to a vote, the process already individualized what had been a collective issue. In either case, from the perspective of Frente members, voting did not enable a more democratic process; it was used to legitimate a spurious one.

Neither of these conflicts over political parties or elections necessarily challenges the foundations of liberalism that emerged from the eighteenth century. Elections could be held without campaigns, for example, and candidates could be pushed forward by their constituencies (as they are in the cargo system) rather than going around knocking on doors. The competitive self-interested individualism associated with protagonismo is a twentieth-century neoliberal exaggeration of eighteenth- and nineteenth-century liberal ideas of individual freedom and autonomy. The liberal ideals of John Locke, Mary Wollstonecraft, and John Stuart Mill, for example, as distinct as they are from each other, are also far from celebrating the kind of competitive, self-interested individualism that activists such as Humberto and Ignacio del Valle criticize. If the hyperbolic individualism of early twenty-first-century neoliberalism were reduced to the size of its eighteenth- or nineteenth-century liberal roots, would anti-neoliberal activists be content? If the same democratic processes were carried out under a different ethical sensibility, would the democratic processes be transformed? Based in the perspectives surrounding the critique of protagonismo of many Atenco activists, I don't think that they could. I argue that ideas of protagonismo go straight to a foundational contradiction in the eighteenth-century liberal democratic model: its emphasis on individual freedom obscured deeply hierarchical relationships, based on conceptions of moral interdependence, with African slaves, indigenous peasants, and women. This hierarchical morality is not an unfortunate inconsistency in ideas of liberal citizenship but is a foundational characteristic.

In liberal revolutions, bourgeois men achieved self-governance and autonomy from the state as well as from other bourgeois men, but they retained deeply hierarchical relationships based on ideas of dependence and moral duty in their households. Around the turn of the twentieth century, women and abolitionists in the Americas fought new political battles, largely on the terms of liberal democratic constitutions, to liberate slaves, grant citizenship rights to women, and create universal suffrage. However, suffrage for women and racial and ethnic minorities did very little to transform the moral basis of racial, ethnic, and gendered hierarchies.

In the mid-twentieth century, decades after universal suffrage was won, the contradictions between the official political discourse of citizen equality and the unequal moral reality came to the fore in a series of important social movements often referred to as New Social Movements: civil rights for women, Black people, gay people, indigenous people, and other minority groups. In order to transform relationships between people to create more effective equality, the New Social Movements worked hard to bring about cultural change: trying to redefine the social and cultural meanings of the identities that had been the bases of their oppression. Some feminist thinkers even attacked the individualism of liberalism. Eisenstein, for example, wrote,

> Today's feminists either do not discuss a theory of individuality or they unself-consciously adopt the competitive, atomistic ideology of liberal individualism. . . . Until a conscious differentiation is made between a theory of individuality that recognizes the importance of the individual within the social collectivity and the ideology of individualism that assumes a competitive view of the individual, there will not be a full accounting of what a feminist theory of liberation must look like in our Western society. (Eisenstein 1981, 5)

In other words, even activists and scholars who had some sympathy with liberal ideas (Eisenstein's book is entitled *The Radical Future of Liberal Feminism*) were critical of ideas of liberal individualism.

The critique of protagonismo circulating among many social movements in Mexico argues that the liberal conception that people are free, autonomous individuals is simply not an accurate description of what human beings are or ought to be. This critique implies that the basic unit of society is not the individual, but complex moral relationships among people. As Ignacio del Valle told me, "This supposed modernity makes us very individualistic. It makes us egotistical; more than human beings have as a natural condition." He argues that the idea that people are autonomous individuals and should seek freedom from interdependence and social responsibility is unethical and corrupt.

The model of indigenous social movements that the Frente has followed is a departure from the liberal political pattern of the other New Social Movements. Instead of struggling for the individual rights usually afforded to straight, light-skinned men, indigenous movements largely have been arguing for *collective* rights, including collective property. Rather than asking the concept of individual freedom, autonomy, and private property to privilege all humanity, indigenous movements have asked those free white men who had individual autonomy to become as self-sacrificing as the women and slaves who supported them. In short, the ethic of anti-protagonismo, or what I am calling compañerismo, challenges people to embed themselves further into moral relationships of interdependence rather than attempting to extricate themselves from them.

As a consequence, the form of citizenship loosely attached to being a compañero/a is an ethical regime describing people who selflessly dedicate themselves to the collective benefit. They are willing to serve their communities but recognize that service is a burden of personal sacrifice rather than a vehicle for personal advancement or a leadership opportunity. A great deal of effort should go into ensuring that relationships of mutual dependence among people are nonhierarchical (unlike the moral duties of patriarchy, white supremacy, or the divine right of kings), but the way to ensure these relationships are nonhierarchical is continual purposeful monitoring of the relationships, not liberation from them. In short, ideas of compañerismo and liberal citizenship are in considerable, perhaps incommensurate, tension.

The tension between the two is not a battle between two different kinds of political subjects: state citizen voters on one hand and members of radical leftist social movements on the other. Instead, it is an ethical struggle within individuals who are caught between their simultaneous subjectification to each form of citizenship. "Falling into" protagonismo is the process through which one allows an ethical regime of neoliberal individual self-interest (state citizenship) to overtake one's better nature (virtuous compañerismo). State citizenship is associated with immorality and corruption, and the practices of state citizenship are likewise tainted. Voting is not an ethical practice of being a good citizen; it is a spurious activity that legitimates corruption. Electoral politics are not systems that channel the will of the people; instead they provide a platform for power-hungry elites. In short, falling into protagonismo is the process of becoming the kind of political subject that creates unjust political processes: a liberal subject.

Even as compañerismo has a firm idea of what it means to be human based in interdependence and collectivity, it presents no clear political alternative to liberal (or neoliberal) democracy. This lack of clearly articulated utopian political organization is possibly its most radical characteristic. In clear contradiction with their ethical conception of self, compañeros/as even continue to use a language of democratic citizenship (rights, democracy, etc.) when struggling with the state. In part this is because that language is the de facto political language, but it is also because they are still in the early stages of creating a new language. The development of the idea of protagonismo as a specter for community policing is a significant step toward developing this new vocabulary.

For example, Subcomandante Insurgente Marcos, on the eve of the collective creation of La Otra Campaña in 2005 (the new iteration of Zapatismo I referenced in the Introduction), wrote an article telling the story of Pingüino (Penguin) to help address criticism of the new EZLN declaration (Marcos 2005). In his retelling, El Pingüino was a very odd chicken who was among a group of chickens held by Marco's EZLN unit in the jungle of Chiapas. Marcos's military camp needed to move, and so they began to eat all the chickens that they had been keeping. Among the chickens, though, was a strange one who didn't behave much like a normal chicken. It walked upright. Someone noted that it looked like a penguin, and so everyone began calling it Pingüino. Having a name and being different seemed to save it from being eaten, and in the moment that the encampment had to depart, instead of leaving Pingüino behind (in the rain no less), a soldier (la Insurgenta Toñita) wrapped up Pingüino in her rain poncho and held him on her lap. In the next encampment, Pingüino always seemed to come around when the soldiers were studying and talking about politics under their processes of collective schooling and political formation. Little by little, it seemed that Pingüino was becoming less and less like a chicken and more and more like a soldier. It stopped eating in its corner, insisting instead that it should eat with the soldiers. It stopped sleeping by itself, preferring to sleep in the same space as the soldiers. At some point, someone gave it a white cloth to hang around its neck to increase the impression that it was a penguin instead of a chicken. (So the opossums in the jungle would not confuse it with a chicken and eat it, Marcos jokes.) Pingüino also became the mascot of the EZLN soccer team. Marcos ends his account with the moral of his (true) fable:

> It occurs to me now that we are like Pingüino, forcing ourselves to walk upright and make a place for ourselves in Mexico, in Latin America, in the world. As if the journey that we are embarking on is not in our anatomy. Surely we will lose our balance when we walk, unsteadily and clumsily, causing smiles and jokes. Although perhaps, like Pingüino, causing some kindness and someone, generously will wrap us up and help us, walking with us, to do what all men, women, or penguins have to do. That is, try to always be better in the only way possible: struggling.

The fable reminds the reader that, while it seems impossible for a chicken to become a penguin (or a soldier), the only recourse for a chicken who wants to be a penguin or a soldier is to begin to try even if it appears ridiculous. Marcos equates political struggle with the struggle to reinvent or slowly convert the self into a different kind of being. For him, the political body is the same as the individual body. He also implies that it is unclear what the end result will be. We might become penguins. We might become soldiers. We might simply look ridiculous. We might die trying (as Pingüino undoubtedly did). It might even be undesirable to have a firm idea of what the end result might be.

This uncertainty about the future coupled with a radical dedication to political process, often to the exclusion of concrete political or legal goals, can be found throughout the scholarship of twenty-first-century social movements.[8] These movements ask activists to behave "day-to-day as much as possible in the way that you envision new social and economic relationships: the way you would want to be" (Sitrin 2012, 4). The context of prefigurative politics that these scholars and activists describe means that in the contemporary context, the important activist question "What can we do to change the world?" overlaps significantly with "How do we need to *be* in order for the world to change?" This *being* is not a precondition for subsequently making instrumental legal changes to government institutions, but an end in itself. This end is to cultivate in oneself characteristics of horizontality, collectivity, and selflessness in the face of a political, economic, and ethical regime that values competiveness, individuality, and self-interestedness. According to this political vision, structural change can come about only as a result of the cultivation of this ethical way of being.

This prefigurative ethical strategy means that these anti-neoliberal movements are not threatening to overthrow or destabilize a particular state, but are instead undermining the legitimacy of liberal democracy, as well as neoliberalism, on ethical grounds. This means that much of the political activity of this prefigurative strategy would seem to fall outside the traditional realm of political activity at all. Cultivating a new ethical sense of self would seem to happen almost entirely in the realm of what a liberal political framework would consider to be the private sphere. Cultivating the selfless interdependence of compañerismo in Atenco is a matter of becoming more involved in the existing community life. One can become more involved in any one of numerous community organizations, churches, or work commissions to make the collective life of the community stronger. As numerous members of the Frente continually reminded me, the social fabric of the community is supported by collective festivals, celebrations, and community work. For anyone seeking to become more involved there are the *mayordomias* of the church and numerous local cargos having to do with clean water, maintaining collective parks, managing irrigation systems, and organizing local celebrations surrounding Cinco de Mayo, Carnival, Independence Day, and numerous other festivals. There are even continual communal cooking and eating festivals surrounding weddings, funerals, quinceañeras, and other celebrations in which a helping hand in the kitchen is always welcome. These are the modes of cultural production in small town life anywhere in the world.

Cultivating compañerismo as a middle-class mestizo in Mexico City, like the students at the elite university of the #YoSoy132 movement mentioned at the beginning of the chapter, who are not embedded in all the interdependent opportunities of small town life, is quite another matter entirely. Zapatista teachings are clear that the answer does not lie in urban people putting down their laptops and cell phones and becoming subsistence farmers in rural Mexico (although plenty of activists, including Subcomandante Insurgent Marcos/Galeano have done just that). The challenge that Zapatistas have made to their urban supporters is to use practices of cultural production that they have at their disposal rather than appropriate the modes of cultural production of rural Mexico.

One major mode of cultural production of urban public life is the production of digital media (including documentary film and social media), and so these are the media through which urban people can cultivate a new collective ethic, a new transformative subjectivity. Rather than being a peripheral or "soft" form of activism, the production and circulation of politically committed media become modes of cultural production and collective self-production. Making and circulating media become a creative field in which people can attempt to become penguins and soldiers and compañeros purged of protagonismo. They certainly cannot do these things within the purview of normative liberal democratic citizenship (voting, electoral campaigns, etc.) because these activities are in considerable tension with the ethic that activists are attempting to cultivate and that is crucial for the kind of social and cultural change that they envision. The combined repression of the Frente and La Otra Compaña in 2006 provided an excellent, though tragic, platform to practice this kind of ethical self-production. It is to these urban attempts at film activism that I now turn.

CHAPTER FOUR

Breaking the Siege

Resistance and Autonomy

On May 3, 2006, in Mexico City, Mario Viveros was sitting in the offices of the independent film association Canalseisdejulio, the most well-known independent documentary film organization in the country, with a team of colleagues. The group was simultaneously editing a documentary about a historical student massacre and listening to a radio broadcast about the latest standoff between the Frente and the police, this time outside of Atenco in the nearby city of Texcoco. Although the members of Canalseisdejulio had not previously made a film about Atenco and had no plans to make one before that day, in part because of Viveros, they would soon find themselves partnering with an indigenous media collective named Promedios and many other anonymous media makers to produce *Romper el cerco / Breaking the Siege* (2006), the most famous, most professional, and most widely distributed documentary about Atenco.

Mario Viveros did not imagine himself as a strong ally of the Frente as he sat editing and listening to the radio in 2006. Neither was he an oppositional or "mainstream" listener; he was a committed and unapologetic cultural producer of the Left, at that moment editing a documentary exposing terrible state violence against activists in the 1970s (*Halcones: Terrorismo de estado*, Mendoza 2006). He did not have a sudden shift in consciousness. He was not awoken or converted through shifting public discourse. He, and the possibly hundreds of anonymous people who came together to make and distribute *Breaking the Siege*, became activists allied with the Frente not through having their minds changed (they were already, broadly speaking, convinced of the rightness and goodness of leftist, anti-neoliberal social movements), but through actively participating in the arena of cultural production that a documentary film created.

I met Mario Viveros in 2007 when I first interviewed him as a representative of Canalseisdejulio. We became friends very quickly after our initial conversation, and Mario is still one of my closest friends and colleagues in Mexico City.

In this chapter, I use his experiences in the production and distribution of *Breaking the Siege* as an entry point for discussing and parsing through the complexities of how activist films work. What do they *do*? Do they work in the ways that filmmakers think that they do? How do we know if they do? I seek to challenge an often unexamined assumption behind popular narratives as well as a great deal of scholarship about how activist media works: that the most valuable work of activist media occurs over what Castells calls "the construction of meaning in the minds of people" (2012, 5).

This conception of what activist media does, or should do, is rooted in conceptions that media can act to awaken true consciousness in viewers or that it acts on a more collective level to counter or resist hegemonic, or mainstream, discourses. The former conception (individual consciousness-raising) can be loosely labeled a Marxian framework, and the more collective process (a change in mainstream public opinion) can be termed a Gramscian framework. Both Marxian and Gramscian frameworks privilege the idea of conversion—changing the way people think—as the primary utility of activist media. They are not necessarily in tension with each other; I make the distinction only to draw attention to individualized and collective ideas of conversion. Both models are embedded in ideas of activist resistance: speaking out, speaking up, demonstrating against. Marxian and Gramscian understandings of activist media assume that an activist film's primary responsibility is to resist or contest mainstream/dominant/hegemonic discourses either in the consciousnesses of individuals, or in the collective consciousnesses of societies.

The converse of these models means that if an activist film is seen only by those who already agree with it, the film may be said to do no good, or that it was only "preaching to the choir": talking to those who needed no convincing. In this chapter, I do not claim that activist media does not or cannot awaken consciousness and transform hegemonic discourses. On the contrary, I think that they often can and do. However, in privileging the idea of conversion or resistance, media scholarship also misses some other very important aspects of how activist media can be a useful tool of social transformation. In this chapter, I argue that autoconsumo (self-consumption or "preaching to the choir") is a valuable political and organizational tool; an ethical-political practice that helps produce new senses of individual and collective self even if a film or other media work is never seen by an audience that disagrees with its messages. In short, I argue that media circulation among populations who might be considered "self" or "the choir" to activists and filmmakers can build infrastructures and discourses that are autonomous from mainstream/hegemonic/dominant ones. In the next chapter,

I will go on to connect these self-making processes to the ideas of compañerismo presented in the previous chapter.

I delve into the specifics of the production and distribution of *Breaking the Siege* as a case that can tell us a great deal about two divergent approaches to film activism: strategies based around ideas of resistance (Marxian/Gramscian activist media frameworks and the Canalseisdejulio model of production), and strategies based around ideas of autonomy (as followed by Promedios). *Breaking the Siege* highlights how an autonomy strategy of activist filmmaking can work. The production and circulation of the film formed the basis for individual and collective self-making practices, even if "outside" audiences never saw it.

However, in the mixture of resistance and autonomy strategies out of which *Breaking the Siege* emerged, there also emerged an incongruity between how the film was used as a medium for political action (providing people a way to *do something* in the wake of the violence) and the language of the film, which remained very focused on a resistance strategy of conversing with and attempting to counter mainstream ideas. The particular language of the film is inspired by a human rights framework that emphasizes physical harm to people. The effect is that the film describes the violence of the state in horrific detail, likely conveying the message the perpetrators of the violence would have wanted to convey: participating in social movements is dangerous and can get you beat up, raped, or killed. In short, the terrifying language of the film would seem to dissuade viewers from political action even as it urges them to act. The fact that the filmmakers purposefully chose an autonomy strategy mode of production and circulation, but never seemed to question the resistance language of the film, suggests that shifts in ethical activist practice are more nimble than shifts in language when it comes to innovating new ways of utilizing filmmaking as an activist tool.

Their unquestioned use of the autonomous, nonproprietary mode of production also poses significant challenges to the neoliberal assumption that capitalist markets are the most efficient means of production and distribution. In this case, the nonproprietary, noncommercial production and circulation model of IndyMedia centers was unquestionably the more nimble and efficient means of producing and distributing the documentary. The observation is perhaps obvious to media makers locked in a continuous struggle with pirates and freebooters to capture more profits from their work, and yet the observation is no less radical for being self-evident.

I conclude the chapter by using the example of *Breaking the Siege*'s autoconsumo to challenge what has become a contemporary truism of social media activism: changing one's profile image or posting links on social media may make users feel like they have done something but is actually useless. This kind of "inside" circulating discourse has been criticized in some theorizing of activist media as "slacktivism" (Morozov 2009, 2014), creating "echo chambers" (Sunstein 2007, Jamieson and Cappella 2010), or even connected to social media algorithms that create "filter bubbles" (Pariser 2011).[1] Shedding Marxian and Gramscian understandings of activist media can allow us to see this kind of activism as helping to build autonomous languages and infrastructures that are very useful organizing tools.

Repression, Resistance, and Autonomy

On May 3, 2006, while the crew of Canalseisdejulio was listening to the radio and editing scenes of police violence from thirty years before, police had attempted to arrest several of the most visible leaders of the Frente. The day before, the Frente had helped mediate a meeting between some flower vendors and local officials. The officials were attempting to prevent the vendors from selling flowers on the sidewalk outside of the central market where they had sold for decades.[2] In the end, officials had agreed that they could sell the next day.[3] Suspecting that the officials might not keep their word, several members of the Frente arrived with the vendors early in the morning. When they arrived, the sidewalk and street was inundated with riot police. In the ensuing scuffle, some of the flower vendors and several of the most visible members of the Frente retreated and hid in a nearby building. With the vendors and Frente members sequestered inside, the police surrounded the building, and helicopters circled overhead. It seemed inevitable that police would storm the building to arrest the activists. This breaking news spectacle consumed the national media as residents of Atenco blocked the highway that connected Atenco with Texcoco in protest and began to clash with police. As had happened in clashes with police in 2002, both protestors and police took prisoners in the confrontation. The protestors were successful in making the police retreat from the scene, but police returned with reinforcements early the next morning and perpetrated one of the most significant cases of police violence in Mexico's history. An explanation of this violence and the role that commercial news media played in the violence became the topic of *Breaking the Siege*.

The police violence came at a crucial intersection of politics in Mexico that is a necessary part of understanding the stakes involved in the production of the film and the remarkable bridging of political ideologies and accommodations that had to occur between the various filmmakers. The violence was not only about flower vendors, or even only about the Frente. The confrontation occurred in a quite tense moment of electoral and revolutionary politics in Mexico's history.

The term of Mexico's first democratically elected president, Vicente Fox, was nearing its end.[4] In the buildup to the July elections to replace Fox, it seemed within the realm of possibility that, after several years of relatively conservative leadership, the very popular left-leaning mayor of Mexico City, Andrés Manuel López Obrador (also known as AMLO) might win the presidency representing the left-of-center PRD (Partido Revolucionario Democrático, or Democratic Revolution Party). The rise of the PRD would have signified to a large portion of Mexico's left-leaning public that significant political change was possible through established democratic means.

The Zapatista movement, a more radical symbol of social change from the Left, was also increasing its level of activism. In 2005, the EZLN (Ejercito Zapatista de Liberación Nacional, or Zapatista Army of National Liberation) released a public announcement called La Sexta Declaración de la Selva Lacandona (the Sixth Declaration from the Lacondon Jungle, or just La Sexta), an invitation to social movements throughout Mexico "from below and to the left" to convene in Chiapas and help form a new network of social movements throughout the country. The invitation to come to this event outlined their vision of the world's political situation, in which neoliberal corporate interests from the United States and Mexico were selling Mexico to enrich themselves at the expense of the people of Mexico. La Sexta outlined how political parties from the Left and the Right were putting themselves at the service of foreigners instead of their constituents. The declaration argued that the system of electoral politics is useless because "it does not take people into account." Instead, "it just approaches them when there are elections" (EZLN 2005, official English translation). As a result, La Sexta invited people and organizations from the Left and all over Mexico to take part in a new national campaign "for building another way of doing politics, for a program of national struggle of the left, and for a new Constitution." La Sexta also called on people throughout Mexico "who are good of heart and intent" to state publically that they supported La Sexta and supported creating a new form of politics outside of political parties. The implication was to encourage people to publically state they did not support the PRD, but supported a way forward outside of political parties.

The campaign that resulted from activists and political organizations from all over the country convening to plan a new kind of politics came to be named La Otra Campaña (the Other Campaign). The name evoked the "otherness" of those who are usually excluded from civil society and political decisions: indigenous peoples, rebel teenagers, queer people (Anonymous 2005). Much like the Black Power movement or the queer movement, La Otra Campaña attempted to reclaim the terms of their marginalization from mainstream Mexican politics by appropriating its own language of "othering." However, instead of reclaiming one characteristic (skin color, sexual orientation), it reclaimed the idea of marginality itself, turning otherness into unity, and disenfranchisement into autonomy: the Other. The name also implied that the effort was an alternative to the electoral campaigns unfolding in Mexico at the same time: this movement was the *Other* Campaign. The name also was an attempt to extend the spirit of autonomy fomented in the autonomous Zapatista communities to a more varied audience. For those who are not subsistence farmers as the Zapatista communities are, it is difficult to create completely autonomous communities according to their model. However, a wide variety of people could become autonomous from the mainstream in small, but significant ways. La Otra helped and encouraged people to cultivate these small autonomies. They were not the countercampaign or the resistance campaign. They were the autonomous campaign: the Other One. The result of the congress in Chiapas was a physical tour of La Otra Campaña throughout Mexico in 2006, headed by the famous masked, pipe-smoking Subcomandante Insurgente Marcos.[5]

In other words, the months leading up to the July 2006 presidential elections was a significant and exciting time for mainstream left-of-center (reformist) politics because of the very real possibility that AMLO could become president.[6] It was also a very exciting and hopeful time for the more radical revolutionary politics of the Zapatista movement and its network of supporters because of La Otra Campaña. AMLO's presidential campaign held the potential of social change through institutional, reformist, and democratic means, while the EZLN's Other Campaign represented the potential of a more radical change through a network of social movements calling for a new national constitution. Rather than working together to create a unified but diverse wave of leftist politics, however, the specifics of the two campaigns worked at cross-purposes. AMLO needed votes to win the election, and La Sexta encouraged people not only to not vote, but to state publically that voting and electoral politics were useless. According to the campaign, voting in the election was consenting to unjust rule. It argued that the concentration on electoral politics was obscuring the fact that no politicians and no political parties were working for poor and marginalized Mexicans. As often happens in the tensions between reformist and radical politics, La Otra Campaña saw AMLO's campaign as merely another oppressive regime that would not represent any real change, and AMLO's campaign saw La Otra Campaña as a political force that was simply convincing people who would otherwise vote for AMLO not to vote at all.

In the abstract, the political lines were quite clear, but there was a quite sizable portion of the population who felt affinity for both AMLO and the EZLN. Many non-campesino, left-leaning urban residents felt deep fondness and support for the Zapatista movement and wanted to support La Otra Campaña at the same time that they also supported the PRD and AMLO as a way forward (and to the left) for the country.

Mario Viveros, one of the two central filmmakers responsible for *Breaking the Siege*, was part of this conflicted population. Since 1999, Viveros had dedicated his life and talents to working for a company founded in part to support the candidacy of another PRD politician, Cuauhtémoc Cárdenas. At the same time, he was also a college student who supported the EZLN in the 1990s when it rose to prominence. As a filmmaker, he had even helped make a very important documentary series about the EZLN for Canalseisdejulio, *Zapatistas: Crónica de una rebelión* (2003) and so had even spent time in Chiapas with the EZLN and residents of the autonomous communities that the EZLN protects.

There were also strong supporters of La Otra Campaña who were not that far removed from more mainstream politics. Nicolas Défossé, for example, was a French national who had been working with the media organization Promedios: Comunicación Comunitaria (Promedia: Communitarian Communication) in Chiapas since 2001. Promedios is an organization that provides video equipment and training to the autonomous (Zapatista-protected) communities in Chiapas. Défossé helped edit many of these projects and in 2005 had received a grant from the French government that allowed him to purchase a camera and some recording equipment. Although working with a media organization with such strong ties to La Otra, he was not opposed to collaborating with others further removed from La Otra, or even receiving a government grant for his work.

The paths of these two filmmakers crossed (not for the first time) in the context of the Frente, which was working within its own set of restrictions and local issues at the intersection of revolutionary and reformist politics. Since 2002, when the Frente successfully fought against the expropriation decree, it had remained a formidable political force. Frente activists continued to try and hold government officials responsible for their actions and were actively involved in politics. One of their primary concerns was to help hold local officials accountable, and they often did so using the same direct action tactics that they became famous for in the airport struggle. In April 2006, Frente members met with an official concerning the misappropriation of funds intended for a local medical center for disabled children. For political leverage, the Frente retained a local official in his office, preventing him from leaving until he called his supervisor, who could account for the misattribution of funds.[7] The confrontation quickly escalated when the police became involved, and the Frente confronted a few additional officials. After a standoff that lasted several hours, the police retreated, the officials were released, and the activists left. The supervisor was never reached, and the activists never received a satisfactory answer.

Days after this confrontation, and only a week before the confrontation in Texcoco over the flower vendors, the Frente hosted La Otra Campaña in a widely publicized and well-attended solidarity and organizing visit. Ignacio del Valle of the Frente appeared with Subcomandante Marcos before a large enthusiastic crowd, and members of the Frente provided protection for Marcos, a human chain of people holding hands around him. Many people told me that the Frente was also charged with providing Marcos with protection while he was visiting Mexico City over the next week (see Figure 4.1).

Leading up to this solidarity event, both the Frente and La Otra were experiencing increasing opposition from authorities at various levels. Although the Frente had been advocating about local issues and pressuring officials for years, this time the state was processing warrants for the arrests of several key figures of the Frente connected to allegations about the children's hospital issue.[8] Activists told me that police merely used the certainty that central figures of the Frente would be in Texcoco on May 3 to carry out warrants for their arrest already issued.[9] Défossé, as a journalist and filmmaker with Promedios following La Otra, told me that as La Otra came closer to Mexico City, they faced rising opposition from local authorities.[10] The campaign was increasingly facing small skirmishes with authorities wherever it went. Défossé and others paying attention to La Otra's progress told me that tensions were rising as the campaign came closer to Mexico's capital.

On May 3, all these tensions came to a crisis point. While Viveros and the Canalseisdejulio filmmakers were editing and listening to the scene in Texcoco play out on the radio, Marcos and his caravan were making solidarity visits with social movements in Mexico City. A very visible member of the Frente, América del Valle, was accompanying Subcomandante Marcos in Mexico City as her father, Ignacio, was trapped in a building in Texcoco surrounded by police.[11] The whole nation watched as Atenco residents blocked the highway in protest of the arrest and as police arrived to clear the highway. The confrontation escalated as police stormed the building in Texcoco, violently removing the activists

Figure 4.1. Still from *Romper el cerco / Breaking the Siege* (Canalseisdejulio and Promedios 2006) showing Subcomandante Insurgente Marcos and La Otra Campaña visiting Atenco.

sequestered there, and police in Atenco shot a fourteen-year-old boy in the chest and killed him. Television cameras recorded from the pedestrian overpasses and from helicopters as activists on the highway chased off the police with rocks and sticks. They recorded, played, and replayed moments in which activists beat and kicked police who had been left behind. One image that was replayed over and over was a protestor kicking an unconscious policeman in the groin (through his plastic body armor and codpiece) as he laid spread eagle on the highway.

When news of the scene reached Marcos and América del Valle, they called on supporters of La Otra to go to Atenco to help support the Frente in their standoff with police, knowing that the police would return after being forced to retreat. Members of La Otra Campaña helped populate barricades erected to prevent police from entering the town. However, the ranks of the police ballooned much beyond the ranks of activists. One human rights report estimated that there were thirty-five hundred state and federal police involved in the incursion (OMCT

2007, 17). In comparison, the total population of San Salvador Atenco at the time was around seventeen thousand (INEGI 2011, 36). When the police entered the town by force in the early hours of the morning on May 4, they did not stop with opening the barricades and chasing off activists in the streets. Numerous human rights reports, testimonies, and films document that police arrested and beat anyone they could find, entering people's homes, overturning furniture, and pulling everyone out (see Urirarte and Silva Forné 2006, CCIODH 2006, Méndez Cruz 2006, CCIODH and UNAM 2008, Centro ProDH 2012). They arrested journalists, human rights observers, and bystanders. Testimonies recount that police beat and loaded people on pickup trucks before stacking them, some lying unconscious in pools of blood, on busses. In what has become some of the more widely publicized instances of violence, police terrorized and sexually assaulted many of their detainees on an unnecessarily extended journey to prison. Human rights reports count two deaths (Francisco Javier Cortés Santiago, the boy shot in the chest, and Alexis Benhumea, a college student killed by a head wound inflicted by a tear gas canister) and 211 arbitrary arrests over the two days of repression, including forty-seven women, most of whom who were subjected to sexual assault at the hands of police (CCIODH 2006, 75). Locals in Atenco told me that the number of sexual assaults was in fact much greater and was not limited to women. Several cases of sexual assault are still being adjudicated through the Inter-American Court of Human Rights in 2018.

Nico Défossé and members of Canalseisdejulio heard of the conflict on the news and both went to Atenco on the morning of May 4 to cover the conflict, then in process. As Viveros commented to me, "We didn't know what was going to happen, but we suspected that something could happen." They arrived just in time to capture some of the bloodier instances of police violence. Défossé and the Canalseisdejulio crew recognized each other from their earlier work together on the Zapatista film but did not initially think of collaborating on a project together. Promedios would, of course, cover the events as part of its coverage of La Otra Campaña.[12] On their part, Canalseisdejulio had not initially thought of doing any film about the violence; they were merely collecting footage for their archives. A few years later, in 2009, Viveros described to me how and why they decided to make a film:

> I remember that we were in a moment of—a little rediscovery of the Internet, so we were looking for all the information [about the Atenco police repression] on the Internet that Medios Libres publishes, and IndyMedia, etc., etc. And we began to find much more information. And we thought we could do

something very small, like five minutes, a denunciation, and upload it to the Internet page. This was the first idea that we had. Later, in some moment in the afternoon, I saw . . . a list of *desaparecidos*, of people who were missing; I found the name of Valentina Palma. And this was the trigger for doing *Romper el cerco*. Valentina Palma is a compañera, a film student. I've known her since '98 or '99.

Palma's detention was significant to Viveros because he had been there when she had almost been detained in Cancún in 2001 while filming the World Trade Organization protests. On that occasion, her status as a foreigner in a tourist destination (she is from Chile) had provided her a degree of protection. In Cancún, the police removed her from the scene and released her, assuming that she was a tourist who had mistakenly gotten caught up in the confrontation. Seeing her name on the list in 2006, Viveros knew that she had not been so lucky this time.

So when I see the name of Valentina Palma, the Chilean, lost there, I said, "Fuck [*puta*]." Valentina doesn't know how to react in the face of eventualities like that. She isn't the one who runs the fastest. She doesn't know how to react. So I said, "Oh, my god, [*la torre*], no." . . . It took on a more personal nature. It is someone you know. It is someone, in addition, with whom you share an occupation. And the first thing [I thought] was, "if they harm her, they harm all of us" [*si la tocan a ella, nos tocan a nosotros*]. So this has to be denounced quickly.

Viveros also knew that the consequences would be severe for Palma because she was not a Mexican citizen. It is illegal in Mexico for foreigners to demonstrate against the government, and if she were arrested during a political action, she could be deported and be unable to return to the country for five years.[13]

Since Viveros knew that people from Promedios were also at the scene and had footage, he contacted Défossé through another shared contact and invited him to use the equipment and resources of Canalseisdejulio to help put together a denunciation. He also contacted his boss, Carlos Mendoza, founder and head of Canalseisdejulio who was on vacation at the time, to approve the project and their plans for moving forward. As news of their collaboration spread, other commercial and independent media makers who had footage and images of the repression arrived to work on the project and contribute content for the film. Initially imagined as a very quick video denouncing the violence, the project blossomed into a feature-length film.

Friends and colleagues, both Viveros and Défossé are political filmmakers from the Left with a very similar set of politics: among other issues, an affinity for Zapatismo, a broad critique of neoliberalism, and a detailed knowledge and critique of mainstream electoral politics. However close they were interpersonally and politically, they were also members of filmmaking organizations that were at least superficially on opposite sides of the line that La Otra Campaña was attempting to draw between the presidential campaigns and the Other Campaign.

Canalseisdejulio had been deeply embedded in electoral politics, and specifically the conversation around the PRD (AMLO's party) since its birth in 1988. Although entirely independent, and sometimes deeply critical of the PRD, Canalseisdejulio emerged as an organization in 1988 to tell the story of the first viable PRD presidential candidate, Cuauhtémoc Cárdenas, who Carlos Mendoza thought was not getting fair coverage in the national commercial news. The name of the organization (Channel July 6) is a reference to the date of the presidential elections in 1988 that Cárdenas is widely believed to have lost only because of electoral fraud. Additionally, the topics of Canalseisdejulio films are often deeply entrenched in national electoral and party politics. Carlos Mendoza describes the organization's main mission as one to disseminate "counterinformation" (Mendoza 2006), or as resistance to the hegemony of mainstream commercial media. Canalseisdejulio as an organization was profoundly embedded in a set of politics that saw its "counterinformation" as a tool advancing democracy through engaging mainstream public discourse and formal democratic processes. In short, their film activism followed a classically Marxian/Gramscian model of activist media.

In contrast, Promedios was intensely committed to the Zapatista mission of autonomy that was at that moment attempting to form a movement around the idea that the more effective agent of change lay outside of electoral party politics. Promedios as an organization was deeply embedded in more radical autonomist politics of the EZLN since its inception in the 1990s. It was founded within the Zapatista experience of creating autonomous communities that operate according to different political and economic structures as autonomous as possible from the rest of the country. La Otra Campaña was attempting to spread their experience of autonomy out of the Lacondon Jungle and into small towns and cities around the country. In contrast to Canalseisdejulio's media strategy of breaking hegemonic discourse and politics, La Otra was based on a more radical agenda that sought to completely ignore mainstream politics and create something new from the ground up.

I am emphasizing the differences between Promedios and Canalseisdejulio because I am interested in what a collaborative project like *Breaking the Siege* can tell us about these two distinct media strategies: one based in resistance politics (as Canalseisdejulio generally is) and the other autonomist politics (as Promedios generally is). However, in practice, neither Défossé nor Viveros described to me tension or friction between them as individuals and filmmakers. They are, in fact, quite good friends. However, the distinct strategical foundations of their filmmaking practices had some interesting consequences for *Breaking the Siege* that can teach us a lot about the diverse ways that activist media can work as a political tool.

Breaking the Siege

Défossé and Viveros both told me that the analytical focus of the film came about as a compromise between them. If he had been doing the film by himself, Défossé told me, the film would have concentrated on analyzing the violence as a means of repressing La Otra Campaña and its affiliated social movements. If the Canalseisdejulio team were doing the film own their own, Viveros told me, the film would have concentrated on the violence as a means to scare people away from voting for AMLO and the PRD in the upcoming elections. In other words, they would have concentrated on the political alliances of their respective organizations. Through the collaboration, the film came to speak on the shared common ground between them, making an argument about the role of the media in criminalizing social movements, presenting visual evidence of human rights abuses, and naming those responsible for the violations. It argues in part that through dwelling on images of protestors running police off and literally kicking them when they were down, the commercial news media justified (and in some instances literally called for) violent state interference to "restore order" in Atenco.

The film builds this argument using the compositional qualities for which Canalseisdejulio is known: a combination of recorded commercial news coverage, original recorded material of some of the same events, and testimonial interviews. This footage is brought together and supported with a strong voice-over narration delivering political analysis in the authoritative, satirical tone characteristic of almost all Canalseisdejulio films. It begins with a description of the escalation of events on May 3 and 4 and gives a detailed time line of what happened when. The time line is frequently punctuated with detailed testimonials from victims of the police violence, some of them journalists, describing physical injuries inflicted on them. One woman describes how, on the six hours they spent on a police bus, "I looked to my side and saw that the bodies that were at my side were almost like corpses, totally open, swollen, full of blood. The cries of pain, the smell of blood was terrible." Another recounts that "they told us that we were going to die, and I heard the women shouting out, 'Stop touching me. Please stop,' and they said 'Open your legs, you fucking bitch.'" An older woman shows a cameraman her home, ransacked by police. She cries out painfully about how the police took her children and how she does not want to remember the violence by recounting it again to the camera. Another man describes how his son was hit in the head with a tear gas canister and was trapped in a house for eleven hours without medical attention because the police would not let the Red Cross pass.[14]

There are interviews with a few experts, presenting their analyses of how police plan and carry out such attacks, as well as how and why commercial media play a role in constructing public opinion about political violence, justifying its necessity. The film names the officials who called for and carried out the attacks. It draws interpersonal connections among them, their political histories, and the branches of the police and military units that they headed. It demonstrates with visual and medical evidence that the fourteen-year-old (Francisco Javier Cortés Santiago) killed on May 4 died of a bullet wound of the same caliber as police-issued weapons rather than a firework as official accounts had claimed. Chillingly, it also presents the anonymous video testimony of three state police officers who detail how they were called to participate in the violence and how one of their colleagues shot and killed Javier Cortés Santiago at point-blank range because he discovered where police were hiding. At times the film lingers on violence: a policeman entering Atenco at a jog casually tries out his billy club by bringing it down hard on the skull of a dog who happened to be on the sidewalk; a group of six or seven policemen chase down and beat a man running away from them in a scene reminiscent of the Rodney King beating; lines of detainees come off of a police bus and are forced to walk into prison through a double line of police beating them over the head with billy clubs. Ominous music plays as the camera lingers on a close-up of a woman's eye, clouded with blood, seen through the bars of a jail cell.

Near the end of the film, one of the media experts (Carlos Fazio) explains that this type of operation is meant to "generate terror, paralyzing fear, throughout the population." "The message is," he says, "don't get involved. If you get involved, the same thing could happen to you as happened to the women arrested in San Salvador Atenco." Because of this, he continues, "it is important to overcome fear and terror." The film presents a montage of political demonstrations organized in support of Atenco all over the world: Seattle; Athens; Madrid; Rome; Paris; Berlin; Chicago; Wellington, New Zealand; London; Quito; Vienna; Montreal; San Diego; Vancouver. The film ends with comments from a few people from Atenco that they are scared to go back to their homes, but plan on rebuilding bit by bit. The last message of the film is that none of the responsible parties have been punished for the violence.

Breaking the Siege's title was coined by a man named José Luis Mariño who both worked as part of Canalseisdejulio helping to distribute official copies of its films and also self-identified as a member of La Otra Campaña. Mariño and Viveros both told me that there are three "sieges" to which the title of the film refers: a siege of biased national media that was isolating and strangling the truth, a physical police siege of social movements that was preventing them from acting, and a third siege created from the first two: a siege of fear. "The fear that provokes you, that paralyzes you," Viveros told me in 2008,

> [*Breaking the Siege*] was a call to the people to say, "Let's break the fear, let's break the misleading propaganda of the electronic media, and let's break the fear- the siege of the police too." In moments [like this] that are so critical, that are so strong, you become a little more militant. There are other moments in which you can be more analytical and things, but in these moments suddenly you are like, "Let's call to action," and the action was, "Don't be afraid." It has to be said. It has to be denounced. One can't let these things repeat in this country. This was the motivation to do this video.

Later in the same conversation, I asked Viveros why it was important to denounce abuses, and, citing a range of affronts to independent media makers in 2006 including the arrest of Valentina Palma Novoa, he told me, "If you don't do anything, if you stay silent, the only thing that you are doing is allowing everything to go unpunished. . . . We can't stay silent as documentarians."

It is striking that Viveros intended the film to "break the siege of fear" because the great majority of the content of the film argues, in horrifying detail, the level of devious, conspiratorial, murderous retribution that the state is prepared to bring down on innocent citizens and well-meaning social movements. *Breaking the Siege* is filled with images of police beating people, carrying blood-covered bodies, and stacking them on top of one another in trucks. The soundtrack powerfully evokes emotions of fear, danger, and sadness. It is difficult to imagine how the film could have presented the repression in any other light because of its violent nature. Even so, the overwhelming tone of the film stands in sharp contrast to its producers' intentions to communicate the message "Don't be afraid." Instead its tone seems to collude with the intended purpose of the repression, emphasizing the power of the state and intimidating people into not participating in social movements. Through detailing the violence of the state it communicates the message the state desired: if you become involved in anti-state protests, this is what can happen to you. The film gives the viewer no reason to fight against repression other than the fact that the violence was horrible. Undoubtedly, this horror can inspire viewers to act, but it seems quite likely to also make them afraid of doing so.

Its human rights framework, focusing on the physical damage to people's bodies as the primary locus of violence, is problematic in the context of making a film that aligns itself with anti-neoliberal social movements.[15] Essential to popular as well as scholarly critiques of neoliberalism is the idea that it is an individualizing ethical regime that has difficulty imagining collective actors and collective rights (Sawyer 2004, Yashar 2005, and Ong 2006 for example). Because liberal and neoliberal democratic frameworks imagine the basic unit of society to be the individual, physical violence against individuals is an expedient means to make powerful juridical arguments in a neoliberal/liberal democratic context.

However, the focus on individual bodies it is not one that most members of the Frente probably would have chosen as the best way to represent their experiences of the repression. It is telling, for example, that the only on-camera testimony in Breaking the Siege by a resident of Atenco is broken when the woman cries out that she doesn't want to remember. There were none from Atenco who participated in the film's focus on violence against individual bodies.[16] The concentration on the physical evidence of abuses on individual bodies ("Here are images of my bruises, my broken arm, the wound where the bullet entered.") is grounded in a human rights framework that has historically concentrated what Tate (2007), critically but sympathetically, has termed, "counting the dead." In bringing legal cases of state violence to justice, physical documented evidence of violence is paramount in establishing that violence empirically occurred. In the wake of official state denials of violence, images of specific incidents of violence can be powerful, visceral proof of what occurred. In part, Breaking the Siege was an attempt to argue a human rights case in the public imagination and prove to all who see the film that the police violence was horrible and unlawful. Presenting empirical, physical evidence was not just metaphorical: lawyers handling the human rights cases on the national level told me that Breaking the Siege, among other films and images, were admitted to court in human rights cases as evidence of abuses.

In my discussions with people from Atenco about the violence, people were certainly deeply impacted by the physical nature of the repression, but they also tended to emphasize the damage that it did to their relationships and sense of community. Instead of showing me physical wounds, people were much more likely to describe the fact that a detained man missed his daughter's wedding, a fifteen-year-old boy had to become the man of the house, or a daughter could not forgive her father for his activism because it resulted in police raping her.[17] People emphasized that the repression broke a sense of community in Atenco: people became suspicious of their neighbors or no longer felt safe in their homes. The film's focus on the violation of individual bodies, it became clear, was largely the framework of the Frente's urban and non-campesino allies, mostly members of La Otra Campaña who came to Atenco to help protect it. Some of these outspoken allies specifically identified themselves in the wake of the violence as human rights observers (see *Atenco: Un crimen de estado* (Atenco: A crime of the state) by Colectivo Klamvé, 2006). This is not to say that the emphasis on individual bodies was completely imposed from the outside or by the filmmakers. Many of the people detained, beaten, and sexually assaulted were, in fact, urban non-campesino allies and are certainly entitled to their experience of the repression as well as their means of responding to it. The film is also about them, after all, not just about Atenco.

Unfortunately, it seems that the human rights framework has not been particularly effective in the case of the Atenco/Texcoco violence. In 2010, Mexico's Supreme Court ruled that human rights violations had been committed in May 2006, but that the perpetrators could not be punished because the individual police officers who committed the offenses could not be identified. The sexual assault cases are still being processed through the Inter-American Court system and awaiting judgment in 2018. In short, at least on the national level, the concentration on individual bodies of victims had the effect of defining the perpetrators as individual abusers (the man who made this specific bruise). Therefore, individual police officers were to blame, not a systematic, ordered attack against a collective actor or community of people.[18] This individualized explanation for the attacks is contrary to the popular, even commonsensical, explanation of the repression, which was a repressive state attack again La Otra and the Frente, and possibly to send a message to all other social movements challenging the state. It is true that the individual bodies of police and residents were used to carry out this attack, but they were beside the point. In short, the human rights framework in the case of the Atenco/Texcoco police violence may have been useful to a certain extent, but it also misses the social nature of the violence that for local people in Atenco was the most salient, and it hasn't been particularly effective in punishing the perpetrators of violence.

The portrayal of physical violence against individuals may also have been counterproductive to the long-term goals of the Frente. More than ten years after the events, the testimonies of people have not been enough to adjudicate individual police officers. Meanwhile, most people in Mexico have been exposed to images of Atenco that depict the community and social movement as a series of abused, bleeding, and victimized bodies. Even unflattering commercial media portrayals before the repression had depicted them as powerful and strong, if frightening. These depictions of strength survived through many occasions of police violence including dramatic arrests and bleeding protestors. After the repression, commercial and independent media, including *Breaking the Siege*, colluded to redefine the Frente, if unwittingly, as crippled and victimized. This victim status has done very little to help the Frente struggle against unwanted development projects or the violence Atenco has experienced as a community.

My aim is not to portray *Breaking the Siege* as a bad or flawed film. To its credit, the film also spends considerable time naming the names of those officials who orchestrated the repression and attempting to make them visible. The partnership of Canalseisdejulio and Promedios was simply using the language available to them at the time to reach as broad an audience as possible in as short a time as possible. They were also using the preferred framework (concentration on individual acts of violence and the physical evidence of abuses) of those who were speaking up the loudest about the abuses after the attack. Neither Viveros nor Défossé hinted to me that they ever considered using a different emphasis to describe the violence. The language of human rights is very widely accepted (most countries in the world have signed the Universal Declaration of Human Rights of 1948), is largely considered nonpartisan (political parties and administrations from the Right and the Left are quick to prove that they uphold human rights), and is easily communicated and understood (the idea that one has a right not to be arbitrarily beaten and raped by police officers is quite commonsensical). I believe in the case of *Breaking the Siege*, the use of the human rights framework (broadly conceived) was a simple unexamined reflex. Even so, the language of human rights exists in part because activists, media makers, and artists helped innovate and develop it as a popular language for talking about state violence and repression. If media makers, artists, and activists do not innovate new and better languages to describe systems of oppression and injustice, no one else will.[19]

The attempt to use physical evidence to build a case and prove to an audience that terrible violence did happen fits firmly in the tradition of "counterinformation" of Canalseisdejulio and a framework of resistance politics. The film is battling with and engaging the official story that there was no excessive use of violence. It is possible that *Breaking the Siege*, along with the other allied films and media, succeeded in creating the dominant popular narrative of the events as a demonstration of horrific state violence meant to repress social movements. (This was a near unanimous popular opinion of postrepression media about Atenco, although it is nearly impossible to empirically establish something as slippery as public opinion or collective consciousness.) I do not wish to argue that changing public opinion was not a worthy pursuit. However, it is unclear what the tangible benefits of this narrative have been to Atenco or La Otra Campaña, and there have also been some equally questionable consequences. It may have permanently established Atenco and the Frente as a victimized population needing the intervention of others more powerful than themselves in order to create justice. It may have also helped establish that the Mexican state is not to be crossed under pain of violence and sexual assault.[20] It is possible that the shift in narrative was worth it, but it should certainly not be uncritically assumed to be positive.

Purposeful Filmmaking Practice

The "call to action" the filmmakers intended with *Breaking the Siege* is much more apparent in the collective production and distribution of the documentary rather than in its specific messages. For Viveros, making the film was something that he could *do* in the wake of the violence against his friend and colleague Valentina Palma Novoa. Inviting media makers from La Otra to use the facilities of Canalseisdejulio was something else that he could do. In 2008, Viveros told me how he got in touch with Défossé to invite him to collaborate:

> So Nico [Défossé] came and brought a whole group of guys from other places who came with footage [*material*]. So we began to make a network; we began to share material. I began to use contacts from the *Canal* to get more material, like Univision, like La Jornada. . . . And we began to put it together [*armarlo*]. . . . And a lot of information started to come out. A lot of people began to collaborate. So the project started to transcend. . . . It became a very cool phenomenon. The web began to work.

For Viveros and his colleagues, working on the film amounted to *doing something*, taking action against state attempts to systematically silence social movements and their allied independent media. Viveros and Défossé both described this collaborative process to me as almost magical. Nearly a year after I spoke to Viveros, and three years after the events he was recounting, Défossé described the process from his perspective:

> From being on the [La Otra Campaña] tour, we had the network of alternative media. So there were compañeros who gave me images of inside [Atenco] on the fourth in the early morning. . . . And later word gets around that we're doing this video. People even came without us asking, to leave more material. . . . There is a collective dimension of this work that is very strong. . . . It was a lot of people, and the process was very beautiful [*bonito*]. . . . The little rivalries that there are in whichever medium, [and] that are here too, even though they are activist media [were put aside]. There was a lot of collaboration here.

The practice of making the film itself opened a space for acting against the repression. Once the space was opened, it provided an arena for others to collaborate on the project and act against the repression as well. Many people began to collaborate on the film; some providing images, others subtitles in different languages, still others copying and distributing the film.

I have argued elsewhere (Hinegardner 2009) that *Breaking the Siege* and films like it are a constitutive arena for political action quite apart from the specific message or knowledge that the film communicates. Participating in the production and distribution of an activist documentary implicates the participant in the struggle. It is a risk and a demonstration of support not unlike marching in a political demonstration. It is an act of transformative solidarity: one goes from being a bystander to being a participating activist.

Because collaborating on the film was a kind of activism and action in itself, the ethical nature of that participation mattered a great deal. Viveros and Défossé decided to produce and distribute the documentary according to the collaborative, nonhierarchical, nonproprietary, noncapitalist ethic of production and distribution of Promedios, an indigenous community-based media organization, and the IndyMedia networks closely related to La Otra Campaña in Mexico.[21] For Défossé, these production and distribution practices were a necessary condition of their collaboration with Canalseisdejulio. This meant that while the language of the documentary was rooted in Canalseisdejulio's resistance strategy of "counterinformation," the production and distribution of the documentary was unambiguously grounded in the autonomist strategy of La Otra Campaña and Promedios.

At first glance, it would seem that the production and distribution practices of Canalseisdejulio and Promedios were nearly identical. Both organizations recorded their own material as well as obtaining material from allies. The vast majority of the products of both organizations were effectively distributed through informal video vendors and activists giving and selling unauthorized copies to each other. However, they came to these processes through very different perspectives. Canalseisdejulio often purchased audiovisual material from repositories to use in its products and would have preferred to have entirely commercial (though fiercely independent) products. Carlos Mendoza, the head and cofounder of Canalseisdejulio viewed the informal means of distribution as politically helpful, but unfortunate. He told me in 2007 that he realized that video pirates allowed many more people to see their films than Canalseisdejulio could have reached on their own, but because Canalseisdejulio owed its continued existence to video sales, he also deeply regretted the loss of revenue. At the time, all Canalseisdejulio films began with a generous but firm message thanking video pirates for their work distributing its documentaries, but reminding the viewer that the organization lives off of the profits of its films and so to please send some funds back to Canalseisdejulio.[22] The sentiment of this message is quite different from the official threat of legal action that most commercial films carry, but it is also a far cry from the "Watch, discuss, and distribute this video" message that was placed at the beginning of *Breaking the Siege*.

Although Viveros certainly took the lead on this film and could therefore be seen to be in tension with Mendoza's vision for Canalseisdejulio's production and distribution practices, Mendoza easily assented to its method of production and distribution. For someone to take charge of the project for the advancement of their own career or for their own financial benefit would have been distasteful (perhaps even seen as protagonismo), and it seems that Mendoza also recognized this ethical responsibility under the circumstances. Mendoza had taken this stance himself in 1982 and again in 1984 when he refused accept the very prestigious Ariel award for his work.[23] This collaborative mode of production was never questioned as the most appropriate for the occasion even though Canalseisdejulio had never utilized this production and distribution model before. No individuals were credited as the filmmakers on the project, and no author's rights were claimed.

The nonproprietary mode of production is significant for two reasons. First, because it demonstrates that in a time of crisis in which rapid and wide distribution seemed to be of the utmost priority, the collaborators on *Breaking the Siege* used the noncommercial, nonproprietary model of IndyMedia, knowing it would help distribute the documentary further, wider, and quicker. They did not use the professional independent commercial model that would have placed films in bookstores and newsstands throughout the country (like some of its other widely distributed products). Instead, it and indigenous media networks placed the film online for free. The assumption that the nonproprietary model was more nimble and efficient is, of course, in direct tension with neoliberal assumptions that capitalist markets and their associated forces of supply and demand are the most effective means of production and distribution. In this case, defiance, righteous indignation, and compassion were the forces that initially helped produce and distribute the film. (I discuss this kind of distribution practice in the next chapter as an ethical practice in anti-neoliberal self-making.) That the informal means were more efficient came as no surprise to the Canalseisdejulio team, of course, because that is effectively how their films have as wide a distribution as they have.

Based on web presence and its ubiquity among street vendors in the years after the repression, I suspect that *Breaking the Siege* had the widest national distribution of any film Canalseisdejulio had made at that point, but because of the largely informal means of distribution, this would be extremely difficult to demonstrate conclusively. It is certain that the film had more international distribution than any other film they had made. Most Canalseisdejulio films do not carry subtitles in different languages, and *Romper el cerco* was translated into at least five different languages.[24] Well into 2018, the film was available for streaming or download in numerous places online. If the goal was to produce quickly and distribute widely, in short, the collaborative model seems to have worked.

This mode of production and distribution is also significant because it suggests that production and distribution practices are more nimble and accessible to purposeful change than the conceptual framework, or language of a film. Thought, of course, did go into the analytical focus of the film, but never in the years that I have known Viveros and Défossé, or the many conversations we have had about *Breaking the Siege*, have they ever revealed ambivalence about detailing the many violent human rights abuses that they do in the film. Indeed, this was a primary reason to make the film: to expose the extreme violence of the state. In contrast to the difficulty of creating a new language to describe state violence without relying on neoliberal conceptions of individual harm was difficult—it was never questioned—and yet Viveros, Défossé, and the other collaborators could quite easily discuss and decide on what Buddle (2008, 135) has referred to as the "alternative economies of practice" associated with indigenous video and cultural production. Practice was simply more visible as a purposeful project than language.

Autoconsumo, or "Preaching to the Choir"

The three sieges referred to in the title *Breaking the Siege* reveal several intended audiences for the film. These distinct audiences demonstrate how the filmmaking team thought of how this film would operate as an arena constitutive of political power. The first siege is a physical siege of social movements that prevents them from acting. This siege implies an audience of the officials and politicians who had a hand in the repression, or who have had a hand in other repressions. It is primarily to them that participation in the production and distribution of such a documentary represents a defiant act. This is the "they" that wins if people stay silent in the wake of such repressions: the actors who make up the state.

The second siege refers to a siege of biased media strangling the truth. Implied in this siege is a general audience that is victim to the misinformation of commercial media. They are the general audience whose hearts and minds are struggled over as commercial and activist media vie to convince them of their perspective. Mazzarella (2013) uses the image of the "pissing man" to describe how censor boards in India imagine the popular audiences of Bollywood films. The pissing man is an unsophisticated, illiterate moviegoer who uncritically urinates where he is told. He is in contrast to more educated, sophisticated viewers (like the educated filmmakers and censors themselves) who have the critical analytical capacity to know what is appropriate and what is not. It is unclear if the pissing man really exists, but it is his image (a man who might rape if he sees a rape in a movie, or who might kill someone if he sees murder) that justifies film censorship in the minds of censor board members in India as an unfortunate necessity to keep the social order.

In the activist imagination implied by the idea of a siege of truth (or even in the more mainstream idea of a particular politically biased media), the average viewer is as malleable as the pissing man but is not potentially violent and needing to be shielded. Instead, he or she is a viewer who is easily duped by the conservative biases of commercial media and potentially "won over" through activist media. If average viewers knew the truth they might sympathize and identify with social movements rather than the state. According to a Gramscian view of hegemony, these are the minds at play in the struggle over meaning (see Hall 1981, Lipschutz 2005, Castells 2012). As Carlos Fazio (the same media scholar interviewed in *Breaking the Siege*) has written, "during the events of Atenco ... the majority of the news media, and more than a few of the 'star' hosts, columnists, and editorialists, came together in a lynching campaign oriented toward forcing before public opinion an image of the Atenquenses as intrinsically violent and rebellious." (2013, 297). According to Fazio and many other critical news consumers in 2006 (including Viveros, Défossé, and Mariño, all contributors to *Breaking the Siege*), they did this "with the goal of altering and controlling opinions, ideas, and values" (Fazio 2013, 298) so that the general public would interpret the ensuing state violence against people in Atenco as necessary.[25] Under this roughly Gramscian idea of activist media, Canalseisdejulio's "counterinformation" is a counterhegemonic force attempting to resist a dominant construction of La Otra Campaña and the Frente as uncontrolled and dangerous.

The more radical construction of this imagined malleable audience conceives of it as a population of potential activists. In this more Marxian imagination, the general public are manipulated and oppressed into a false consciousness (identifying with interests that are not their own) and need the wool pulled from their eyes in order to see the true nature of their oppression.[26] A film, or a series of mediated experiences, can be the catalyst for individuals to awaken to the reality of their own oppression. This more Marxian perspective is not at odds with the Gramscian idea of struggle over meanings; it merely has a slightly different focus: individual conceptualizations of self and consciousness rather than public discourse and social understandings. In this understanding, activist films are attempting to recruit new activists, not just beat back mainstream or oppressive discourse. In both cases, the siege of biased media referred to in the title *Breaking the Siege* prevented a malleable and impressionable public from either gaining true consciousness of themselves as political actors or simply feeling kindly toward La Otra Campaña and the Frente. Both of these overlapping scenarios are at play in this imagined general audience of an activist film. This imagined audience is the battleground over which mediated political struggle takes place.[27]

These two intended audiences, the oppressor and the malleable mainstream public, are very important. However, the third audience is the one that I find the most compelling, in part because it makes up the vast majority of the actual viewers of a film like *Breaking the Siege* at the same time that it faces the most criticism. This is the siege referred to in the siege of fear that is created from the police and media sieges. It is an audience that conceives of itself as part of the same population that was repressed on May 4: an international "inside" network of social movements and independent media producers that (1) wanted to know what was going on behind the "siege" of biased media coverage, (2) faced physical lines of police that prevented them from acting, and (3) might be afraid because of the media and physical barriers erected against them. This population might be afraid, unsure of what just happened, and struggling to come to terms with and understand the events. In other words, this is also the same population of activists that encompassed both Viveros and Défossé, even though neither of them was involved with the Frente specifically.

Many activists consider this third "inside" audience to be problematic. Défossé, for example, told me that mostly "what happens is that these projections [of *Breaking the Siege* in Europe] stay in the same circle of people as always, that certainly does not need to be convinced." I often heard this criticism of activist media from urban, non-campesino allies of the Frente: the same people as always show up for screenings and to meetings. The complaint is rooted in an idea succinctly articulated by Manuel Castells: "the most important source of influence in today's world is the transformation of people's minds" (2013, 27). If people's minds are not being transformed by a film (because they already agree with the film), then the film has not accomplished anything. In English terms, the film is "preaching to the choir," addressing only those who do not need to be addressed. In Mexico, the term is "autoconsumo" (self-consumption). It is a problem because new audiences are not reached to be converted.

However, this Gramscian or Marxian view is not the only way of conceiving of how activist media can work. I first became interested in this concept as I began to realize that I continuously heard complaints about autoconsumo from my non-campesino friends and colleagues in Mexico City whenever the topic of activist media arose, but I absolutely never heard these complaints from anyone from Atenco. Instead, members of the Frente seemed consistently almost overwhelmed with help and offers from people they considered to be outsiders. One of their greatest organizational challenges was not how to reach and convert outsiders, but how to know which of the unsolicited offers pouring in from outsiders were genuine (versus attempts to spy on or sabotage the movement), and how to best communicate with those offering support and utilize their offers.

A dramatic illustration of the Frente's general attitude toward outsiders was the feeling expressed to me by one of the only members of the Frente who refused my request to interview him. Since he seemed critical of my project in general, I asked him if there was ever a use for researchers such as myself for the

Frente. "No," he replied. "Everyone who needs to know about the Frente already knows." This was an attitude corroborated by many people who also quite openly granted me interviews. They did not feel that there was much harm in answering my questions but did not think I could do much to help the Frente either. They graciously granted me time and related their experiences and wisdom, not for the sake of the Frente, but out of simple kindness to me.

Why, then, were the urban non-campesino activists nearly obsessed with autoconsumo as a political obstacle? One reason is the significant blurring between ideas of "insiders" and "outsiders," involving many layers of interlocking associations with other social movements and communities. For many members of the Frente, urban sympathizers (and the population in my experience most likely to complain about autoconsumo) *are* the exterior population they are attempting to reach. The urban sympathizers simply do not consider themselves to be outsiders and so don't recognize that they are the target "outside" audience.

However, it is not simply a matter of the definition of "insider." There is another, deeper, aspect to the difference between how the Frente was conceiving of organizing through film and how the urban allies concerned with autoconsumo viewed media activism. The vision of how the Frente's Communication Commission was to work was explained to me by Eduardo Ríos in 2009 when I asked him about what success would look like for the commission. He answered,

> I think that the social process is complex. The thing is that you are getting consciousness, and the community is also. Your individual participation and your private consciousness [is forming], but the community itself is developing collective consciousness . . . reencountering itself, valuing [itself]. . . . The thing . . . that we have to learn as a commission is to try to transmit to the interior and the exterior. To remind ourselves, and remind the people, that there we are, that we exist, and that we are not going to let up.

In other words, for Ríos, making films is not an exercise in communicating something outward toward an audience who needs to be awakened. It is instead about finding and building a conception of the self, both a collective self and an individual self. He didn't answer my question about success even within the realm of communicative strategy, but instead as a social process. For Ríos, this is a long, continual, collaborative process that works toward an indefinite end. Consciousness is not something that you "get" through film, or a sudden awakening, but something that you develop and slowly form through participation and practice. He is not overly concerned with conversion or conversing with mainstream ideas. Filmmaking for Ríos has been a process of building an idea of himself, and his community building a collective idea of itself as an independent "we," rather than sending or receiving an already fully formed idea of what that self is. Ríos's vision of media activism is closer to a community-based media model that sees itself as autonomous from mainstream media because it has distinct goals, rather than being resistant to it.

The division between resistance strategies and autonomy strategies is exactly the division that La Otra was making between the electoral campaign and the Other Campaign. One might also see it as the difference between a reformist agenda and a radical one, or the difference between establishing dominance and "changing the world without taking power" (Holloway 2002). The autonomy strategy is, of course, deeply informed by Zapatismo. Cristina, a self-identified member of La Otra Campaña in 2008 and a filmmaker who collaborated on a film about the 2006 repression called *Atenco: Un crimen de estado* (Atenco: A Crime of the State, Colectivo Klamvé, 2006), elaborated on the idea of autonomous media strategy when I asked her if her film collective produced counterinformation along the lines of Canalseisdejulio:

> No. I don't think so. Because this is to give a kind of validity to the information of the other, as if that one was the good [one] and we were the opposite, or the counterinformers. I personally think that what it is about is to generate our own media, our own networks, our own channels, our own professional codes for our information, for our information needs. So I think that to say "counterinformation" is to place yourself—like counterculture too, it's the same concept—to place yourself not only against, but outside, below.

Here, Cristina articulates quite clearly the difference between using filmmaking as a practice in resistance and using it as a practice of autonomy. La Otra Campaña was uninterested in taking over or impeding the operations of mainstream institutions. It strove to be simply unconcerned with them and make its own institutions that operated according to a different set of political ethics rather than having to first contend with mainstream politics. The job of the media makers identifying with La Otra Campaña then, was not to push back and resist mainstream media, but to provide media for "our own networks." They were attempting to create a distinct, autonomous body of work (an Other media) rather than a countermedia.

Although I am making a sharp distinction between autonomy strategy and resistance strategy, in practice the two can overlap considerably, and they did in the case of *Breaking the Siege*. Even as the film was self-consciously providing a counternarrative to the repression in the tradition of Canalseisdejulio's counterinformation, in practice it was also creating autonomous networks and channels of communication. *Breaking the Siege* provided a platform for activists to *do* something in the wake of the repression: they could collaborate on a project helping to bring together an expansive network of activists spreading throughout Mexico into the United States and Europe. Much like Mario Viveros, none of these activists needed very much convincing of the virtue of the Frente or the evil of a state repression. It is quite possible that very few people ever saw *Breaking the Siege* that weren't already horrified by the repression. They were not hearts and minds to be won in a Marxian or Gramscian sense, but they were an "outside" audience according to the Frente's conception of outsiders. To someone like Eduardo Ríos, both Mario Viveros and Nicolas Défossé, along with their entire audience of sympathetic allies, are all outsiders, not to be converted, but to be organized. Additionally, taking part in the production and distribution of the documentary formed part of their own individual process of forming themselves as ethical and political subjects as well as forming a part of a larger, more collective process of forming a sense of "we" in concert with the Frente. The imperfect nature of the human rights language of the film that I detail above—human rights language not quite fitting with how the Frente usually saw itself—is an example of some of the difficulties that the Frente faces in trying to communicate with and organize these "outside" supporters.

Even if no one's consciousness was suddenly awoken by *Breaking the Siege*, it doesn't mean that the film wasn't a step in a continual process of developing consciousness in the sense that Ríos describes. My friend Mario Viveros as an excellent example. Although he was vaguely sympathetic to the Frente on May 3, 2006, he was also critical of some of the things that Ignacio del Valle was saying in his speeches at the time. He thought, for example, that del Valle's speech the day before the repression was perhaps a bit too radical and removed from the practicalities of Mexican politics. However, the events of the repression touched him personally. At first, he was just going to produce a short piece and lend resources to a compañero. This step led to another, which led to another, which led to a feature-length film that is firmly allied with a social movement that he had been wary of a month before. The story of *Breaking the Siege* is, in some sense, a story of consciousness building and awakening, but not in the sense that resistance communication models imagine it. Before making *Breaking the Siege*, Viveros was already an activist and a partisan. He did not need his consciousness to be awakened. The film did not convert him, but it did provide a platform for him to participate, to *militar*, in alliance with the Frente. He became more militant and practiced an ethical form of filmmaking that he hadn't before, and his politics and political practice shifted as a result.

Even if not one person has ever been convinced of the arguments of *Breaking the Siege*, helping make the film changed Viveros's politics, even if it was slightly. He became better friends and colleagues with Défossé. He may have cemented friendships and working relationships with the other journalists and activists who contributed to the project. He pronounced himself a more committed ally to the Frente and La Otra Campaña in a way that he had not before. In short, being involved in the production and distribution of the film enabled Viveros to *do* ethical activist practice that had consequences for himself politically as well as for others. He developed his own consciousness as a compañero activist and provided opportunities for others to do the same.

And although Viveros was perhaps more central to the production of the film than others, his story of the film bringing him closer in to a network of militating allies and activists is widespread. At the end of 2008, I attended the première of a film called *Atenco: A dos años* (Atenco: Two years later) (Colectivo Klamvé, 2008) in the cultural center of Coyoacán (a very trendy and traditionally left-leaning neighborhood in Mexico City). The first question after the film ended came from a middle-aged man who stood up and spoke with emotion as he explained he had not seen a documentary about Atenco before, only what he read about in the newspapers, and he was incensed. "How can I help you distribute these films?" he asked. "Everyone I know should watch this." The man's reaction was repeated often in dozens of film screenings that I attended over the course of several years.

Incidents like this could be used to show how films help to raise or awaken consciousness. According to resistance models of activist media, people like this are "converted" or awoken through watching the film. In this case, perhaps this man was. I do not deny that there are shifts of consciousness that can happen through the messages in a film. However, what I find more significant about this kind of reaction is that the first impulse is not to ask, "How can I volunteer to help organize against such injustice?" or "Where can I donate money to support political prisoners?" Instead, the reaction pertains to the documentary itself; the documentary acted on him and inspired him to act as a distributor *of the film*. The film becomes both his inspiration and his platform for action. He is drawn in to a network of activism surrounding the Frente through doing something within the arena of action that the film itself created by nature of being something that can be, and even asks to be, collaboratively circulated. The very next day this man might offer the film to his friends, be rejected by those who have negative feelings about Atenco, and become frustrated because of autoconsumo. He is unsatisfied because he cannot convert others, and yet he himself, within a very short period of time, has come to identify himself as an ally of the Frente willing to act—circulate a film—on their behalf.

There may only be one person out of an audience of one hundred that feels their consciousness shift as the result of a film, but there are many more who will be drawn closer in to an interpersonal network of activism as a result of the same film. They will have met and socialized with a social movement spokesperson at a screening. They will have elevated their casual interest or concern to a very slight level of activism by copying a DVD and giving it to a few of their friends, or organizing a screening at their university. The focus on conversion through discourse obscures the degree to which the film drew this man and others like him (including Viveros and Défossé) into a form of ethical activist practice that contributes to the work of collective and individual transformation.

This happens not because of some special properties of film, but because people in the current moment are drawn to film as a medium. As José Luis Mariño told me in 2008, "It [film] makes horizontal communication. It allows citizens to sometimes get to know each other, or they learn things they didn't know. . . . It is where more people are participating, where most of the young people are in politics and culture. . . . That is to say, that we are working with the symbols, and little by little we are making a small space, a new imaginary, a new conception of reality, a different kind of common sense." His description sounds a lot like a Gramscian processes of creating hegemony except that it is unconcerned with becoming dominant. It is a new and different kind of common sense and collective imaginary that has aspirations, not of taking over the mainstream, but simply being an autonomous space or network.

The space of the film's production and distribution provides opportunities to practice doing and being instead of just feeling and thinking, opportunities to cultivate a sense of self (both individual and collective selves) that can also be transformative. Faye Ginsburg, for example, has described how "social relations built out of media practices are creating new networks of indigenous cooperation" (1993, 575) in Australia. Elsewhere, she describes media production as a practice in "collective self-production" (1997, 120). Kathleen Buddle has argued that indigenous radio production in Canada "calls into being new forms of subjectivity and action, and with them come new collective senses of belonging" (2008, 135). These new subjectivities and new forms of being (new senses of self) occur through the collective process of production and circulation, quite apart from any received messages or relationship with an audience. Flores (2004), for example, even describes how a creative process never produced a completed film, and yet it was an extremely valuable, even transformative, collective experience for a whole community.

A purely resistance perspective of activist filmmaking sees that nothing has happened if discursive, legal, or mental ground has not been won away from the enemy/state/mainstream. It is focused outward. An autonomy strategy of activist media doesn't want to legitimate mainstream structures and trends through acknowledging them. Instead, it is focused inward to a complex long-term processes of transforming individual and collective selves into something otherwise inconceivable. These processes of "inward" collective transformation mean that media is often *doing something* even if it isn't converting people's consciousnesses or shifting the weight of dominant hegemonic discourses. They are creating and strengthening bonds among activists, turning sympathetic bystanders into active participants, solidifying political alliances, and transforming how people understand themselves as political actors. All these things can happen completely independently of the content of a specific film. The specifics of how circulation practices become transformative ethical practices is the focus of the next chapter.

Under this conception and strategy of activist media use, the media practices that are often derided as "slacktivism" (Morozov 2009) or empty gestures (changing one's profile picture in solidarity of a cause, reposting a video, retweeting a political slogan) take on a new light. It doesn't matter if a social media post on Facebook or Twitter converts no one or is seen by anyone who disagrees with it; it will have been a small political and ethical practice of cultivating an individual and collective sense of consciousness and self. For the individual, it is a significant step of participating and declaring oneself implicated. It is the virtual equivalent of stepping off of the sidewalk watching a demonstration passing by and into the street to join it. For the collective, the accumulation of myriad small participations helps create and crystallize activist networks of allies. *Breaking the Siege* began as the impulse to upload a short denouncement to a web page, an act that may have been defined as an instance of "slacktivism," and within a month became a crucial part of a process of transformation for possibly hundreds (perhaps even thousands) of people newly willing to act in solidarity with the Frente. Furthermore, this happened not because the message of the film was so convincing, but because the film, through its collaborative mode of production and circulation, invited and enabled people to *do something* within the framework of making and producing a film.

CHAPTER FIVE

Distribution and Organization

At the beginning of 2009, the Frente launched a new campaign along with many partnering organizations called Libertad y Justicia Para Atenco (Liberty and Justice for Atenco) dedicated to the release of the last of the political prisoners from the 2006 repression. The vast majority of the more than two hundred detainees from May 3 and 4 were released shortly after their capture. At the time that they launched the campaign, there were only thirteen people still in prison and three *perseguidos*, or those in hiding because of outstanding warrants.[1] There were ten people being held in the state facility in Texcoco (Molino de Flores), and three being held in the nation's highest-security prison, known as El Altiplano, or La Palma.[2] The three in El Altiplano were Ignacio del Valle, Felipe Álvarez, and Héctor Galindo Gochicoa. All three had had warrants for their arrest issued before the repression and were arrested in the police standoff in Texcoco on May 3 that began the repression. The perseguidos were issued warrants for the same alleged crimes but were not there on the morning of May 3 to be arrested. Felipe and Héctor were sentenced to more than sixty years of prison for a variety of charges related to the retention of officials in April 2006, and Ignacio del Valle was sentenced to more than one hundred years. His sentence was so exaggeratedly long that, according to one of his lawyers, many of the charges against him were never followed up on because it was impossible that he would live long enough to serve the sentences that he had already.

The goal of the Campaign for Liberty and Justice for Atenco was to have all the political prisoners released and all the outstanding warrants against people revoked. Throughout the winter and spring of 2009, there were press conferences, solidarity marches, and media events with famous allies staged at the respective prisons. This was also a time in which the Mexican Supreme Court was hearing the human rights cases of May 3 and 4. As part of these renewed efforts, in April 2009, I accompanied a small commission of the Frente on a weekend solidarity trip to the southern state of Oaxaca. The trip was meant to build solidarities between the Frente and Oaxacan social movements as part of the campaign, specifically the APPO. The APPO (Asamblea Popular de los Pueblos de Oaxaca, or the Popular Assembly of the Peoples of Oaxaca) was a social movement that emerged almost immediately after the political repression in Atenco. At the end of May 2006, the teachers' union of the state (el Magisterio) went on strike to renegotiate their contracts for the following year, as they always did at the end of the school year. As part of the strike, the teachers erected a plantón, or occupation, in the center square of the capital city. This too, was a yearly occurrence. In a dramatic historical shift, however, the governor Ulises Ruiz Ortiz was not negotiating with the union representatives, and the teachers had been camped in the central plaza for over a month when in the early morning hours of June 14, state police attempted to displace the plantón by force. A helicopter flew overhead shooting tear gas canisters into the square, and riot police came from all sides taking down banners and cutting down tents. For a lot of city residents, this police action was the last straw in a series of very unpopular actions taken by the governor, and by nine o'clock the same morning, the teachers, with the help of a massive popular outpouring, took back the central plaza and forced the state police to leave the city. By the afternoon, the APPO was formed as a unification of the Magisterio and dozens of other local political groups, community organizations, and residents of Oaxaca City. The APPO served as a de facto government for the capital city from June 14 until November 25, when federal police overwhelmed the APPO in a demonstration of violent repressive force that rivaled that of Atenco six months earlier.

Under the APPO's organization, a time often referred to as the Oaxaca Commune (Esteva 2008), life in the city went on more or less as normal for most local people except for the erection of barricades in the streets at night by community organizations (allied with the APPO) to keep the police from returning, and the near constant series of political marches demanding the removal of the state governor. Activists from the APPO and allied media makers who spent time in Oaxaca during the commune unanimously described the time as a magical, uplifting time of intense feelings of togetherness and productivity. Famously, the APPO had its own media outlets, including pirate radio stations and the takeover of several commercial stations and the public television station.

Atenco and Oaxaca are often spoken of together because so many mobile activists and media makers traveled directly from covering the repression in Atenco to covering the Oaxacan Commune (see Gibler 2009, for example). Oaxaca in the summer of 2006 was an incredibly powerful generator of powerful political art and media and as a result (coupled with the heavy presence of foreigners in the city) has been extensively documented and analyzed in scholarship and film.³ By 2009, the APPO as a designation was more an idea than an active cohesive social movement, but the solidarity event with the Frente was referred to in some promotional materials as a meeting of the APPO and the Frente.

When the six of us arrived early in the morning to Oaxaca City, our hosts picked us up and drove us to the collective house where we would be staying for the weekend. This collective house was an attempt to bring together a dozen or more young people who had been involved in social movements (some of whom had been political prisoners in the past) in a communal living and working situation. Our hosts explained that the house was under constant police surveillance and that police had attempted to break in twice under the pretext that residents were trafficking in drugs. Both times, residents and neighbors were able to drive the police off, but as a result they were trying to open up the house as much as possible through activities open to the public. These activities (including film screenings, performances, and a small shop that sold the arts and crafts of political prisoners) brought more and varied people into the house, providing protection for those who lived there and legitimating the space as a center for cultural and social activities.

Almost immediately upon arriving at the house, Virgilio, who seemed to have been central to organizing the trip, produced from his backpack a packet of three documentaries about the Frente on DVD, and he presented them to our host as a gift.⁴ The Frente has a long history of giving films as gifts in similar circumstances, to the extent that Salvador Díaz proudly claims that his first Atenco film was used as their "calling card" during the original struggle against the airport. These films were also screened at various points in public places during the time that we were in Oaxaca, and sold to passersby at various points (although not by members of the Frente). Much like most political events of the Left throughout the country, activist films formed a constant material presence and activity, more invisible for their ubiquity rather than a conscious effort on the part of any of the organizers or activists.

In this chapter, I use this one solidarity visit in Oaxaca to examine how the Frente utilized films as a tool for social organizing. I argue that three key ways that these films were used—gifting, screening, and selling—facilitated or mediated autonomous ethical political economies. The social practices of media circulation and consumption assisted in producing new ethical (noncapitalist, non-neoliberal) ways of doing and being. Gifting, screening, and selling activist documentaries (within and beyond this single solidarity visit) are noncapitalist economic practices that, much like film production, provide opportunities to purposefully cultivate and strengthen ethical-political senses of individual and collective self.

Media and Cultural Production

> The medium is the message. This is merely to say that the personal and social consequences of any medium ... result from the new scale that is introduced into our affairs by each extension of ourselves, or by any new technology.... For the "message" of any medium or technology is the change of scale or pace or pattern that it introduces into human affairs.
> Marshall McLuhan 2003 [1964], 19–20

Today, Marshall McLuhan's argument, "the medium is the message," is a cliché that signifies how the ever-increasing speed and scale of digital technology is making the world smaller and more connected. McLuhan's argument is that there is a social aspect to media production and distribution that tends to organize people in certain ways. He conceptualizes media production in the same light as other general modes of production such as agriculture or industrialization. All are large-scale economic and social activities that "have some obvious social patterns of organization as a result" (McLuhan 2003 [1964], 34). In this conceptualization, agriculture produces food, but it also helps produce and support a certain kind of social organization that tends toward permanent settlements, higher population densities, and job specialization. These modes of production are certainly not deterministic, and anthropologists have long discredited any strict relationship between a mode of production and a particular categorization of social organization. However, it is also a certainty that any large-scale economic activity, such as a shift from agriculture to industrialization, will have social consequences. McLuhan argues that the production and distribution of media, just like the production and distribution of food, has social consequences. McLuhan was generally concerned with scale. I invoke his conception that "the medium is the messages" to highlight shifts in how people can use media to arrange social organization in substantive, qualitative ways.

Cultural production is usually conceived of as referring to the production of material culture (art, film, music). However, any contemporary social movement is also involved in attempts to purposefully produce "culture" in the traditional anthropological sense of a nearly undefinable, ever-changing, fluid sense of being and doing. I argued in Chapter 3 that ideas of compañerismo are often incompatible with political practices associated with liberal democratic citizenship. As a result, activists have little choice but to find other political arenas, such as filmmaking, to develop and practice the ethic of being the kind of political subject that they wish they were. Likewise, many economic activities (selling, buying, consuming) are inconsistent with the anti–corporate capitalist ethic of the Frente, and so activists seek out and create new ethical economies to innovate and practice being the kind of economic subjects they wish to be. In this way, producing and distributing documentaries becomes a creative project, nor oriented as much toward the film itself, but using the film as a platform to innovate social, cultural, political, and economic ways of doing, organizing, and being. The Frente and its allies, to the extent that such a diverse landscape of people and movements can be generalized about, were broadly trying to build new cultures (plural) in which corporate capitalism, neoliberalism, and a host of other social, political, and economic forces that they saw as damaging were socially and culturally devalued in favor of a new set of ethics and values.

In her work with aboriginal Australian television networks in the 1990s, Faye Ginsburg found that media production mediated (facilitated, or provided an arena for) the production of indigenous identities as well as indigenous content (1995). She argues that "analysis [of media] needs to focus less on the formal qualities of film and video as text and more on the cultural *mediations* that occur through film and video works" (Ginsburg 1995, 259). Ginsburg's television producers purposefully used their television station to cultivate indigenous identities, both among themselves and for a larger, national, largely white Australian audience. She argues, "when other forms are no longer effective, indigenous media offers a possible means—social, cultural, and political—for reproducing and transforming cultural identity among people who have experienced massive political, geographic, and economic disruption" (Ginsburg 1995, 266). This reproduction and transformation of identity did happen through the development of content for the television station about aboriginal people, but it also happened through the economic and political structures that came about as a result of the television station. The station mediated professional training programs, interpersonal connections between aboriginal artists, and connections between videographers and performers. According to her conceptualization, aboriginal Australians had used in the past, and continued to use, other forms of mediation (oral histories, traditional dances and ceremonies, even legal pathways) to help mediate identity, but television production became one means of working toward collective social, cultural, and political goals. In short, the station represented a "change of scale or pace or pattern" that had social consequences according to McLuhan's conceptualization. Her reframing of media and activism brings processes of social, economic, and political transformation out of the Habermasian realm of rational dialogue in which things happen because we talk about them, and into a realm of practice and human relationships in which things happen because we create new social, economic, and political cultures and structures.

I argued in the previous chapter that through the process of making the film *Breaking the Siege*, my friend Mario Viveros went from being a skeptical bystander to being one of the key players in the construction of the Frente's ally network on an international scale. This was a personal transformation, but it also cemented his friendship with Nicolas Défossé and others involved in the production and distribution of the film. These relationships are important because they create new professional and personal bonds that can spring into action in times of need. Anyone who has ever taken part in the production of a play knows, from the backyard theater of a group of children to the largest and most expensive Broadway production, the collective process of making theater creates bonds between people that can last a lifetime. Collectively producing a film can similarly create lasting human bonds. However, these human relationships are not only created in the production process; they are also created in the process of circulation and consumption.

In his foundational ethnological work *The Gift* (1990 [1950]), Marcel Mauss argues that economic transactions around the world and throughout time are based on a principle of creating relationships among people. Systems of what he calls "total social phenomena," such as the *potlaches* of the indigenous peoples of the Pacific Northwest and the Kula Ring of the Trobriand Islands are not shrewdly rational, self-interested economic systems based on the idea of accumulation of wealth. Instead, he argues, they are meaningful activities that help create relationships among people. In one of his classic examples, based in the work of early anthropologist Bronislaw Malinowski (2002 [1922]), people do not brave the open waters of the Pacific Ocean in a canoe simply to obtain valuable goods. They do so in order to create and maintain relationships with people on other islands. The circulation of things only provides the excuse for (mediates) relationship-building excursions. According to Mauss, the social obligations to give, to receive, and to reciprocate provide one of the most elemental structures for creating relationships of trust, solidarity, and interdependence among human beings throughout time and space.

Amplified and expanded by anthropologists such as Marshall Sahlins (2017 [1972]) and Richard Lee (2012 [1984]), Mauss's conclusions are almost commonsensical today. Buying your friend a beer creates a small obligation between the two of you, an intimacy of dependence and future obligation that deepens your friendship in the present and invites opportunities for other relationship-building beers in the future. The point of buying someone a drink is not the drink, but the human face-to-face interaction that takes place over the drink. Mauss calls such systems "total social phenomena" because the transaction is not merely economic. It is also moral (the obligation to reciprocate is based in social ideas of fairness), juridical (a contract is made), aesthetic (enjoyable and tasty), magically symbolic (a five-dollar bill would not create the same effect), and structural (gifting beers depends on a whole infrastructure that would make such an activity possible) (Mauss 1990 [1950], 79). In short, the exchange of things is "one of the human foundations on which our societies are built" (1990, 4) and permeates everything that we do. We exchange sacrifices for blessings and favors from God, and we demonstrate love for our families through gifts of food. Sometimes we demonstrate superiority through paying the bill, and entire nations dominate others through economic debt.

Mauss's arguments are political as well as academic. He laments that "the brutish pursuit of individual ends is harmful to the ends and the peace of all" (1990 [1950], 77). Mauss was a severe critic of what his uncle, Émile Durkheim, called the "cult of the individual" (1973 [1898]), a phrase Subcomandante Marcos used in the speech I discussed in Chapter 3. He urges his reader to resist the modernist (not yet neoliberal) impulses toward self-interested individualism, and instead to emphasize a politics of civility (and although he does not use this word, we might say "ethic") of "mutual respect and reciprocating generosity" (Mauss 1990 [1950], 83). The implication is that since systems of exchange are total social phenomena, they can also be significant agents of total social change: cultural change. As economies become more self-interested, individualistic, and ruthless, so will our societies by extension. If we form economies based on generosity, horizontality, and mutual dependency, cultures with these characteristics will follow.

The "culture" in the term "cultural production" is usually conceived of as material culture: art, film, music, theater. However, any mode of production (industrialism, for example) is also a generator that produces culture conceived of in less material terms (ways of doing, being, and knowing). The cultural transformations that take place through processes of industrialization are *mediated* through the economies of industrial production of things. The terms "media" and "cultural production" take on new and deeper meanings if we see film/video/radio/theater/art as substrates that facilitate creative human practice, and the purposeful production of culture as something that activism *does*.

Filmmakers are very literally producing a *medium* of human interactions—a substrate or a context—that helps *produce a culture* outside of neoliberal economies and neoliberal morality. A change in mode of production can be a powerful engine of cultural transformation. Activists tend to be focused on the "mode" as significant, but in order to have a "mode," one also needs some form of "production." It could be anything, but creative pursuits like filmmaking are powerful because people get excited about them. As I quoted José Luis Mariño saying in the last chapter, "It is where more people are participating, where most of the young people are in politics and culture." Creative pursuits like filmmaking have a great deal of flexibility built into their mode so that they work well in terms of experimentation (as I argued in the previous chapter). In short, films certainly produce discourse and messages, but they also operate on a social level of human interaction, creating social, economic, and political structures that can be culturally transformative. The basic economic practices of gifting, screening/watching, and selling films can be reinvented to structure relationships in new ways and quite literally help to produce culture.

Gifting Films

For Mauss (1990 [1950]), gifts are the most elemental human transaction. I first became interested in the practice of giving films as gifts because it is a primary channel through which social documentaries seemed to be distributed in Mexico. These quite obscure films can only occasionally be found in bookstores, rarely come out in theaters, and cannot be found in video rental stores. They are much more likely to be bought at a political march from a pirate video vendor and then copied for friends who might be interested. In 2009 in Mexico, the personal, face-to-face transaction of one person handing another a film on a physical DVD (like Virgilio gifting these three films to our hosts in Oaxaca) remained a primary way that films gained new audiences and were distributed to new places. The official film of the campaign was not in distribution in Oaxaca before we arrived. Even I had not seen it before that trip. Through physically bringing it to Oaxaca and gifting it to an ally, it was assured that the film would be copied and distributed in the area. At first, it might be found only in the small store in the collective house. Then it would appear in the collection of pirate street vendors, and soon it would find its way into the inventories of the personal libraries of dozens of people who burn copies for their friends, who then burn copies for their friends, thereby spreading the film among a considerable audience.

Gifting films carries all the positive, Maussian relationship-building attributes of a gift: they help build relationships and solidarities. Much like bringing beer or wine to a party or purchasing small gifts for one's family while traveling, the existence of activist films as a material good that is enjoyable, politically appropriate, and giftable is a primary way that the films are helpful to the Frente. Throughout our time in Oaxaca, lots of media changed hands in the form of music, books, DVDs, web addresses, and e-mails, simply as a result of sharing interesting or cool information with friends. DVDs are desirable and meaningful because they are one of the few products that a social movement produces. They help mediate face-to-face relationships based on sharing resources and knowledge. It is an added advantage that the films can be reproduced infinitely and very cheaply, both by the Frente and by recipients of the gift.

The films of the movement make a politically and ethically appropriate gift because they were not produced for profit, they have explicit political messages, they can be consumed collectively, and they support social movement networks of cultural production. In the case of the three DVDs presented to our Oaxacan hosts, a gift of media helped both movements. The Frente received wider exposure whenever the films were screened, and the Oaxacan collective acquired some content, both for film series and possibly to copy and sell in their small store as a means of support. In the case of Atenco (which has considerable social capital), this small Oaxacan collective also received the privilege of associating themselves with a nationally famous successful social movement.

Virgilio's gift of the films was also a personal and political practice tied to his own cultivation of ethical practice. I argued in Chapter 3 that filmmakers are able to use making films as a creative practice of cultivating a particular ethical disposition oriented toward collectivism rather than self-interest, profit, and individualism. Circulating films also mediates the cultivation of these same qualities. Gifting or sharing documentaries is an act that defies a neoliberal sense of economic activity. In the case of many social documentaries, it is not illegal because there are no rights reserved on the films. This, in itself, was a practice of cultivating compañerismo on the part of the filmmakers. It does not recognize the conception of private property or utilize exploitative labor. Instead it helps support an autonomous political and moral economy of independent filmmakers, social movements, and distributors who are working outside of neoliberal corporate capitalism. In short, it is exactly the kind of economic practice that Marcel Mauss imagined as a total social phenomenon with moral, juridical, economic, political, and even religious or magical components. Gifting films creates human relationships between people and helps support an entire autonomous infrastructure of leftist social movements.

Screening Films

Later in the evening of our first day in Oaxaca, after several public appearances of the Frente commission, we returned to the collective's house for a film screening. A projector and screen were set up in one long room, with enough folding chairs for forty people to attend. People of all descriptions and ages came to watch the film, including a small French film crew (who recorded the speeches made afterward), and a young indigenous man who had traveled all day from a teachers' college in a rural area. The film they had planned to screen was *Atenco: Un crimen de estado* (Colectivo Klamvé, 2006), which was introduced simply as "a film about Atenco." A few minutes into the film, however, the image froze and would not recover. After several minutes of playing with the DVD player and projector, Virgilio put in a recompiled film called *Atenco recargado* (Atenco recharged), which didn't have any difficulties.[5]

After the film, the four members of the Frente's commission said a few words to the small crowd and invited the audience's participation. The French film crew recorded. Several people stood to express their support and solidarity with the Frente and offer their assistance. The speeches and conversation went on for at least an hour after the film had ended, meaning that the crowd had been sitting in their metal folding chairs for almost four hours. Afterward, people did not leave but stayed around drinking the refreshments provided by the collective and exchanging e-mails, phone numbers, and stories.

This event was very much like the multitude of other social documentary screenings that I attended in 2008 and 2009 in venues throughout Mexico City, Atenco, and Oaxaca. Film screenings of political and social documentaries are a ubiquitous part of political and social organizing in Mexico. Sometimes these screenings were in cultural centers (like the Casa de Cultura in Coyoacán), free public centers (like the José Martí theater in a downtown metro station), "autonomous" spaces (like the Café Ramona, a Zapatista space, or the Auditorio Che Guevara at UNAM), university classrooms, independent bookstores, and even bars. During the yearlong occupation in support of AMLO in Mexico City, there was often a tent erected in the plantón labeled Cine del Pueblo (Cinema of the People), which showed political documentaries on a small television. Often films were projected onto the sides of buildings after dark, or on large portable screens in central public places. The day after the screening in the collective house, for example, a screening was arranged on a large portable screen in the central square of Oaxaca City as part of the daylong occupation. These screenings are nearly always free, introduced by a member of the movement or someone quite familiar with the movement, and followed by a question and answer period (see Figure 5.1).

Much like the gift of DVDs, these film screenings are firmly embedded in a set of ethical and political practices associated with leftist social movements and a left-leaning public in Mexico. Attending free public screenings of social documentaries is a form of consumption that is not burdened with much corporate capitalist or neoliberal ethical baggage. It is a practice of consuming that supports an autonomous, non–corporate capitalist moral economy of activism and transformation. In short, audience members get to practice/embody/perform what consumption might look like in a world not ruled by neoliberalism. It is free, collectively oriented, educational, and wholesome.

But these events aren't only about consuming media. They also mediate a certain kind of human interaction. In the case of both screenings in Oaxaca, the films provided a forum through which local people could meet members of the Frente, ask them questions, and build relationships with them. This could have happened without a film, of course, but the film was preferable to the Frente and the collective house for a variety of personal and political reasons. When I asked Virgilio why they screened a film instead of just talking about the Frente, he replied that it gets very repetitive to tell the same stories over and over, and it is traumatic to relive political violence again and again in speeches and presentations. Each of the members of the commission left the room during the screening in the collective house. Virgilio and a man I will refer to as Carlos spent most of the screening outside. When I asked Carlos why, he said that it was too personally difficult for him to see portions of the film. I also suspect, from hearing Virgilio talk about his own experiences with violence, that there is a fear of crying or showing emotion while telling these stories, especially for men. Conversely, if it is not traumatic and they do not show emotion, it may not convey the intensity of their experience and the urgency of the issues that they are talking about. A film has the benefit of having a precise tone, never losing its emotional intensity, and sparing members of the Frente from having to repeat (and relive) many of their experiences for an audience.

For the collective house, the screening mediated a political event much like a plantón or an occupation, but with an extremely low barrier for entry and risk. The people who came to the house were showing support for the Frente and the local collective through their presence at the screening, much like one might

Figure 5.1. Solidarity film screening. Photo by Livia K. Stone.

show support by coming to a political march. As I mentioned above, the house was under constant police surveillance, and the presence of more than forty people, including foreigners and a film crew, was a display of strength and legitimacy for the house. Unlike a political demonstration or occupation, however, the film screening provided an innocuous activity for such a display of solidarity and strength. It would be very difficult for the police to claim that a film screening was dangerous or illegal, even though organizing and attending such an event was essentially a political act. In other words, the screening mediated a very low intensity, low commitment political event that was open to a wide range of people and that made connections among a wide variety of people and organizations. It helped produce a cultural idea of what non-neoliberal consumption might look like: a free informative film and getting to know a group of potential allies and friends over political discussion and hot chocolate.

Selling Films

The Sunday of our weekend solidarity visit to Oaxaca, the collective we were staying with and its allies had planned a daylong occupation of the central plaza of Oaxaca City.[6] The central plaza of nearly any town or city in Latin America is very important space because it is the literal geographic center of public life (see Low 2000, for example). Central plazas all over Mexico are continually embroiled in struggles over the kinds of activities that should be taking place on them. One of the many reasons that the governor of Oaxaca was so unpopular in 2006 is that he had renovated the central square, spending a large amount of money removing large trees and repaving the square. The changes were deeply unpopular.

On Sundays during the Frente's solidarity visit in 2009, the main event in the plaza was a classical music concert organized by the city government. From the perspective of our Oaxacan hosts, this classical music concert was an excuse to make illegal any political demonstration in the central plaza on its most busy day. The concert prevented any large party from gathering in the largest open area of the square because this is where the musicians sat, and anyone making noise or speaking over a loudspeaker could be removed under the premise that they were interrupting the concert. In effect, our hosts felt that the classical music concert was a physical and auditory government occupation of the (ostensibly public) central square. This occupation was made all the more significant because the concert was a display of European (colonial) music and a reminder of the deep class and ethnic hierarchies in Oaxaca that enabled only a small percentage of the population to be familiar with European classical music. In short, while for the many tourists and wealthy Oaxacans in the square on a Sunday, the concert was an innocuously enjoyable treat, for others the concert was a dramatic performance of symbolic violence not unlike a police barricade. The situation provided an excellent opportunity to create a dramatic confrontation and replace the colonialist music with more accessible and less hierarchical performances.

The plan was to mobilize a large number of people very early in the morning in the plaza to erect a tent to prevent the concert from setting up. Throughout the day, musicians and artists allied with the movements performed in the tent, and there were panel discussions about the concerns of the Frente and other social movements throughout Mexico. In the evening, after the sun went down, the new film that Virgilio brought was shown on a large outdoor screen. In this way, a film screening became part of the plaza occupation.

Another trend in the restructuring of central plazas in Oaxaca as well as Mexico City has been the criminalization and forceful removal of small vendors from central public spaces. The removal of small vendors from the sidewalk in Texcoco, of course, is precisely the struggle that catalyzed the 2006 repression in Atenco. The city didn't want flower vendors selling on the sidewalk in central Texcoco, only one block removed from the central plaza. This is possibly a struggle that has been going on since Spanish colonization (Low 1995, Jiménez 2006). It seems quite likely that in pre-Hispanic times, the primary use for many of these central public spaces was commerce. In Bernal Díaz del Castillo's firsthand account of the Spanish conquest on Mexico, for example, he describes the center of the great city as a marketplace at the base of the large temples (Burke et al. 2012, 208–11). Just because these central plazas were markets in central Mexico doesn't necessarily mean that they were in the Zapotec region of what is now Oaxaca. However, just as the central plaza in Oaxaca is now often referred to as the *zócalo*, even though this is a word that used to exclusively refer to the central plaza in Mexico City (Dixon 2010, 125), so have some of the struggles over space in Oaxaca mirrored other struggles throughout the country.

Elite attempts at modernization and formalization of informal economies would prefer that small vendors sell in official markets (Walker 2013). According to this perspective, businesses should have names, addresses, and premises and should pay taxes. There is a general idea that central plazas should look like European gardens, with artfully crafted topiaries, scenic pathways, and carefully controlled open spaces. According to this vision, they should not be nearly permanently occupied by very poor people selling things off of blankets and tarps. The removal of these poor vendors and the encouragement of large, formalized businesses certainly has a modernizing effect, but it also has the effect of literally ejecting small, local businesses from the public square in favor of large, corporate ones. It also has the effect of ejecting indigenous peoples in favor of mestizo people and even foreigners. For many local people, pushing the vendors out of the central public square represented a political statement that the square belonged only to local elites with the money and resources to open restaurants and stores in the commercial buildings lining the plaza and tourists who could afford to shop and eat in these expensive locations.

Mirroring this struggle over who has the right to sell and how, aiding in the weekend occupation of the Oaxacan plaza was a large association of independent vendors who normally were not allowed to sell their goods in the plaza. According to one independent vendor, only a very few plaza vendors remained in 2009, those who sold particular goods and who paid large fees to the government.[7] During the daylong occupation of the square, the vendors could take advantage of the new temporary regime to make some money, the movement would have more bodies and physical things preventing anyone from removing them, and the commercial activity would draw passersby (including tourists) into the political event. More tourists not only meant more people and more customers for the vendors; it also meant that the police were less likely to forcibly remove the occupation for fear of scaring away future tourism. The tourists, on their part, were unlikely to even know that they had unwittingly become part of a political demonstration as they listened to the performances and perused goods laid out on blankets on the stone surface of the square.

The products of these independent vendors that Sunday in the plaza were not unlike the products of other outdoor markets throughout the city. Their goods included indigenous textiles, handmade indigenous-style clothing and bags, homemade toys and sculptures made out of potato chip bags and soda cans, wood and stone carvings, and handmade jewelry made out of stones, wire, and hemp fiber. There were also vendors selling Che posters, used books of political philosophy, and handmade photocopied booklets of Noam Chomsky speeches and the writings of Ricardo Flores Magón.[8]

There were also several vendors of social documentary films. The largest of these vendors wore a T-shirt with a large Canalseisdejulio logo across the front (he was not from Canalseisdejulio) and had set up a table stacked high with dozens of copies of fifty or more distinct films. A small television and DVD player screened the films and demonstrated the quality of the images. Other vendors sold a few documentaries off of tarps on the ground alongside photocopied political pamphlets of speeches or philosophy; indigenous-looking handicrafts such as jewelry or handmade notebooks; stickers, patches, or pins with Zapatista imagery, or handmade mantels embroidered with Zapatista images and slogans.

Films as material objects are a ubiquitous part of the material culture of leftist social movements throughout Mexico. Any political march or plantón (occupation) will have people selling documentary films on DVD spread out on a tarp or blanket. Even the collective house where we were staying in Oaxaca had a small store where they sold social and political documentaries on DVD alongside the artwork of political prisoners. Although it depended on the vendor, the films usually sold for around twenty pesos (about US$1.70 at the time) (see Figure 5.2).

The vendors selling political or social documentary films fit into a thriving culture of informal DVD sales in Mexico. Certainly, there are the vendors who sell pirated Hollywood films and seasons of American television shows from their sidewalk stalls and tarps, but in Mexico City there are also the sidewalk stalls outside of the Balderas metro stop that sell art house films that are usually found only in university libraries. The films of Dziga Vertov, Federico Fellini, Alejandro Jodorovsky, Ingmar Bergman, and Luis Buñuel can all be found easily and cheaply, sold by men on the sidewalk who seem to know as much about film studies as college professors.[9] There are the vendors outside of the Facultad de Ciencias Sociales y Políticas (Department of Social and Political Sciences) at UNAM who sell recorded speeches (sometimes given at UNAM) of Noam Chomsky, Gilles Deleuze, Slavoj Žižek, and other contemporary thinkers. They also sell obscure political and social documentaries from around the world. Other vendors sell political documentaries and anarchist films outside of the Facultad de Filosofia y Letras (Department of Humanities) at UNAM. Vendors outside of the Cineteca Nacional (National Film Center) sell art house fictional films and professional documentaries from around the world. Still others specialize in anarchist and punk films that they sell alongside zines at the back of the weekly El Chopo punk market. Documentaries, important historical films, and art house films are extraordinarily accessible in Mexico City. It is a film scholar's paradise.

Disregarding copyright restrictions, as most of these vendors do, is a complicated political issue. Large US corporations like Disney, who have played a significant role in creating the copyright laws in the United States, are clearly against this kind of distribution of their products because they can't recuperate funds for pirated material. Copying and distributing a Disney film can become a protest against the unjust laws that line the pockets of large transnational corporations, disadvantage small local business owners, and are at the heart of neoliberalism. However, it also hurts small political documentarians like Carlos

Figure 5.2. Street vendor of documentary films at a political march. Photo by Livia K. Stone.

Mendoza, whose filmmaking activities depend on recuperating some money from the sales of their products. There are other filmmakers like Salvador Díaz or Eduardo Ríos who are content to sell a few DVDs themselves so that they can recuperate some expenses but are mostly happy to have pirating operations and activists alike help spread their messages and make a living in the process. They have made a political and ethical decision not to attempt to make money off of their political products. In this way, the circulation of documentaries becomes part of a political practice creating a smarter, healthier, and more ethical marketplace according to an anti-neoliberal sensibility, even if no one precisely agrees on the ethical foundations of that economy.

More obscure historical documentary and art house films are a special case. Certainly they are distributed without permission from the copyright holders, but it seems a little unfair to call them "pirated." A significant reason that one cannot buy Luis Buñuel and Salvador Dalí's (1929) surrealist film *Un Chien Andalou*, Robert Gardner's (1963) ethnographic film *Dead Birds*, or Sam Green and Bill Siegel's (2002) documentary *The Weather Underground* at large, commercial bookstores is because a distributor couldn't sell enough copies to make it worth their while. However, a small vendor on the street outside of Balderas metro isn't hindered by such economic constraints. Neither is he hindered by the legal constraints of having to deal with the distribution company and the high prices associated with small commercial runs of films. These film vendors made obscure, highbrow films much more accessible to the general public than they would have been otherwise, and certainly more accessible than they were in the United States at the time.

Mexico City's film market could be held up as a thriving example of why free market capitalism, unhindered by government regulation, is much more efficient at delivering the products that people want at the cheapest price. However, the informal market in art house films and social documentaries is firmly planted in the material culture of the political Left in Mexico. I have never seen Fox News documentaries, photocopies of Ayn Rand books, or translations of Adam Smith's (1776) *The Wealth of Nations* being sold on the street in Mexico City. The idea seems ludicrous. I have seen PBS documentaries, photocopies of Ursula LeGuin novels, and translations of Pierre-Joseph Proudhon's writings. Documentaries and art house films are part of what is usually called *difusión cultural*, a phrase that could be translated as "cultural promotion" or even "cultural advancement." The political ethic that surrounds these films is an idea of people educating themselves about politics, art, and history. Films are accessible ways to learn in an environment with a generally low level of education and literacy.[10]

This is the work that my friend Rafael, who I described in the Introduction, conceived of himself doing at his stall selling used LPs and cassette tapes outside of a downtown metro station not far from the Balderas metro. Selling these things, and his unsuccessful attempts to sell political documentaries, was a way that he could make a living in a manner that he saw as contributing to a positive culture of art, education, and leftist politics. It was a way to create relationships and expand the networks and allies of La Otra Campaña and the Frente. When taken from the perspective of an individual having to find a way to make a living, and wanting to do so in an ethical and politically committed way, selling social documentaries (and/or handmade crafts, photocopied pamphlets and books, etc.) is a way to make a living without relying on exploitative labor, supporting large corporations, or encouraging a vapid consumer culture. In other words, it is a way to make some money partially outside of the sphere of neoliberal corporate capitalism.

This is also consistent with the motivations of a self-made union of vendors that sold films during political demonstrations in Mexico City called UPCI

(Unión de Promotores de la Cultura de la Izquierda, or the Union of Promoters of the Culture of the Left). This "union" was made up of a group of vendors (usually dressed in red polo shirts with the UPCI logo embroidered on the chest) who began selling DVDs, books, posters, and other media at the massive plantón set up in support of Andrés Manuel Lopez Obrador (AMLO), when he narrowly lost the presidential election in 2006. In 2009, UPCI was still fighting for the rights of their union to sell on the street in the Historic Center, where police have been famously battling informal vendors of all kinds for decades, and could be found most days around the Alameda Central. Although my short interviews with members of this group revealed that they had wildly different political beliefs and practices, they all believed that they were helping to create and strengthen a network of social movements through selling media. One slogan written on a sticker advertising the union was "For the right to work and freedom for the people!" (*¡Por el derecho al trabajo y la libertad del pueblo!*). The slogan combines the idea of popular liberation with workers' rights.

In many ways, films are a kind of flexible commodity that are uniquely equipped to play with and experiment with different conceptions of private property, economic value, and marketplace ethics. However, DVDs are also deeply problematic as non–corporate capitalist commodities. Although I never heard anyone refer to it, even noncopyrighted DVDs are, in fact, made with a great deal of exploitative labor and are firmly embedded in neoliberal industrial capitalism. The computers that they are burned and copied on were made by transnational corporations. So were the actual plastic blank DVDs that they were burned on to. The same is true for the plastic sleeves, the paper inserts, the copy machines that made the paper inserts, the cameras that recorded the footage, the computers that edited the footage into a film, and even most of the software used to edit, burn, and copy. Virtually every aspect of the material production of such films are deeply embedded in neoliberal corporate capitalism. The only thing that separates them are the lack of regard for private property in terms of honoring copyright restrictions, the educational nature of their content, and the indifferent commercial value of them as commodities (always cheap, sometimes free, and quite likely to be copied and passed around among friends).

Critics can easily point to these aspects of film circulation as a political/ethical contradiction. I think it is a contradiction that doesn't occur to most people engaged in film circulation for reasons that are unclear even to me. I once found myself talking to a film collective made of three men from three different Latin American countries (Brazil, Argentina, and Mexico) who were filming a political event in Mexico City. They had just returned from a prolonged experience in the autonomous Zapatista communities in Chiapas, and the Brazilian man was staying with friends for the night. He had no idea how to get around Mexico City or how to find his friends, so I showed him how to get to where he was going. On the way, he saw a Walmart outside of the metro station and insisted on ducking inside to purchase more MiniDV tapes for his camcorder. I was shocked that he, a man spending his life dedicated to anti-neoliberal activism, who was wearing combat boots made in the Zapatista factory in Oventic, would consider buying something in a Walmart. He was completely untroubled by it. The tapes, he explained to me, could be found only at Walmart, and if he didn't get them, they couldn't make the politically committed documentary. He pointed out to me that the Zapatista communities drink Coca-Cola and that activists cannot allow themselves to be paralyzed into inaction through attempts at political or moral purity. It is a significant mark of our age, and the enormity of what the Frente and other anti-neoliberal social movements were attempting, that even the most basic activist work (even painting a sign or giving a gift) is difficult to accomplish without utilizing commodities produced by transnational corporations.

Selling DVDs of social documentaries may not be seen as generally problematic, but activists themselves selling anything at all in the context of activism is considered problematic. It would have looked very bad if the Frente appeared to be selling things in order to make a profit. In distributing films, as well as making them, making a profit is an indication of self-interested *protagonismo* likely to incur a great deal of caustic gossip, both within the movement and from critics of the movement. When talking with people in Atenco who were critical of the Frente, for example, I often heard reference to how much money Ignacio del Valle's family took in from international allies.[11] One woman spoke very harshly to me about the Frente once, telling me in no uncertain terms, "The social movement is a profitable enterprise." In the context of an activity that the Frente might participate in as an entity, making a profit discounts their assertions that they are selflessly working toward the betterment of all people. For this reason, although selling homemade DVDs in the street is an integral part of the way that social documentaries are distributed, and the distribution of social documentaries is very good for the movement, they are almost never sold by the movement directly. I never saw Eduardo Ríos, for instance, personally selling his documentaries of the Frente. He sold only his documentaries of community festivals. Otherwise, he might be seen to be making a profit off of the movement. Salvador Díaz did sell some copies of his films, but only after a few free public screenings of the films when they were produced. The vast majority of the copies were given as gifts by the Frente or sold by people only allied with the Frente.

Even so, activists do sometimes sell things at marches or plantones out of necessity. Activism is expensive and takes up a lot of time that could otherwise be spent working.[12] However, because it is problematic, they tend to do so surreptitiously or step out of their role as an activist for a moment in order to do business. For example, on a very similar occasion several months later in which the Frente sent another commission to Oaxaca, a member of the Frente brought out and sold (very quickly) a dozen or more copies of a DVD out of his hands. The vendor told me that these sales would help pay for bus tickets back to Atenco after the event. On another occasion during an event at a university in Mexico City, a man whose normal business was selling homemade yogurts, puddings, and gelatin deserts (a common category of street vendor) in the street in Texcoco separated himself briefly from the event to sell his normal wares in the immediate vicinity. When he had sold nearly everything he brought (in a terrifically short period of time during a student lunch rush), he joined the group again and distributed his last few deserts among the activists from the Frente delegation. I didn't hear anyone criticize either man for selling something while representing the Frente at an event, but in dozens of political events I attended with the Frente over the course of years, these were the only two times I ever saw someone explicitly from the Frente selling anything. On the contrary, they were often giving out free food to supporters as part of the large communal meals they brought with them on their bus.

Selling documentaries is thus an ethically fraught practice for central activists, but not for more marginal figures. And much like film screenings, the practice of selling creates face-to-face human interactions that build relationships and strengthen networks, albeit on the peripheries of the movement. My first step in making contact with La Otra Campaña and the Frente, for example, occurred through a vendor selling DVDs and Zapatista handicrafts in 2006. Although he was selling pirated DVDs, he also gave me the address and told me how to get to the offices of Canalseisdejulio. Rafael, the vendor I describe in the Introduction, made contact with a man who he fondly thinks of as a teacher and mentor at the punk market El Chopo where the mentor, a significant presence in Mexico City's anarchist scene, was selling records and DVDs. Throughout my research, I frequently utilized a sales transaction to find out about film screenings, marches, political events, organizing meetings, or even simply the current political fears and desires circulating among members and allies of various social movements. By spreading a blanket on the ground with an array of political paraphernalia, vendors identify themselves with social movements and open themselves up to discussions about politics and the efforts of social movements. By showing interest in what they have for sale and asking questions, customers and vendors identify one another as friends and allies and share information, literally over (standing above and on either side of) social documentaries. The documentaries have mediated a human connection, and non–corporate capitalist political, economic, and social networks by doing nothing more than lying on the street.

Transformative Alternate Capitalisms

Every technological advance in media technology produces a wave of excited utopian speculation about how the new technology (radio, television, VHS, fax machines, the Internet, YouTube, Twitter) are going to revolutionize our society. Much of this speculation echoes Marshall McLuhan's idea of the media *being* the message. It is not so important *what* you are tweeting, for example; the utopian imagining surrounding Twitter is about is the scale of interaction between people that the medium brings. Within several years the Twitter/fax/VHS revolutions turn out to not be as profound as we thought, life goes on much as it always has, and we begin to get excited about the next technological revolution. The difference that filmmaking and film circulation makes in terms of social transformation and cultural production is not any inherent property of the medium. This story of transformative economies of film is one of people using the creative tools they are interested in to help transform themselves and produce new cultures of production and consumption.

Gifting films helps mediate human relationships based on material and moral economies of what Escobar has called "alternative capitalisms" (2008, 100–105). Selling these films provides opportunities to imagine and play with new conceptions of what commodities and markets can be. Precisely because it is an ethically fraught practice, selling films becomes a site of creativity and innovation through which new kinds of markets can emerge. It is also a practice through which people can bring together (however imperfectly) their commitment to living a life free of exploitation, domination, and neoliberal capitalism, with their pragmatic need to earn money to live.

Much like gifting films, screening them is a small transformative practice in cultural production. It mediates human interactions according to an alternate, noncapitalist (or at least less capitalist) economy of consumption and reciprocity. Screenings provide a forum for the Frente to broaden their network of friends and allies through face-to-face human interactions. Screenings also enable all the audience members to engage in an ethical practice of noncapitalist consumption. Watching social documentaries (for free in a collective house, community center, etc.) helps support noncapitalist cultural production and helps create a culture of noncapitalist consumption. Not unlike buying organic, locally grown food, attending a social documentary is an ethical practice of supporting an alternative economy through consumption. The alternative economy of locally grown organic food largely operates under a logic of consumer demand and profit margins, however, while an alternative economy of social documentary films operates under a noncapitalist logic. All attendees can use the occasion to cultivate an ethical disposition of compañerismo through participating in noncapitalist economic and political practices.

Film is not the only media through which this kind of cultural production happens. Film is perhaps not even among the most important. Political marches, plantones, meetings, political coalitions, festivals, music, and a host of other organizational activities and media are also significant forces of cultural production. Films are a strong force only as long as they are a medium that people are interested in. They take advantage of economic activities everyone desires in the contemporary age (giving valuable gifts, consuming media, buying products) and transforms these activities into a means of cultivating non-neoliberal individual and collective selves.

CODA

Ignacio del Valle, Felipe Álvarez, and Héctor Galindo Gochicoa were released from prison and exonerated in 2010. Returning home, they faced a very different Frente and a very different political climate than in 2006 when they were arrested.[1] The ejidos of several of the surrounding communities had already voted to privatize their parcels of land, and a federal agency (CONAGUA) had already purchased many parcels, telling ejidatarios that they were going to build a federal ecological park with the land (Salinas Cesáreo 2011). Members of the Frente in 2009 told me that the ecological park was a smokescreen and that when the state had purchased enough land, the airport project would continue as it was planned in 2001. This is more or less what has happened.

Enrique Peña Nieto, the man who had been the governor of Mexico state in 2006 and is often credited with orchestrating the May repression, was elected president of the nation in 2012. In 2014 he announced renewed plans to construct NAICM (Nuevo Aeropuerto International de la Ciudad de México, or the New International Airport of Mexico City) in the Texcoco area (Lagunes Gasca 2016). He promised that the airport plans would not affect the Atenco ejido, but by 2016 it seemed clear, based on the erection of a fence around the project and the movement of large machinery, that at least some of the communal lands of Atenco would be inside the perimeter fence of the airport project. As of this writing in 2018, Atenco's streets have become the usual pathways of construction trucks involved in building the airport.

The Frente continues to attempt its multifaceted legal, direct action, and multimedia campaign against the airport (see *atencofpdt.blogspot.com* for updates). Unfortunately, the Frente in 2018 is not what it was in 2001. There is no one reason that it is not as strong. Many people have passed away in the last fifteen years. (The Frente was never a movement of young people.) Others were successfully intimidated and repressed by the 2006 violence. Others have become exhausted through continual activism. Still others have been the victims of personal circumstances having to do with family and businesses that have brought them away from the Frente. Some of these "personal circumstances" are undoubtedly orchestrated campaigns of fear, intimidation, and manipulation meant to weaken the Frente and local opposition to the project. In a press conference statement in 2017, the Frente gave a long list of tactics supporters of the airport were using: "manipulation and buying favor, corruption of municipal and ejido authorities; campaigns of fear; rumors and divisiveness; disinformation and the fabrication of lies; . . . not to mention the permanent repression of those who openly oppose the deadly airport." Recent history has been divisive enough that many point out to me the "social fabric" of the community has already been broken, regardless of whether or not the airport comes. For all these reasons and more, there is a general feeling of inevitability about the renewed airport plans among local residents I continue to be in contact with in 2018. It seems that this time the airport will be built.

This might seem a depressing note on which to end a book mostly dedicated to arguing for the utility of film production and distribution as a means of social change. However, 2018 is simply a moment in a struggle over the land and people of Atenco that has been continually waged at least since Spanish conquest more than five hundred years ago. If the airport is built or if it isn't, the Frente's struggle will not end because it isn't only about the airport. The airport was only ever one concrete issue on which to hang more profound concerns about oppression, dignity, and morality. In 2012, a much more optimistic moment than 2017, I was in Atenco and bumped into the man that I call Humberto. In conversation, I lamented not being able to stay for the social movement convention being held the next week in Atenco to strategize against Peña Nieto's recent election. I asked Humberto how he thought it would go. He answered with a sudden sharp severity that startled me and made me think I had offended him with the question. "When do we stop fighting?" he demanded. I think he noticed on my face that I was suddenly afraid of getting the wrong answer. Before I could say anything, he rescued me. "Never, *güera*," he told me, now smiling, "Never." Seeing definitive success or failure is an impulse that belongs to reformist politics and capitalist production metrics. It is not a conception at the heart of social movements like the Frente. Even so, the construction of the airport will be a crushing blow for all those who have worked so hard over the past nearly twenty years to prevent it, to say nothing of those who gave their lives in the struggle.

The superficiality of a success/failure perspective is perhaps seen more easily in the human rights cases of the women sexually assaulted in the 2006 repression. Their case has passed to the last stage of the Inter-American Court of Human Rights in 2018 and seems likely to be adjudicated soon. It will unquestionably be a victory if the court rules in their favor, and yet will justice have been served? What would justice mean in this case? The court can demand that the Mexican state give the women money and resources, but it cannot restore them to their former selves. It can put pressure on Mexico to discourage the use of sexual violence as a political and military weapon. However, it cannot prevent future violence. If future military, police, and political leaders take sexual assault out of the repertoire of military and police violence in Mexico, it is not the court ruling that would have accomplished this. It will have to be the simple fact of superiors not encouraging sexual violence as a tactic and soldiers / police officers not using it. The court can help to focus attention to the issue and pressure institutions and individuals, but ultimately any court "win" is a limited success, just as any court "loss" does not negate the cultural, social, and political work that the Atenco women have done over the past eleven years drawing attention to the use of sexual violence as a form of torture and political repression. Success and failure, much like political awakenings or transformations of self, are always partial and processual. The law, just as a film, is but a medium for change. It is not change itself.

The number of full-length documentary films about the Frente have had a sharp drop-off since the political prisoners were released in 2010. By 2012, YouTube was widely used in Mexico, and the Frente was incorporating short online videos into their communication repertoire. One might think that there was a lot of optimism about the political potential of the platform, but I have yet to hear much enthusiasm about YouTube among my filmmaker and activist friends and colleagues in Mexico. Many of them use it, but seemingly reluctantly.

In 2012, Eduardo Ríos and I chatted specifically about the Frente's use of YouTube. He told me that, in order for a short video to make a difference, it needs to go viral. He continued that videos have to be very concrete, have a definitive purpose, and be "morbid" and "biting" in order for people to reproduce them and to reach a lot of people. I could tell he was not enthusiastic about online video, but when I pushed him, he insisted that YouTube, Facebook, Twitter, and the other social media platforms have their uses and were often very effective. They are useful for "certain ends: asking for the liberation of a certain person, ask for help, ask for solidarity or something. It is like sending a very particular message." "We use it," he assured me, without enthusiasm and possibly a bit defensively, "We use it when something is happening. . . . We have to use it, and we use it."

In contrast, Ríos as well as Ignacio del Valle were very excited about a dream project of digitizing, archiving, and cataloguing the hundreds (thousands?) of hours of video that had been captured about the Frente over the last fifteen years and establishing a library of the material for public use. They had various offers to adopt and process all the material as part of a larger existing library (offers that the Frente saw as appropriation) but had not encountered much help to enable the Frente itself to do the work and house the library. At one point, they had received a substantial grant from a South American institution for this purpose, but according to Ríos, when Peña Nieto was elected the grant was withdrawn for fear of political reprisal. This project, Ríos told me, would be useful for the use and strengthening of a whole network of social movements interested in the lessons of the Frente. The implication was that creating more robust face-to-face connections with people in a physical new library space was much preferable to the kind of limited alliances over particular issues and concrete campaigns that social media and online video encouraged.

The global politics of neoliberalism has also changed significantly since 2009 when I was living in Atenco. The administration of Felipe Calderón (2006–2012) intensified the drug war in Mexico and resulted in increasing the national level of violence. The election of PRI candidate Peña Nieto in 2012 seemed to be a signal that the nation preferred the old PRI regime that pacified the cartels through coming to understandings with them rather than fighting against them. The 2014 violent disappearance of forty-three indigenous students in Ayotzinapa, Guerrero, reminded the nation of the terrible liabilities of this strategy. When the violence of the state colludes with the violence of organized crime, it is often social movements who suffer because they are the state's biggest challenger.

The US economic crisis of 2008 seemed at the time to be a defining moment in the history of neoliberalism, and the last many years have shown that initial impression to be true. Outside of Mexico, the #Occupy movements in Spain, Argentina, and the United States were a moment of bringing the lessons of the World Social Forum and Zapatismo to national and local politics. Activists turned to working on ever more local and concrete issues in subsequent years. Both the political Left and Right seemed to be turning toward more local, rather than global politics. A series of antiglobalization movements erupted all over Europe and the United States, culminating in the bizarre developments of 2016: the UK's exit from the European Union and the US election of Donald Trump. Just as the United States and the UK were the first powerful generators of neoliberal reform in the Reagan/Thatcher era, so are they at the forefront of retreating from these policies in 2018 in the Trump/May era. Oddly, it is now the mainstream political Right that is holding the banner of anti-neoliberalism instead of the more radical Left in the UK and United States. This confluence of events is in some way a victory for anti-neoliberal activists, but it is also very confusing. The anti-neoliberal rhetoric of the Right is mixed with anti-immigrant racism and xenophobia. It is not the anti–corporate capitalism of the World Social Forum.

These developments have drawn the moral and ethical dimensions of neoliberalism into stark relief against its economic principles. The figure of Donald Trump especially demonstrates this contrast. At times as vehemently anti–free trade as Subcomandante Marcos, Trump is the prototypical protagonista. A fictional caricature could not be a more exaggerated illustration of the principles of protagonismo that I outline in Chapter 3: self-interested, self-involved, profit-driven, individualistic, competitive. The popularity of Donald Trump is a graphic illustration that while the economic principles of neoliberalism may be waning on a global scale in the wake of the financial collapse of 2008, neoliberalism as an ethical and moral regime is as strong as ever. It is as if the Right, long smuggling neoliberal subjectivities in alongside economic policies, has suddenly abandoned their economic philosophy but deepened their reverence for neoliberal ideals as an ethical and moral regime.

The struggle against him and his administration also drives home the importance of ethical practice as a transformative political process. It would certainly be a victory for the Left if Donald Trump were impeached, but his removal from office will not change the entrenched racism and xenophobia of rural, white Americans. Neither will his presence or absence in office do much to change the very serious economic plight of rural Americans who are indeed also looked down on, demeaned, and to some degree oppressed by urban (largely left-leaning) elites. People will become less racist only when they practice being less racist, and our economy will benefit rural Americans only when we focus economic efforts on benefiting rural Americans. The law is one medium through which these practices may occur, but it is not the only one, and it might not be the most direct. To the extent that the act of making and circulating films facilitates people practicing something—being nonhierarchical, or creating an economy that benefits the rural poor—it is every bit as useful.

NOTES

Introduction

1. Eduardo Ríos is a pseudonym.
2. Because the word *pueblo* can mean either "town" or "people," the name could also be translated as "Towns United in Defense of Land." In Spanish, of course, it means both simultaneously.
3. Rafael is a pseudonym.
4. Emiliano Zapata was an important military leader during the Mexican revolution (1910–1920). He was a peasant farmer from the state of Morelos who was an influential proponent of the idea of redistributing large landholdings as communal farmland for peasant farmers (the land reform that resulted in the *ejido* system). He was killed in 1919, just before the end of the revolution. His name and image are a mainstream part of Mexican patriotism but are often the part of Mexican nationalist symbolism taken up by agrarian and indigenous social movements in Mexico, including the Ejercito Zapatista de Liberación Nacional (EZLN) of Chiapas that took over San Cristóbal de las Casas in 1994 and has maintained a standing army and the autonomy of some indigenous villages ever since. Because the international notoriety of the EZLN has surpassed the notoriety of Emiliano Zapata himself in the contemporary era, "Zapatismo" is usually used to refer to the philosophy and extended network of the EZLN rather than Emiliano Zapata.
5. See Mahmood's (2012) characterization of the difference between Bourdieu's and Aristotle's conceptions of habitus.
6. A brief bibliography of this important literature would include Holloway (2002); Sitrin (2006); Juris (2008); Graeber (2009); Lindholm and Zúquete (2010); and Mitchell, Harcourt, and Taussig (2013).
7. See Melucci (1989), Taylor and Whittier (1992), Laraña et al. (1994).
8. Like the Combahee River Collective of the 1970s Black liberation movement, the founders of #BlackLivesMatter are queer Black women who critique the larger Black liberation movement for being patriarchal, heterosexist, and ableist.
9. Although the connection between consensus-based, leaderless political organization and indigenous communities is taken as a truism in contemporary leftist social movements in Mexico (and throughout transnational anti-neoliberal movements), this connection is hard to establish in scholarship. It is true that the cargo system and consensus-based community decision-making processes that I discuss in Chapter 3 are associated with indigenous political organization in Mexico. However, the fact that such a large diversity of indigenous groups use these same methods suggests that the practice is, at least in part, a result of colonial rule. There was also significant influence of European

anarchist and communist political models in the ejido system and peasant organizing that arose out of the Mexican revolution (1910–1920). However, the "authenticity" of their origins notwithstanding, the ideals of horizontal, consensus-based political organization have been associated with rural and indigenous political organization in Mexico for at least one hundred years.

10. See also Harvey 2005, Gershon and Alexy 2011, Giroux 2011, Ganti 2014, Freeman 2014.

11. Although the distinction between film and video was useful when actual 35mm film was a professional medium and VHS was a popular one, in this age when virtually everyone (professionals and amateurs alike) is using digital video, I do not find the distinction to be useful. I generally use the terms "film" and "video" interchangeably throughout the book.

12. I use the word "popular" here in Nestor García Canclini's (1995, 187) sense of the word to mean something that is emergent and accessible to people in general, not what is produced by a culture industry for massive capitalist consumption (see also Williams 2010, Adorno and Bernstein 1990).

13. This was part of the rationale at the time. However, a series of various development projects have been proposed for the same land by various government agencies since 2001. At various points, locals have been encouraged to break up ejidos and sell because of an ecological park, a tourist corridor, and a Ciudad Futura (City of the Future) among other projects. Most people in the Frente believe these other projects are a cover for a continued airport plan and accompanying commercialization around the airport. Whatever the "development" plan, the land is a desirable and relatively close region for the city to expand into.

14. This incident has been documented in numerous human rights reports. See Urirarte and Silva Forné 2006, CCIODH 2006, Méndez Cruz 2006, OMCT 2007, CCIODH and UNAM 2008, Centro ProDH 2012.

15. In May 2006, only weeks after the Atenco repression, the governor of Oaxaca staged a violent repression of a teacher's strike that resulted in the formation of the Asamblea Popular de los Pueblos de Oaxaca (the Popular Assembly of the Peoples of Oaxaca, or APPO), which occupied the city of Oaxaca throughout the summer. The APPO is another historic and transformative social movement with a close relationship to media production and circulation. Filmmaking, occupying radio stations and a television station, and producing content was an integral part of the APPO. See Stephen (2013) and Gibler (2009) for a more thorough accounting of these events. There are also some excellent documentaries made by and about the APPO, including Jill Freidberg's (2007) *A Little Bit of So Much Truth* and Mal de Ojo TV's (2007) *Compromiso Cumplido*.

Chapter 1

1. *Ejido* refers to communally held land, and the Ejido Commission is a kind of farmers' cooperative that manages the communal lands. I describe the ejido system, created after the Mexican revolution (1910–1920), in greater detail later in the chapter.

2. See Vásquez Castillo (2004) for a concise introduction to the establishment and slow dismantling of the ejido system in Mexico.

3. The woman pictured on the cover of this book is sitting on these steps and in front of the mural as she is filmed.

4. "Tierra y Libertad" is a slogan from the Mexican revolution, often associated with the anarchist revolutionary Ricardo Flores Magón, who wrote a play by that name in 1917. The slogan may have been lifted from anarchists from Barcelona who had a magazine by that name in the nineteenth century. Probably the most familiar contemporary reference to the slogan in central Mexico at the time was the magazine of the same name published by Spanish anarchists exiled in Mexico throughout the latter half of the twentieth century. It is a revolutionary slogan, but usually one with an anarchist association.

5. President Fox's interview was shown on the television program *Círculo Rojo*.

6. Most activists nearly always used the word *detener* (to detain) when referring to the state arrests of activists, and *retener* (to retain) for referring to activists keeping government officials from leaving their offices or the Casa Ejidal. However, Humberto was a man who prided himself on being blunt and did not make any distinction between the detentions of the state and the retentions of the movement.

7. Many other people told me that in the beginning, people marched with all kinds of farm implements, including tractors, hoes, pitchforks, and scythes, but over time the machete just became the preferred symbol. However, this more common accounting for the machete is not necessarily in tension with Humberto's version.

8. See Kleinman and Kleinman's (1996) work on elite uses of images of suffering.

Chapter 2

1. For a more comprehensive exploration in English, see Wortham (2013).

2. I use the terms "filmmaker" and "videographer" interchangeably here, although Ríos identifies himself as a videographer and not a filmmaker. The distinction is useful in some contexts, but the production and circulation practices of these three individuals are similar enough as to make these distinctions meaningless.

3. There is also the incredibly valid point that films like these help to counter state hegemony, or change dominant narratives. This is undoubtedly one of the ways that films work as social and political tools. However, it is also an effect that is incredibly difficult to demonstrate. Even if, for example, we could state definitively through popular opinion polls that the majority of people in Mexico saw the events of May 3 and 4, 2006, as an illegal violent repression of social movements and serious violations of human rights, how could we trace this general opinion to particular films? Films undoubtedly help and add to a general impression of public opinion and are a significant reason to make them, and yet here I would like to concentrate on what we can see and definitively say about the impacts of activist filmmaking.

4. See Feldman (1997), Aretxaga and Zulaika (2005), Tate (2007).

5. Although I have spoken with Ríos's wife on various occasions, she did not wish to be interviewed.

6. The music-only version of this album is widely available online for free in 2018.

7. These images can be seen in the two-volume documentary *Zapatistas: Crónica de una rebelión* (La Jornada and Canalseisdejulio, 2003). Lynn Stephen (2002) also presents images of these convoys.

8. My interviews with Greg Berger were conducted in English, as this is the first language of both of us.

9. Article 33 of the Mexican Constitution states simply, "Foreigners cannot involve themselves in any way in the political affairs of the country" (*"Los extranjeros no podrán de ninguna manera inmiscuirse en los asuntos políticos del país"*), and "the executive of the Union has the exclusive power to make any foreigner whose residence it judges inconvenient leave the national territory immediately and without previous judgment" (*"El Ejecutivo de la Unión tendrá la facultad exclusiva de hacerse abandonar el territorio nacional, inmediatamente y sin necesidad de juicio previo, a todo extranjero cuya permanencia juzgue inconveniente"*). Foreigners have been deported under this article in the context of Atenco. Five foreigners were deported in 2006 (see my description in Chapter 4), and seventeen US citizens, most students of Evergreen University, were deported in 2002 for holding machetes and chanting in a Frente protest (Ross 2006).

10. This is the journalist mentioned in Figure 2.1 to whom the film series was dedicated.

11. Many of these can be found on his YouTube channel, *www.youtube.com/user/saldeubas/videos* (accessed June 16, 2018).

12. I don't believe that Díaz would place Greg Berger in this category.

13. See James C. Scott's (2009) book about cultural forms developing to eschew capture by the state.

Chapter 3

1. This movement was connected to the Frente. Peña Nieto was governor of the state of Mexico during the 2006 human rights abuses in Atenco and played a role (possibly a significant one) in orchestrating the police operation.

2. Wolf's characterization of the moral distinction between egalitarian indigenous peoples and power-hungry mestizos is almost precisely the same moral distinction that Ramirez-Valles (2011) makes fifty years later between Latinos and Anglo-Americans living in the United States. In his work, shallow and contractual relationships of white and gay men in the US are in stark contrast to the "solidarity among equals" (2011, 9–10) of Latino men who enjoy sex with one another. These men also refer to one another as compañeros rather than identifying with the label "gay" as their white counterparts do.

3. The term "cult of the individual" is most often associated with nineteenth-century French sociologist Émile Durkheim (1984 [1893], 1973 [1898]) as connected to the rise of a modern society, even as the concept predates him (Giddens 1971, 72). The phrase arose at least a century before the EZLN protested individualism as a part of neoliberalism. As he is a scholar and a former university professor, it seems quite likely that Marcos has read Durkheim's ideas about organic versus mechanical solidarity in which Durkheim argues that the "cult of individualism" replaces religion in a modern society based on organic, specialized solidarity (see Marske 1987 for a concise summary of these ideas).

4. See Sawyer's discussion of how neoliberal reforms in Ecuador unintentionally produce "transgressive subaltern subjects" (2004, 93). James C. Scott has also noted that leaderless political organizations may have been purposefully created in Southeast Asia to avoid state control (2009, 207–8).

5. For example, the #YoSoy132 movement referenced at the beginning of this chapter emerged because a student movement protesting against the presidential candidate Enrique Peña Nieto was accused (by the candidate) of being made up of activists paid for their activities by the opposition. The slogan "I am [one of the] 132 [students protesting]" began as a Twitter hashtag as protestors posted their student IDs on Twitter to prove that they were legitimate, registered students of the university who were protesting under their own convictions.

6. See also Gutmann (2002).

7. As of September 2016, there was an *amparo* against the decision, meaning that a judge has ruled that the assembly decision should not be implemented until a further court decision. However, there have been increasing physical skirmishes between members of the Frente who are protecting the physical land and people they identify as PRIistas (members of the PRI) who are physically trying to intimidate them into leaving.

8. See Holloway (2002), Juris (2008), Graeber (2009), Sitrin (2012).

Chapter 4

1. See also Flaxman, Goel, and Rao (2016) for a review of the more scholarly literature on this debate.

2. May 3 is a Catholic feast day, Día de la Cruz, in which people celebrate by decorating large crosses with flowers. Therefore, it is an important and lucrative day to sell flowers. These vendors had used this space to sell for decades, but the rumor was that the city was planning to close the market, made up of dozens of independently owned stalls, to put in a large chain grocery store. Therefore, the turf war over the sidewalk was also a turf war over small local businesses and corporate capitalism.

3. A video of this meeting can be seen in the documentary *Atenco: Un crimen de estado* (Colectivo Klamvé 2006).

4. Presidents serve only one six-year term of office in Mexico.

5. Marcos attempted to take on the title Delegado Zero (Delegate Zero) for the campaign as a satirical parallel to the presidential delegates also touring the country.

6. AMLO ended up narrowly losing the presidential elections in a contested result reminiscent of the 2001 Bush/Gore election. AMLO's supporters occupied the historic center of Mexico City for months after the election to protest the official result that installed Felipe Calderón, a member of the same PAN party as Vicente Fox, the previous president.

7. Within the discourse of the Frente, this kind of action is referred to as a "retention" because officials are being retained in the space that they already occupy; the Frente was just preventing them from leaving. Sometimes the term was also used for cases in which the Frente took officials out of their offices and kept them (at times for days) in the offices of the local ejido. The word creates a distinction between the "detentions" of the state (arresting people) and the "retentions" of activists.

8. There is evidence that the children's hospital dispute was simply a stand-in for a more general annoyance with the Frente. Ignacio del Valle, for example, was issued a warrant for the confrontation when he wasn't even in the state of Mexico at the time. Although the official order stated that he helped orchestrate the plans from afar, this casts significant doubt on the strict correlation between the April retentions and the reason for the arrest warrants.

9. In my limited experience with the law in Texcoco, this public ambush tactic of the police was not uncommon. In another case involving acquaintances in Atenco, two women were involved in a dispute over the inheritance of a piece of land. One woman charged another with a criminal offense because she plowed land that didn't belong to her. Instead of coming to her house to arrest her, police waited until they knew she had a court date having to do with the dispute and ambushed her outside the courthouse. The ambush tactic was explained to me as a way of ensuring that they had arrested the right woman. In this case, police knew that the leadership of the Frente would be accompanying the flower vendors because they had told officials they would be there the day before in a meeting. Ambushing them would be a way of ensuring that they arrested the correct people. The state was probably correct in estimating this would be an issue: no one with warrants issued for the same offenses in April who were not in Texcoco on May 3 were successfully arrested.

10. The original concept behind Défossé's grant was for people from the autonomous communities to use this equipment to follow La Otra Campaña and record their activities. This proved to be difficult, however, and instead Défossé, along with a longtime colleague of his, took turns recording the events of the campaign.

11. There is footage of América del Valle and Marcos speaking in Mexico City during this time in a video called *Todos somos Atenco* (We are all Atenco) (IndyMedia Mexico, 2006).

12. Promedios's resulting film is called *A Very Big Train Called the Other Campaign* (Chiapas Media Project and Audiovisuales de los Caracoles Zapatistas 2007). Défossé also made an independent film called *Viva Mexico!* (2009).

13. Palma was deported and did lose her place in film school in Mexico City.

14. This young man, Alexis Benhumea, died as a result of his injury.

15. The language of human rights has come to be criticized within activist and scholarly contexts for quite a while (see Messer 1993 and Goodale 2006 for reviews). One of the significant criticisms is that the human rights framework is Eurocentric and bourgeois. The indigenous movement networks in which the Zapatista movement, and hence Promedios, were embedded have also had an uneasy relationship to human rights discourse. See Stephen (2002, 28–32) for an excellent, concise discussion as relates to Zapatismo.

16. There are women from Atenco who are part of the human rights case brought to the Inter-American Court of Human Rights. The Frente was also very interested and supportive of the human rights case that was brought before the Supreme Court of Mexico in 2009. However, even as the Frente drew attention to the case by protesting in front of the court while it was in session, its public language was not about bringing justice to the abuses of individuals, but bringing justice to Atenco as a community and making families whole again.

17. The only time that someone did show me the evidence of a physical wound he had received at the hands of police (Humberto, as described in Chapter 1), he showed it to me laughing, as a battle scar he was proud of.

18. This evasion strategy of the state was predicted by the human rights organization Centro de Derechos Humanos Miguel Agustín Pro Juárez (abbreviated as Centro ProDH) in a statement they release shortly after the violence and that is reproduced in *Breaking the Siege*. The man presenting the report at a press conference holds the report in the air for emphasis as he says into a microphone, "Here we want to emphasize and underscore that there is a responsibility that the state has; not of an individual officer, not of a subordinate functionary who gets out of control."

19. See Stone 2015 for an example of an alternative framework that the Frente itself has used in its own documentaries that is based on what I call "productive confrontation."

20. The casual North American reader of these words might easily be thinking that, of course, both of these things are true: poor and disenfranchised people *do* need the help of privileged outsiders, and the Mexican state is indeed violent and scary. However, the former claim does nothing to dismantle the kind of neocolonial oppression that social movements like the Frente are fighting against. The latter belies the fact that Mexican social movements successfully beat back police, storm into offices, take back land, negotiate new contracts, and generally get what they want quite frequently. Arguably, neither of these assertions serves the interests of poor and disenfranchised people so much as they serve the interests of an elite political Left who would like to displace an elite political Right as a better, kinder elite to be in charge. This, of course, is precisely the political point that La Otra Campaña was attempting to make about the national elections.

21. It should be pointed out that IndyMedia emerged in force through the 1999 anti-WTO protests in Seattle but were deeply inspired by Zapatista's use of media (see Kidd et al. 2003, Coyer 2005).

22. I once asked Carlos Mendoza if anyone had ever done this, and, laughing, he said that no one ever had.

23. Mendoza won but refused to accept the very prestigious Ariel award for his documentary *El Chahuistle* in 1982 and for his part in the documentary *Los Encontraremos* in 1984.

24. The five languages on the official DVD are English, French, Italian, German, and Portuguese. It is certain that the film was seen by people who speak all those languages because someone had to have actively volunteered to make the subtitles in that language. Therefore, they must have had greater distribution. Also, in the time that I was living in Atenco, a commission of the Frente toured France, where the French organizations that brought them screened *Breaking the Siege* as part of their solidarity visits. People from the Frente told me that they had been on a few tours through Europe over the years with *Breaking the Siege*. This is very unusual for a Canalseisdejulio film.

25. There is a wealth of literature regarding this kind of symbolic violence that constructs some humans as more worthy than others. Lynn Stephen has called symbolic violence against indigenous peoples in Mexico a "cultural packaging of violence" (2002, 28) that is a significant means through which the Mexican state justifies violence.

26. The foundation of the idea of "false consciousness," or a proletariat population who identifies more strongly with the interests of the bourgeoisie rather than their own material interests, can be found in Marx and Engels's *The German Ideology* (Marx and Engels 2010). The scholars of the Frankfurt School (Walter Benjamin, Theodore Adorno, Max Horkheimer, Herbert Marcuse) largely believed that a capitalist "culture industry" took the means of symbolic production out of the hands of everyday people and turned it into a means of pacifying and controlling them. The activist implication is that through criticism, one can be awakened or develop consciousness of the reality of one's oppression.

27. It is worth pointing out that a possible audience that is not mentioned at all is an international audience that might be leveraged to shame the Mexican state into no longer committing human rights abuses, or that might help adjudicate abuses. See Hinegardner (2009) for my discussion of this audience.

Chapter 5

1. Within a very short period of time after the campaign was launched, one of the men in Molino de Flores was released, and one of the perseguidos received an *amparo* (suspension of the warrants against him), which allowed him to come out of hiding.

2. The ten detainees in Texcoco had a variety of sentences and backgrounds. Every time I attempted to get to know their stories from local members of the Frente, or even the lawyers involved in the new campaign, I received vague answers. Through suggestion and innuendo, a sense emerged that they were people who simply came to be caught up in the action and had very little to do with the Frente or La Otra Campaña. Some,

it seemed, refused to be represented by the Frente's lawyers. That may have been a significant reason that they were still in prison. A few people whispered to me that some may have been working for the police. Regardless of their chosen affiliation, three years later there was still a group of young people who self-identified as members of La Otra Campaña who were occupying a corner of the parking lot outside the prison twenty-four hours a day to draw attention to the remaining political prisoners and provide them with support. La Otra had claimed them, even if they did not claim to be part of La Otra.

3. See Davies 2007, Osorno 2016, Martínez Vásquez 2007, Sotelo Marbán 2008, Castro Sánchez 2009, Denham 2009, Martínez Vásquez 2009, Bolos and Estrada Saaveda 2013, and Stephen 2013. Some of the many films about the commune are Consorcio Oaxaca and Mal de Ojo TV 2006, Vanguardia Proletaria 2006, Mal de Ojo TV 2007, and Coladangelo 2009.

4. These were probably actually VCDs, discs that in the United States were usually sold in 2009 as data storage discs. I use the term DVD because in 2017, it has lost its connotation of video encoding and is generally recognized as the way of referring to video files on a disc.

5. This is a film that is frequently sold at political demonstrations and is probably edited by an enterprise specializing in pirating videos. It is a compilation that begins with long pieces of Klan Destino's *La rebelión de los fulgores* and ends with the entirety of Klamvé's *Atenco: Un crimen de estado*. Because it is a compilation, I do not consider it a unique feature documentary even though this compilation under this unique name is a widely distributed DVD.

6. The central plaza of any town or city in Latin America is traditionally a large open square with a church on side, government buildings on another, and the other two sides of the square given over to either shops (usually framed in a series of arches), or more public government buildings. This space in Mexico is often called the *zócalo* because the largest central plaza in Mexico, the plaza in the historic center of Mexico City, for many years had in its center a gigantic plinth, or statue base, referred to as a "zócalo." (According to the historic models of the tourist displays in the metro station at the zócalo, it was the plinth of a statue removed in the nineteenth century.) It is unclear how the word came to signify other central plazas throughout Mexico. In Texcoco, for example, this space is referred to as *el jardín* (the garden), and in Atenco as simply *el centro* (the center). I suspect that the central square of Oaxaca is often referred to as the zócalo (by tourists and locals alike) because of the large flow of tourists coming through Oaxaca who have recently passed through or are from Mexico City and don't realize that the word for "plaza" is not "zócalo."

7. In 2009 these vendors included a newspaper stand, a hamburger/hotdog stand, an *elote* (corn on the cob) stand, and a few men who sold large balloons for children to play with in the square. Although the other vendors were "relocated" and able to sell things in other spaces in the city, including other public plazas, they have not been allowed to return to the central plaza.

8. A Mexican anarchist from the early twentieth century.

9. These vendors are all that is left of what was a very popular art house theater near this metro. The theater itself closed down, but the vendors remain.

10. In 2009, films were sometimes distributed online through streaming sites such as YouTube and Vimeo, and for download on some independent media sites like IndyMedia, Salon Chingón (a now defunct site), and *Archive.org*. However, most people still accessed the Internet in busy Internet cafés and college computer labs. These spaces are not very conducive to immersing oneself in streaming a movie, and while downloads are possible, the large file sizes can mean long periods of time waiting, each minute of which might be counted and charged in the Internet café. Using computer power offline to copy DVDs was a much more reasonable option in 2009. However, most of these films could be obtained for free by anyone with relationships (even somewhat marginal ones) with people in the movement because of gifting and sharing networks. The fact that they could quite easily be obtained for free meant that the price of the DVDs more closely resembled a convenience fee for providing the film at the right time in the right place, or simply an excuse to give a donation to a member of a worthy cause or support the livelihood of a compañero. Additionally, no attempt was made on the DVDs to protect them from being copied and distributed even further. Putting a pirated DVD into a computer makes it very easy to transfer the files to a hard drive, copy the film for your friends, or burn more DVDs.

11. I don't know if this is true.

12. The solidarity trip to Oaxaca was partially funded by passing hats around for donations at the Magisterio meeting at which the Frente delegation spoke.

Coda

1. Héctor Galindo is not from Atenco and so did not return there. When he was arrested, he was an activist lawyer who had worked his way to the front of the Frente's activism much after the airport struggle. Since his release from prison in 2010, I don't have any evidence to show that he continued his activism with the Frente.

REFERENCES

Adorno, Theodor W., and J. M. Bernstein. 1990. *The Culture Industry: Selected Essays on Mass Culture*. London: Routledge.
Alcayaga, Cristina. 2002. *Atenco: El peso del poder y el contrapeso de la resistencia civil*. Mexico City: Miguel Angel Porrúa Grupo Editorial.
Anderson, B., and J. D. Cockroft. 1966. "Control and Cooptation in Mexican Politics." *International Journal of Comparative Sociology* 7 (1): 11–28.
Anonymous. 2005. "La otra campaña ya comenzó." *Rebeldía* 33: 1–2
Atton, Chris. 2002. *Alternative Media*. London: Sage.
Aretxaga, B., and J. Zulaika. 2005. *States of Terror: Begona Aretxaga's Essays*. Center for Basque Studies, University of Nevada, Reno.
Barclay, Barry. 2003. "Celebrating Fourth Cinema." *Illusions* 35: 7–11.
Bolos, Silvia, and Marco Estrada Saaveda. 2013. *Recuperando la palabra: La Asamblea Popular de los Pueblos de Oaxaca*. México: Universidad Iberoamericana.
Bourdieu, Pierre. 1984. *Distinction: A Social Critique of the Judgement of Taste*. Cambridge, MA: Harvard University Press.
———. 1993. *The Field of Cultural Production*. Cambridge, MA: Harvard University Press.
Buddle, Kathleen. 2008. "Transistor Resistors: Native Women's Radio in Canada and the Social Organization of Political Space from Below." In *Global Indigenous Media: Cultures, Poetics, and Politics*, edited by Pamela Wilson and Michelle Stewart, 128–44. Durham, NC: Duke University Press.
Burke, Janet, Ted Humphrey, and Bernal Díaz del Castillo. 2012. *The True History of the Conquest of New Spain*. Indianapolis: Hacket.
Camacho-Guzmán, Damián Gustavo. 2008. "Atenco: Arma su historia." Master of Rural Development, Universidad Autónoma Metropolitana, Unidad Xochimilco.
Castells, Manuel. 2012. *Networks of Outrage and Hope: Social Movements in the Internet Age*. 2nd ed. Cambridge, UK: Polity.
———. 2013. *Communication Power*. Oxford: Oxford University Press.
Castro Sánchez, Sergio de. 2009. *Oaxaca, más allá de la insurrección: Crónica de un movimiento de movimientos (2006–2007)*. Oaxaca, Oaxaca, Mexico: Ediciones ¡Basta!
CCIODH (Comisión Civil International de Observación por los Derechos Humanos). 2006. *Informe preliminar sobre los hechos de Atenco, México*. Barcelona: Comisión Civil Internacional de Observación por los Derechos Humanos.
CCIODH (Comisión Civil International de Observación por los Derechos Humanos) and UNAM (Universidad Autónoma de la Ciudad de México). 2008. *Chiapas, Oaxaca, Atenco: CCIODH, Comisión Civil Internacional de Observación de los Derechos*

Humanos, sexta visita. Barcelona: Comisión Civil International de Observación por los Derechos Humanos

Centro ProDH (Centro de Derechos Humanos Miguel Agustín Pro Juárez). 2012. *Atenco: 6 años de impunidad, de resistencia*. Mexico City: Centro de Derechos Humanos Miguel Agustín pro Juarez, A.C.

Clark, Jessica, and Tracy Van Slyke. 2010. *Beyond the Echo Chamber: Reshaping Politics through Networked Progressive Media*. New York: New Press.

Coyer, Kate. 2005. "If It Leads It Bleeds: The Participatory Newsmaking of the Independent Media Centre." In *Global Activism, Global Media*, edited by Wilma de Jong, Martin Shaw, and Neil Stammers, 165–78. London: Pluto.

Davies, Nancy. 2007. *The People Decide: Oaxaca's Popular Assembly*. Natick, MA: Narco News Books.

Davis, Charles L. 1976. "The Mobilization of Public Support for an Authoritarian Regime: The Case of the Lower Class in Mexico City." *American Journal of Political Science* 20 (4): 653–70.

Denham, Diana, C.A.S.A. Collective. 2009. *Teaching Rebellion: Stories from the Grassroots Mobilization in Oaxaca*. Oakland, CA: PM.

Díaz, Gloria Leticia. 2013. "Víctimas de tortura sexual en Atenco rechazan "solución amistosa" del gobierno de Peña." *Proceso*, March 14, 2013. www.proceso.com.mx/336249.

Díaz Sánchez, Salvador. 2006. "*La rebelión de los fulgores:* Testimonio de un cineasta texcocano." *Tema y variaciones de literatura* 26: 344–69.

Dixon, Seth. 2010. "Making Mexico More 'Latin': National Identity, Statuary and Heritage in Mexico City's Monument to Independence." *Journal of Latin American Geography* 9 (2): 119–38.

Downing, John. 1984. *Radical Media: The Political Experience of Alternative Communication*. Boston: South End.

Durkheim, Emile. 1973 [1898]. "Individualism and the Intellectuals." Translated by Mark Traugott. In *Emile Durkheim on Morality and Society*, edited by Robert N. Bellah, 43–57. Chicago: University of Chicago Press. First published 1898 as "L'individualisme et les intellectuels."

———. 1984 [1893]. *Division of Labour in Society*. Translated by W. D. Halls. London: Macmillan.

Eisenstein, Zillah R. 1981. *The Radical Future of Liberal Feminism*. New York: Longman.

Escobar, Arturo. 2008. *Territories of Difference: Place, Movements, Life, Redes*. New Ecologies for the Twenty-First Century. Durham, NC: Duke University Press.

Esteva, Gustavo. 2008. *The Oaxaca Commune and Mexico's Autonomous Movements*. Oaxaca de Juárez, Oaxaca, México: Ed. ¡Basta!

EZLN (Ejercito Zapatista de Liberación Nacional). 2005. *Sexta declaración de la Selva Lacandona*. Chiapas, Mexico: Self-published. enlacezapatista.ezln.org.mx/2005/06/30/sixth-declaration-of-the-selva-lacandona.

Fazio, Carlos. 2013. *Terrorismo mediático: La construcción social del miedo en México*. Mexico City: Debate.
Feldman, Allen. 1997. "Violence and Vision: The Prosthetics and Aesthetics of Terror." *Public Culture* 10 (1): 24–60.
Flaxman, Seth, Sharad Goel, and Justin M. Rao. 2016. "Filter Bubbles, Echo Chambers, and Online News Consumption." PUBOPQ *Public Opinion Quarterly* 80 (S1): 298–320.
Flores, Carlos Y. 2004. "Indigenous Video, Development and Shared Anthropology: A Collaborative Experience with Maya Q'Eqchi' Filmmakers in Postwar Guatemala." *Visual Anthropology Review* 20 (1): 31–44.
Foucault, Michel. 1977. *Discipline and Punish: The Birth of the Prison* [Surveiller et punir]. New York: Vintage Books.
———. 1986. *The Care of the Self: The History of Sexuality* [Le Souci de soi]. Translated by Robert Hurley. Vol. 3. New York: Vintage Books.
———. 1988. *The History of Sexuality* [Histoire de la sexualité]. Translated by Robert Hurley. New York: Vintage Books.
———. 1997. *Ethics: Subjectivity and Truth*. Translated by Robert Hurley, edited by Paul Rabinow. Vol. 1. *Essential Works of Michel Foucault, 1954–1984*. New York: New Press/Distributed by W. W. Norton.
Freeman, Carla. 2014. *Entrepreneurial Selves: Neoliberal Respectability and the Making of a Caribbean Middle Class*. Durham, NC: Duke University Press.
Gabriel, Teshome H. 1982. *Third Cinema in the Third World: The Aesthetics of Liberation*. Studies in Cinema 21. Ann Arbor, MI: UMI Research Press.
Galeano, Subcomandante Insurgente. 2014. "Between Light and Shadow." *enlacezapatista*. ezln.org.mx/2014/05/27/between-light-and-shadow.
Ganti, Tejaswini. 2014. "Neoliberalism." *Annual Review of Anthropology* 43: 89–104.
García Canclini, Néstor. 1995. *Hybrid Cultures: Strategies for Entering and Leaving Modernity*. Translated by Christopher L. Chiappari and Silvia L. López. Minneapolis: University of Minnesota Press.
García Martínez, Anayeli. 2016. "A 10 años de Atenco: Tortura sexual, práctica común de la policía mexicana." *Proceso*, May 2, 2016. www.proceso.com.mx/439222.
Garza, Alicia. 2016. "A Herstory of the #BlackLivesMatter Movement." In *Are All the Women Still White? Rethinking Race, Expanding Feminisms*, edited by Janell Hobson, 23–28. Albany: State University of New York Press.
Gershon, Ilana, and Allison Alexy. 2011. "The Ethics of Disconnection in a Neoliberal Age." *Anthropological Quarterly* 84 (4): 799–808.
Gibler, John. 2009. *Mexico Unconquered: Chronicles of Power and Revolt*. San Francisco: City Lights.
Giddens, Anthony. 1971. *Capitalism and Modern Social Theory: An Analysis of the Writings of Marx, Durkheim and Max Weber*. Cambridge: Cambridge University Press.

Ginsburg, Faye. 1991. "Indigenous Media: Faustian Contract or Global Village?" *Cultural Anthropology* 6 (1): 92–112.

———. 1993. "Aboriginal Media and the Australian Imaginary." *Public Culture* 5 (3): 557–78.

———. 1995. "Mediating culture: Indigenous Media, Ethnographic Film, and the Production of Identity." In *Fields of Vision: Essays in Film Studies, Visual Anthropology, and Photography*, edited by Leslie Devereaux and Roger Hillman 256–91. Berkeley: University of California Press.

———. 1997. "'From Little Things, Big Things Grow': Indigenous Media and Cultural Activism." In *Between Resistance and Revolution: Cultural Politics and Social Protest*, edited by Orin Starn and Richard Gabriel Fox, 118–44. New Brunswick, NJ: Rutgers University Press.

Ginsburg, Faye D., Lila Abu-Lughod, and Brian Larkin. 2002. *Media Worlds: Anthropology on New Terrain*. Berkeley: University of California Press.

Giroux, Henry A. 2011. "The Crisis of Public Values in the Age of the New Media." *Critical Studies in Media Communication* 28 (1): 8–29.

Goodale, Mark. 2006. "Toward a Critical Anthropology of Human Rights." *Current Anthropology* 47 (3): 485–511.

Graeber, David. 2009. *Direct Action: An Ethnography*. Edinburgh: AK.

Griffin, Michael, and Jennie Weiss Block. 2013. *In the Company of the Poor: Conversations with Dr. Paul Farmer and Fr. Gustavo Gutiérrez*. Maryknoll, NY: Orbis Books.

Guneratne, Anthony R., Wimal Dissanayake, and Sumita S. Chakravarty. 2003. *Rethinking Third Cinema*. London: Routledge.

Gustafson, Bret. 2009. *New Languages of the State: Indigenous Resurgence and the Politics of Knowledge in Bolivia*. Durham, NC: Duke University Press.

Gutiérrez, Gustavo, Caridad Inda, and John Eagleson. 2014 [1973]. *A Theology of Liberation: History, Politics, and Salvation*. Maryknoll, NY: Orbis Books.

Gutmann, Matthew C. 2002. *The Romance of Democracy: Compliant Defiance in Contemporary Mexico*. Berkeley: University of California Press.

Hale, Charles R. 2009. *Más que un Indio: Racial Ambivalence and Neoliberal Multiculturalism in Guatemala*. Santa Fe, NM: School of American Research Press.

Hall, Stuart. 1981. "The Whites of Their Eyes: Racist Ideologies and the Media." In *Silver Linings: Some Strategies for the Eighties*, edited by George Bridges and Rosalind Brunt, 28–52. London: Lawrence and Wishart.

Harvey, David. 2005. *A Brief History of Neoliberalism*. Oxford: Oxford University Press.

Hinegardner, Livia K. 2009. "Action, Organization, and Documentary Film: Beyond a Communications Model of Human Rights Videos." *Visual Anthropology Review* 25 (2): 172–85.

Holloway, John. 2002. *Change the World without Taking Power*. Get Political. London: Pluto.

Holston, James. 2008. *Insurgent Citizenship: Disjunctions of Democracy and Modernity in Brazil*. Princeton, NJ: Princeton University Press.
hooks, bell. 1984. *Feminist Theory: From Margin to Center*. Boston: South End.
INEGI (Instituto Nacional de Estadistica y Geografía). 2011. *Censo de población y vivienda (2010): Panorama sociodemográfico del Estado de México*. Aguascalientes, Mexico: INEGI.
Jamieson, Kathleen Hall, and Joseph N. Cappella. 2010. *Echo Chamber: Rush Limbaugh and the Conservative Media Establishment*. New York: Oxford University Press. ProQuest Ebrary.
Jiménez, Christina M. 2006. "Performing Their Right to the City: Political Uses of Public Space in a Mexican City, 1880–1910s." *Urban History* 33 (3): 435–56.
Juris, Jeffrey S. 2008. *Networking Futures: The Movements against Corporate Globalization*. Experimental Futures. Durham, NC: Duke University Press.
Khasnabish, Alex. 2008. *Zapatismo beyond Borders: New Imaginations of Political Possibility*. Toronto: University of Toronto Press.
Kidd, Dorothy. 2003. "Indymedia.org: A New Communications Commons." In *Cyberactivism: Online Activism in Theory and Practice*, edited by Martha McCaughey and Michael D. Ayers, 47–70. New York: Routledge.
Kleinman, Arthur, and Joan Kleinman. 1996. "The Appeal of Experience, the Dismay of Images: Cultural Appropriations of Suffering in Our Times. *Daedalus* 125 (1): 1–23.
Knight, Alan, and Wil G. Pansters. 2005. *Caciquismo in Twentieth-Century Mexico*. London: Institute for the Study of the Americas.
Köhler, Axel. 2004. "Nuestros antepasados no tenían *cámaras: El* video como machete y otros retos de la video-producción indígena en Chiapas, México." *Revista Chilena de Antropología Visual* 4: 391–406.
Kuri Pineda, Edith. 2010. "*El movimiento social de Atenco: Experiencia y construcción de sentido*." Ciudad de México: Universidad Autónoma de la Ciudad de México.
Lagunes Gasca, Ricardo A. 2016. "Nuevo aeropuerto: Despojo y ecodicio." *La Jornada*, October 10, 2016. jornada.unam.mx/2016/10/01/politica/014a1pol.
Laraña, Enrique, Hank Johnston, and Joseph R. Gusfield, eds. 1994. *New Social Movements: From Ideology to Identity*. Philadelphia: Temple University Press.
Lazar, Sian. 2008. *El Alto, Rebel City: Self and Citizenship in Andean Bolivia*. Latin America Otherwise. Durham, NC: Duke University Press.
Lee, Richard B. 2012 [1984]. *The Dobe Ju/'hoansi*. Belmont, CA: Wadsworth. First published 1984 as *The Dobe Kung*.
Lindholm, Charles, and José Pedro Zúquete. 2010. *The Struggle for the World*. Stanford, CA: Stanford University Press.
Lipschutz, Ronnie D. 2005. "Networks of Knowledge and Practice: Global Civil Society and Global Communications." In *Global Activism, Global Media*, edited by Wilma de Jong, Martin Shaw, and Neil Stammers, 17–33. London: Pluto.

Low, Setha M. 1995. "Indigenous Architecture and the Spanish American Plaza in Mesoamerica and the Caribbean." *American Anthropologist* 97 (4): 748–62.

———. 2000. *On the Plaza: The Politics of Public Space and Culture.* Austin, Texas: University of Texas Press.

Mahmood, Saba. 2012. *Politics of Piety: The Islamic Revival and the Feminist Subject.* Princeton, NJ: Princeton University Press.

Mahon, Maureen. 2000. "The Visible Evidence of Cultural Producers." *Annual Review of Anthropology* 29 (1): 467–92.

Malinowski, Bronislaw. 2002 [1922]. *Argonauts of the Western Pacific.* New York: Routledge.

Marcos, Subcomandante Insurgente. 2005. "Un pingüino en la Selva Lacandona." *Rebeldía* 33: 10–20.

Marske, Charles E. 1987. "Durkheim's 'Cult of the Individual' and the Moral Reconstitution of Society" *Sociological Theory* 5 (1): 1–14

Martínez Vásquez, Víctor Raúl. 2007. *Autoritarismo, movimiento popular y crisis política: Oaxaca 2006.* Oaxaca, México: Consorcio para el Diálogo Parlamentario y la Equidad: Centro de Apoyo al Movimiento Popular Oaxaqueño: Servicios para la Educación Alternativa (EDUCA): Instituto de Investigaciones Sociológicas de la Universidad Benito Juárez de Oaxaca.

———. 2009. *La APPO: ¿Rebelión o movimiento social? (Nuevas formas de expresión ante la crisis).* Oaxaca: Cuerpo Académico de Estudios Políticos.

Marx, Karl, and Friedrich Engels. 2010. *The German Ideology: Part One, with Selections from Parts Two and Three, Together with Marx's "Introduction to a Critique of Political Economy."* Edited and translated by C. J. Arthur. New York: International.

Mauss, Marcel. 1990 [1950]. *The Gift: The Form and Reason for Exchange in Archaic Societies.* Translated by W. D. Halls. New York: Norton.

Mazzarella, William. 2013. *Censorium Cinema and the Open Edge of Mass Publicity.* Durham, NC: Duke University Press.

McLuhan, Marshall. 2003 [1964]. *Understanding Media: The Extensions of Man.* Corte Madera, CA: Gingko.

Melucci, Alberto. 1989. *Nomads of the Present: Social Movements and Individual Needs in Contemporary Society.* Philadelphia: Temple University Press.

Méndez Cruz, Marisol. 2006. *Informe sobre tortura y otros tratos crueles, inhumanos y degradantes perpetrados en Texcoco y Atenco los días 3 y 4 de mayo de 2006.* Mexico City: Acción de los Cristianos para la Abolición de la Tortura (ACAT-México), A.C.

Mendoza, Carlos. 2006. "Canal 6 de Julio: Documental y contrainformación." In *Documental*, edited by Armando Casas, 39–57. Mexico City: Universidad Nacional Autónoma de México.

Messer, Ellen. 1993. "Anthropology and Human Rights." *Annual Review of Anthropology* 22: 221–49.

Mitchell, W. J. T., Bernard E. Harcourt, and Michael T. Taussig. 2013. *Occupy: Three Inquiries in Disobedience*. Trios. Chicago: University of Chicago Press.

Morozov, Evgeny. 2009. "The Brave New World of Slacktivism." *Foreign Policy*, May 19. *foreignpolicy.com/2009/05/19/the-brave-new-world-of-slacktivism*.

———. 2014. *To Save Everything, Click Here: Technology, Solutionism, and the Urge to Fix Problems That Don't Exist*. London: Penguin Books.

Nash, Manning. 1958. "Political Relations in Guatemala." *Social and Economic Studies* 7 (1): 65–75.

Olcott, Jocelyn H. 2005. *Revolutionary Women in Postrevolutionary Mexico*. Durham, NC: Duke University Press.

OMCT (Oganización Mundial Contra la Tortura). 2007. *Violencia de estado contra mujeres en México: El caso San Salvador Atenco*. Ginebra, Switzerland: Oganización Mundial Contra la Tortura.

Ong, Aihwa. 2006. *Neoliberalism as Exception: Mutations in Citizenship and Sovereignty*. Durham, NC: Duke University Press.

Osorno, Diego Enrique. 2016. *Oaxaca sitiada: La primera insurrección del siglo XXI*. Ciudad de México: Almadía.

Paley, Julia. 2001. *Marketing Democracy: Power and Social Movements in Post-dictatorship Chile*. Berkeley: University of California Press.

Palma Novoa, Valentina. 2006. "They Ordered Me to Lay My Head in a Pool of Blood." *Narco News Bulletin*, May 12, 2006. *Narconews.com/Issue41/article1802.html*.

Pariser, Eli. 2011. *The Filter Bubble: How the New Personalized Web Is Changing What We Read and How We Think*. New York: Penguin Group US.

Pickerill, Jenny, John Krinsky, Graeme Hayes, Kevin Gillan, and Brian Doherty. 2016. *Occupy! A Global Movement*. New York: Routledge.

Ramirez-Valles, Jesus. 2011. *Compañeros: Latino Activists in the Face of AIDS*. Chicago: University of Illinois Press.

Rodríguez, Clemencia. 2001. *Fissures in the Mediascape: An International Study of Citizens' Media*. Hampton Press Communication Series. Cresskill, NJ: Hampton.

Ross, John. 2006. "The 'Dirty War' Returns to Mexico: San Salvador Atenco Attacks Follow Blueprint of Terror from the '70s and '80s." *Narco News Bulletin*, May 18, 2006. *narconews.com/Issue41/article1831.html*.

Sahlins, Marshall. 2017 [1972]. *Stone Age Economics*. New York: Routledge

Salinas Cesáreo, Javier. 2011. "Pretende la Conagua comprar tierras en San Salvador Atenco." *La Jornada*, April 1, 41.

———. 2017. "Impugnan ante la PA al comisariado ejidal de Atenco." *La Jornada*, January 9, 29.

Sawyer, Suzana. 2004. *Crude Chronicles: Indigenous Politics, Multinational Oil, and Neoliberalism in Ecuador*. American Encounters/Global Interactions. Durham, NC: Duke University Press.

Scott, James C. 2009. *The Art of Not Being Governed: An Anarchist History of Upland Southeast Asia*. New Haven, CT: Yale University Press.

Sitrin, Marina. 2006. *Horizontalism: Voices of Popular Power in Argentina*. Oakland, CA: AK.

———. 2012. *Everyday Revolutions: Horizontalism and Autonomy in Argentina*. London: Zed Books.

Sotelo Marbán, José. 2008. *Oaxaca: Insurgencia civil y terrorismo de estado*. México, DF: Era.

Speed, Shannon. 2008. *Rights in Rebellion: Indigenous Struggle and Human Rights in Chiapas*. Stanford, CA: Stanford University Press.

Stephen, Lynn. 2002. *Zapata Lives! Histories and Cultural Politics in Southern Mexico*. Berkeley: University of California Press.

———. 2013. *We Are the Face of Oaxaca: Testimony and Social Movements*. Durham, NC: Duke University Press.

Stone, Livia K. 2015. "Suffering Bodies and Scenes of Confrontation: The Art and Politics of Representing Structural Violence." *Visual Anthropology Review* 31 (2): 177–89.

———. 2017. "*Romper el cerco*: An Ethnography of Transnational Collaborative Film." In *Adjusting the Lens: Community and Collaborative Video in Mexico*, edited by Freya Schiwy and Byrt Wammack Weber, 151–82. Pittsburgh: University of Pittsburgh Press.

Sunstein, Cass R. 2007. *Republic.Com*. Princeton, NJ: Princeton University Press.

Tate, Winifred. 2007. *Counting the Dead: The Culture and Politics of Human Rights Activism in Colombia*. Berkeley: University of California Press.

Taylor, Verta, and Nancy Whittier. 1992. "Collective Identity in Social Movement Communities: Lesbian Feminist Mobilization." In *Frontiers in Social Movement Theory*, edited by Aldon D. Morris and Carol McClurg Mueller, 104–30. New Haven, CT: Yale University Press.

Tenorio-Trillo, Mauricio. 2012. *I Speak of the City: Mexico City at the Turn of the Twentieth Century*. Chicago: University of Chicago Press.

Turner, Terence. 1991. "The Social Dynamics of Video Media in an Indigenous Society: The Cultural Meaning and the Personal Politics of Video-Making in Kayapo Communities." *Visual Anthropology Review* 7 (2): 68–76.

———. 1992. "Defiant Images: The Kayapo Appropriation of Video." *Anthropology Today* 8 (6): 5–16.

———. 1995. "Representation, Collaboration and Mediation in Contemporary Ethnographic and Indigenous Media." *Visual Anthropology Review* 11 (2): 102–6.

Urirarte Borneo, Isabel, and Carlos Silva Forné. 2006. *De Atenco a la reforma policial democrática: Una mirada propositiva en clave de reforma policial democrática y derechos humanos*. Mexico City: Instituto para la Seguridad y la Democracia, AC; Centro de Derechos Humanos "Miguel Agustín Pro Juárez," AC.

Vázquez Castillo, María Teresa. 2004. *Land Privatization in Mexico: Urbanization, Formation of Regions, and Globalization in Ejidos*. Latin American Studies. New York: Routledge.

Viveros, Mario. 2008. "Un trabajo necesario." In *Canal 6 de Julio: La guerrilla fílmica*, edited by Carlos Mendoza, 61–72. Mexico City: Heródotoation
Walker, David M. 2013. "Resisting the Neoliberalization of Space in Mexico City." In *Locating the Right to the City in the Global South*, 171–94. New York: Routledge.
Williams, Raymond. 2010. *Culture and Materialism: Selected Essays*. London: Verso.
Wolf, Eric R. 1959. *Sons of the Shaking Earth*. Chicago: University of Chicago Press.
Worth, Sol, and John Adair. 1972. *Through Navajo Eyes: An Exploration in Film Communication and Anthropology*. Bloomington: Indiana University Press.
Wortham, Erica Cusi. 2013. *Indigenous Media in Mexico: Culture, Community, and the State*. Durham, NC: Duke University Press.
Yashar, Deborah J. 2005. *Contesting Citizenship in Latin America: The Rise of Indigenous Movements and the Postliberal Challenge*. Cambridge: Cambridge University Press.
Zamora, Daniel, and Michael C. Behrent. 2016. *Foucault and Neoliberalism*. Cambridge: Polity.

FILMOGRAPHY

Berger, Greg. 2002a. *Atenco: ¡Tierra sí, aviones no! / Atenco: Land, Yes! Airplanes, No!* Mexico: Gringoyo Productions.
———. 2002b. *Atenco: La rebelión de los machetes / Atenco: The Machete Rebellion.* Mexico: Gringoyo Productions.
Canalseisdejulio and Promedios. 2006. *Romper el cerco / Breaking the Siege.* Mexico: Canalseisdejulio.
Centro ProDH. 2008. *Llamado urgente por la justicia: La voz de las mujeres de Atenco.* Mexico: Centro de Derechos Humanos "Miguel Agustín Pro Juárez," AC.
Chiapas Media Project and Audiovisuales de los Caracoles Zapatistas. 2007. *A Very Big Train Called the Other Campaign.* Chicago: Distributed by Chiapas Media Project/Promedios.
Coladangelo, Claudio. 2009. *El comal ardiente: ¿Qué pasa en Oaxaca? 2006–2009.* Oaxaca: Pueblo Production and AgAgfilms.
Colectivo Klamvé. 2006. *Atenco: Un crimen de estado.* Mexico: Arte, Música, y Video.
———. 2008. *Atenco a dos años.* Mexico: Arte, Música, y Video.
———. 2009. *Atenco 3: La sentencia detrás de la sentencia, la exoneración de los culpables.* Mexico: Arte, Música, y Video.
———. 2011. *Atenco: Crónica de un pueblo rebelde.* Mexico: Arte, Música, y Video.
Comisión Civil Internacional de Observación por los Derechos Humanos. 2008. Chiapas, Oaxaca, Atenco, Mexico.
Consorcio Oaxaca (Consorcio para el Diálogo y la Equidad de Género) and Mal de Ojo TV. 2006. *La rebelión de las oaxaqueñas / The Rebellion of the Oaxaqueñas.* Oaxaca City, Mexico: Mal de Ojo TV.
Cortés, David. 2012. *La herida se mantiene abierta.* Mexico: Bataclán Cine.
Défossé, Nicolas. 2009. *¡Viva México!* Mexico: Terra Nostra Films.
Díaz Sánchez, Salvador. 1982. *El edén bajo el fusil.* Mexico: Centro Universitario de Estudios Cinematográficos.
———. 2002a. *La rebelión de los fulgores.* Mexico: Producciones Klan Destino.
———. 2002b. *Una tierna muralla.* Mexico: Producciones Klan Destino.
Freidberg, Jill. 2007. *Un poquito de tanta verdad / A Little Bit of So Much Truth.* Seattle, WA: Corrugated Films and Mal de Ojo TV.
Frente de Pueblos en Defensa de la Tierra (FPDT). 2002. *La tierra no se vende, se ama y se defiende.* Mexico: Self-published.

Frente de Pueblos en Defensa de la Tierra (FPDT), Campaña Libertad y Justicia. 2009. *Presos politicos libertad: Campaña por la libertad y justicia para Atenco.* Centro de Derechos Humanos "Miguel Agustín Pro Juárez," AC.

IndyMedia Mexico. 2006. *Todos somos Atenco*. Mexico.

Mal de Ojo, TV. 2007. *Compromiso cumplido / True to My Pledge*. Oaxaca, Mexico: Mal de Ojo TV.

Mariña, Victor, and Mario Viveros. 2003. *Zapatistas: Crónica de una rebelión*. Mexico: La Jornada and Canalseisdejulio.

Mendoza, Carlos. 2006. *Halcones: Terrorismo de estado*. Mexico City: Canalseisdejulio.

Olguin, Edgar, and América del Valle. 2010. *Esto no es una elegía*. Mexico: Neta Producciones.

Vanguardia Proletaria. 2006. *Venceremos: La otra historia de Oaxaca*. Oaxaca City, Mexico: Vanguardia Proletaria.

Vicente, Cayo, and Anonymous. 2002. *¿Qué hicimos? ¡Vencimos!* Mexico: Self-published.

INDEX

Page numbers in *italic* refer to figures.

When an entry is preceded by a symbol such as @ or #, the symbol is ignored in alphabetization.

abnegadas (self-sacrificing woman), 97. See also selflessness
accompaniment, 100
activist filmmaking
   compañerismo and, 113–14, 146–47
   as defensive weapon, 15, 60, 61, 62, 70–74, *71*
   DVD sales and, 2–3, 157–64, *159*
   gifting films and, 145–46, 150–52, 164
   mediation and, 4–10, 150
   protagonismo and, 93
   resistance and autonomy strategies and, 113–14, 131–34, 141–42
   role of, 2–3, 13–15, 113–14
   screenings and, 7, 152–55, *154*, *156*, 164–65
   streaming and, 14, 169, 182n10
   surveillance and, 62–64, 69–70
   See also Frente de Pueblos en Defensa de la Tierra (People's Front in Defense of Land)
Adair, John, 6–7
alternative capitalisms, 164
alternative media, 14–15
Álvarez, Felipe, 143, 167
AMLO (Andrés Manuel Lopez Obrador), 17–18, 116–18, 161
Ana María (Frente activist), 29
antiglobalization movements, 170
anti-neoliberal activism, 10–13, 15–20, 105, 170–71. See also Frente de Pueblos en Defensa de la Tierra (People's Front in Defense of Land); Zapatismo
anti-WTO protests (Seattle, 1999), 179n21
Aristotle, 8–9
Asamblea Popular de los Pueblos de Oaxaca (Popular Assembly of the Peoples of Oaxaca, APPO), 174n15. See also solidarity visit in Oaxaca (2006)
Atenco
   ejido system in, 28, 37–38, 39–40, 42, 105–6, 167
   history and political significance of, 27–41, 33
   Sosa Texcoco strike (1995) and, 38–39, 41–42, 48
   as symbol of social movements, 19–20
   See also Frente de Pueblos en Defensa de la Tierra (People's Front in Defense of Land)
Atenco: ¡Tierra sí, aviones no! / Atenco: Land, Yes! Airplanes, No! (Berger, 2002), 74–80, *77*
Atenco: A dos años / Atenco: Two years later (Colectivo Klamvé, 2008), 140
Atenco: La rebelión de los machetes / Atenco: The Machete Rebellion (Gringoyo Productions, 2002), 74–80

Atenco recargado / Atenco recharged (documentary), 152
Atenco: Un crimen de estado/ Atenco: A crime of the state (Colectivo Klamvé, 2006), 33, 138, 152
autoconsumo (self-consumption), 113–15, 134–42

Benhumea, Alexis, 121, 179n14
Berger, Greg, 61–62, 74–80, 82, 83, 85–86, 90
Bergman, Ingmar, 158
Black liberation movement, 173n8
Black Lives Matter movement, 10–11, 89
Bourdieu, Pierre, 8–9
Bresson, Robert, 14
Brexit, 170
Brown Atlantis, 57
Buddle, Kathleen, 5–6, 7, 133–34, 141
Buñuel, Luis, 158, 159–60

caciquismo (authoritarianism), 92, 97–98
Calderón, Felipe, 18–19, 170, 178n6
Canalseisdejulio, 112–13, 115–16, 119, 123–24, 157, 163. See also *Romper el cerco/ Breaking the Siege* (Canalseisdejulio and Promedios, 2006)
cannons, 52–53
caracol (Sosa Texcoco plant), 38–39
Cárdenas, Cuauhtémoc, 118, 123
cargo (burden) model of public service, 92, 96–98
Carlos (Frente activist), 153
Castelao, Odette, 80, 82–83, 84–85, 86–87, 90
Castells, Manuel, 4, 113, 136
Catholicism, 97, 101–2. See also liberation theology
caudillismo (authoritarianism), 92, 97–98, 102

Centro de Derechos Humanos Miguel Agustin Pro Juárez (Centro ProDH), 179n18
Chahuistle, El (Mendoza, 1982), 180n23
Chien Andalou, Un (Buñuel and Dalí, 1929), 159–60
Chomsky, Noam, 158
cine militante (militant cinema), 14, 82–83
citizens' media, 14–15
citizenship, 105–11, 146–47
clientelist politics, 96, 101, 104
collective self-production, 5, 12
collectivity, 95, 96, 108–11
Combahee River Collective, 173n8
community journalism (*periodismo comunitario*), 93
community media, 14–15
compañerismo (activist ethics)
    activist filmmaking and, 113–14, 146–47
    citizenship and, 105–11, 146–47
    concept of, 92, 95–96
    genealogies of, 96–102
    gifting films and, 151–52
    as pragmatic strategy, 102–5
    Viveros and, 140
Compañeros en Salud (Partners in Health), 100
Compromiso Cumplido (documentary), 174n15
consciousness, 95
copyright, 158–59
corporatist citizenship regimes, 92, 101–2, 104
cuetes (large bottle rockets), 52–53, 54
cult of the individual, 99–100, 149
cultural production, 8–9, 146–50, 165

Dalí, Salvador, 159–60
Dead Birds (Gardner, 1963), 159–60
dedication, 58

Défossé, Nicolas, 118, 119, 121–34, 136, 139, 148
Deleuze, Gilles, 158
Díaz del Castillo, Bernal, 156
Díaz Sánchez, Salvador
  on activist filmmaking, 14, 82–83
  background of, 61–62, 80–82
  DVD sales and, 159, 162
  Frente and, 80, 82–87, 145
  PRD and, 85–86
  selflessness and, 90, 96
difusión cultural (cultural diffusion), 2, 160
discipline, 62, 87–90
documental social (social documentary), 15
Durkheim, Émile, 149, 177n3

echo chambers, 115
egoism, 96. *See also protagonismo*
Eisenstein, Zillah R., 107
Ejercito Zapatista de Liberación Nacional (EZLN, Zapatista Army for National Liberation)
ejido system
  Atenco and, 28, 37–38, 39–40, 42, 105–6, 167
  history and overview of, 28
  value and significance of land and, 42–44
Encontraremos, Los (XXX, 1984), 180n23
Escobar, Arturo, 164

false consciousness, 135
Farmer, Paul, 100
Fazio, Carlos, 125–26, 135
Fellini, Federico, 158
film. *See* activist filmmaking
filter bubbles, 115
fireworks, 52–53
Flores, Carlos Y., 141–42
Flores Magón, Ricardo, 175n3

Foucault, Michel, 12, 62, 87–90
Fourth Cinema, 14
Fox, Vicente, 16–17, 42–43, 116
Frankfurt School, 180n26
Freidberg, Jill, 174n15
Frente de Pueblos en Defensa de la Tierra (People's Front in Defense of Land)
  airport activism (2001–2002) and, 3–4, 16–17, 33, 41–47, 55–59
  airport activism (2014–2018) and, 167–68
  barricades and police repression (2006) and, 1, 3, 18–19, 33–34, 69–73, 115–16, 119–21
  Casa Ejidal and, 34–36
  Castelao and, 84–85, 86–87
  compañerismo and, 103–5
  current situation and projects of, 167–68, 169–70
  Défossé and, 118
  Díaz Sánchez and, 83–84, 85–86, 87
  evolution of, 58–59
  films about, 59
  indigenous movements and, 98
  leadership and, 103
  legal justice system and, 55–58
  liberation theology and, 100–101
  Libertad y Justicia Para Atenco campaign and, 1–2, 64, 143
  Marcos and, 119–21, *120*
  media's representation of, 30–31, *31*, 51–52, 58
  origins of, 39, 41–42
  "Paso Atenco" and, 45–46, 47, 70
  presidential elections (2012) and, 19
  research methods and, 20–23
  retentions and, 46–47, 118–19, 178n7
  surveillance and, 62–64, 69–70, 87–90
  use of fireworks and cannons by, 52–53, 54

Frente de Pueblos en Defensa de la Tierra
  (continued)
  use of video and film by, 60–64
  Viveros and, 118
  YouTube and, 169
  Zapatismo and, 98–100, 99
  See also compañerismo (activist ethics);
    machetes; *protagonismo* (egoism);
    solidarity visit in Oaxaca (2006);
    specific films and filmmakers
Frente Democrático Nacional
  (Democratic National Front), 41–42
Frente Popular del Valle de México
  (Popular Front of the Valley of
  Mexico), 41–42
Frente Popular Región Texcoco (Popular
  Front of the Texcoco Region), 41–42

Galeano, Subcomandante. *See* Marcos,
  Subcomandante Insurgente (Rafael
  Sebastián Guillén Vicente)
García Canclini, Néstor, 174n12
Gardner, Robert, 159–60
Garza, Alicia, 10–11
gender expectations, 96, 97–98
German Ideology, The (Marx and Engels),
  180n26
Gift, The (Mauss), 148–49
gifts and gifting, 145–46, 148–49, 150–52,
  164
Ginsburg, Faye, 5, 6, 12, 15, 141, 147–48
Gochicoa, Héctor Galindo, 143, 167
governmentality, 11–13, 98–100
granaderos (riot police), 45, 48
Green, Sam, 159–60
Gutiérrez, Gustavo, 100–101

habitus, 8–9
Halcones: Terrorismo de estado
  (Mendoza, 2006), 112

Hale, Charles R., 23
Harvey, David, 12
Holloway, John, 105
Holston, James, 102
horizontalism, 94–95
Humberto (Frente activist), 21, 41–47,
  48–51, 105, 168

indigenous movements, 6–7, 98. *See also*
  anti-neoliberal activism; Zapatismo
individualism, 96
IndyMedia, 131–33
Inter-American Commission on Human
  Rights, 73
Inter-American Court of Human Rights,
  121, 127, 168–69, 179n16

Jodorovsky, Alejandro, 158
Jornada, La (newspaper), 30, 31
Juris, Jeff, 6

Khasnabish, Alex, 98
King, Rodney, 125
Knight, Alan, 97
Köhler, Axel, 60

leadership, 103. *See also protagonismo*
Lee, Richard, 148–49
leftist social movements, 10–13. *See also*
  anti-neoliberal activism
LeGuin, Ursula, 160
Lewis, Oscar, 22
liberalism and liberal democratic citizenship, 92, 105–11. *See also* neoliberalism
liberation theology, 92, 96, 100–101, 102
Libertad y Justicia Para Atenco (Liberty
  and Justice for Atenco) (campaign),
  1–2, 64, 143
Little Bit of So Much Truth, A (Freidberg,
  2007), 174n15

Locke, John, 106
Lopez Obrador, Andrés Manuel (AMLO), 17–18, 116–18, 161

machetes
　Frente and, 36–37, 48–55, 49–50, 58, 60, 74, 99, 176n9
　Sosa Texcoco strike (1995) and, 48
　Zapatista movement and, 60, 99
Mal de Ojo TV, 174n15
Malinowski, Bronislaw, 148–49
Marcos, Subcomandante Insurgente (Rafael Sebastián Guillén Vicente)
　background of, 111
　on cult of the individual, 99–100, 149
　Frente and, 27, 119–21, 120
　in Mexico, 17–18
　on neoliberal governmentality, 98–100
　on Pingüino, 109–10
　role of, 19
María, Doña (Frente activist), 48, 51
Mariño, José Luis, 126, 141, 150
Martinez, José Alonso, 80
Mauss, Marcel, 148–49, 150–52
Mazzarella, William, 134
McLuhan, Marshall, 146, 147–48, 164
mediation, 4–10, 147–50
Mendoza, Carlos, 122, 123, 132, 158–59
Mill, John Stuart, 106

Nash, Manning, 96
neoliberal governmentality, 11–13, 98–100
neoliberalism
　activist filmmaking and, 114
　compañerismo and, 92, 96, 101–2
　current global politics of, 170–71
　protagonismo and, 94, 96, 171
　See also anti-neoliberal activism
New Social Movements, 10, 96, 107–8
noble savagery, 97

North American Free Trade Agreement (NAFTA), 16, 28, 98
Nuevo Aeropuerto International de la Ciudad de México (New International Airport of Mexico City, NAICM), 167–68

Oaxaca, 174n15. *See also* solidarity visit in Oaxaca (2006)
Obama, Barack, 40–41
#Occupy movements, 11, 170
Olcott, Jocelyn H., 97
Omar (Frente activist), 36–37
Ong, Aihwa, 12
Otra Campaña, La (social movement)
　history of, 6, 116–24
　Marcos and, 17–18, 109–10, 120
　Peña Nieto and, 19
　resistance and autonomy strategies and, 131–34, 138

Palma Novoa, Valentina, 77, 122, 126, 130
PAN (Partido de Acción Nacional, National Action Party), 18
Partido de Acción Nacional (PAN, National Action Party), 18
Partido Revolucionario Democrático (PRD, Democratic Revolutionary Party), 78–79, 81, 85, 87, 116–18, 123
Partido Revolucionario Institucional (PRI, Institutional Revolutionary Party), 16, 19, 87, 170
Partners in Health (Compañeros en Salud), 100
Peña Nieto, Enrique, 19, 91, 167, 170
periodismo comunitario (community journalism), 93
perseguidos (activists in hiding), 143
Pingüino (Penguin), 109–10
pitchforks, 53

plantones (protest occupations), 11
Policia Federal Preventativa (PFP, Preventative Federal Police), 45
PRD (Partido Revolucionario Democrático or Democratic Revolutionary Party), 78–79, 81, 85, 87, 116–18, 123
PRI (Partido Revolucionario Institucional, Institutional Revolutionary Party), 16, 19, 87, 170
Producciones Klan Destino, 80, 81
Producciones Sal de Ubas (Alka-Seltzer Productions), 81
Promedios: Comunicación Comunitaria, 118, 119, 123–24, 131. *See also Romper el cerco/Breaking the Siege* (Canalseisdejulio and Promedios, 2006)
protagonismo (egoism)
    citizenship and, 105–11
    concept of, 91–95
    genealogies of, 96–102
    North American researchers and, 22–23
    Trump and, 171
    See also compañerismo (activist ethics)
Proudhon, Pierre-Joseph, 160
pseudonyms, 21

¿Qué hicimos? ¡Vencimos! (Cayo, 2002), 66, 69

radical media, 14–15
Rafael (vendor), 2–3, 5–9, 18, 160, 163
Ramirez-Valles, Jesus, 176n2
Ramón (Frente activist), 56–58
rebelión de los fulgores, La (Díaz Sánchez, 2002), 83–84, 85
Redfield, Robert, 22
revolutionary tourism, 19–20
Ríos, Eduardo (Frente activist)
    autoconsumo and, 137–38, 139
    background of, 61–62
    Berger and, 76, 79–80
    Castelao and, 82, 86–87
    Díaz Sánchez and, 82, 83, 85–86, 87
    DVD sales and, 159
    on film, 169–70
    as filmmaker/videographer for the Frente, 1–2, 4–5, 9, 64–74
    legal justice system and, 8
    on *protagonismo*, 93, 102
    selflessness and, 90
    on YouTube, 169
    See also tierra no se vende, se ama y se defiende, La (Land is not for selling, it is for loving and defending, FPDT, 2002)
Romper el cerco/Breaking the Siege (Canalseisdejulio and Promedios, 2006)
    "Auditorium Emiliano Zapata" in, 33–34
    autoconsumo and, 114–15, 134–42
    human rights framework of, 126–30
    production and distribution of, 112, 113–14, 115–16, 120, 121–26, 131–34, 148
    resistance and autonomy strategies and, 131–34, 138–41
    tour of Atenco in, 27
Ruiz Ortiz, Ulises, 144

Sahlins, Marshall, 148–49
Salinas de Gortari, Carlos, 28
San Salvador Atenco. *See* Atenco
Scott, James C., 177n4
screenings, 7, 152–55, 154, 156, 164–65
selflessness, 58, 68–69, 90, 95–96. *See also compañerismo* (activist ethics)
Sexta Declaración de la Selva Lacandona, La (the Sixth Declaration from the Lacondon Jungle), 116–18
sexual assault, 18
Siegel, Bill, 159–60

Sitrin, Marina, 93–95, 110
slacktivism, 115, 142
small vendors and markets
  barricades and police repression (2006) and, 1, 3, 18–19, 33–34, 69–73, 115–16, 119–21
  DVD sales and, 2–3, 157–64, *159*
  role and significance of, 156–57
  See also Rafael (vendor)
social media, 169
solidarity, 58
solidarity visit in Oaxaca (2006)
  aim of, 143–46
  DVD sales and, 145–46, 157–64
  gifting films and, 145–46, 150–52
  screenings and, 145–46, 152–55, *154*
Sosa Texcoco strike (1995), 38–39, 41–42, 48
Speed, Shannon, 95
Stephen, Lynn, 29, 60, 70, 176n7, 180n25
streaming, 14, 169, 182n10
substantive citizenship, 102–5
Suprema Corte de Justicia de la Nación (National Supreme Court of Justice), 18–19, 73, 128, 143, 179n16
surveillance, 62–64, 69–70, 87–90

Tate, Winifred, 127
television. *See* activist filmmaking
Tenorio-Trillo, Mauricio, 57
Theology of Liberation, A (Gutiérrez et al.), 100–101
Third Cinema, 14
Thompson, E. P., 47
tierra no se vende, se ama y se defiende, La (Land is not for selling, it is for loving and defending, FPDT, 2002), 2, 65–66, 69
Todos somos Atenco (We are all Atenco) (IndyMedia Mexico, 2006), 178n11
togetherness, 58

total social phenomena, 148–49, 151–52
Trump, Donald, 13, 170, 171
Turner, Terence, 5, 6, 15
Twitter. *See* #YoSoy132 movement

Universidad Iberoamericana (Ibero-American University), 19, 91
UPCI (Unión de Promotores de la Cultura de la Izquierda, or the Union of Promot-ers of the Culture of the Left), 160–61

Valle, América del, 119–21
Valle, Ignacio del
  arrest and release of, 143, 167
  on Berger, 75
  children's hospital dispute and, 178n8
  ejido and, 37
  on film, 169–70
  Frente and, 39, 59
  liberation theology and, 100
  Marcos and, 119–21, *120*
  on *protagonismo*, 93, 94
  Ríos and, 73
  role of, 19
  Sosa Texcoco strike (1995) and, 48
  Viveros and, 139
Vértigo (magazine), 30–31, *31*
Vertov, Dziga, 158
Very Big Train Called the Other Campaign, A (Chiapas Media Project and Audiovisuales de los Caracoles Zapatistas 2007), 178n12
Vicente, Cayo, 66
Virgilio (Frente activist)
  on ejido system, 106
  on people and land, 43
  pseudonyms and, 21
  research in Atenco and, 27, 32, 34–40
  solidarity visit in Oaxaca and, 145, 150–51, 152–53

virtues, 57–58, 63–64, 68–69, 95. See also *compañerismo* (activist ethics); selflessness
Viva Mexico! (2009), 178n12
Viveros, Mario
   on activist filmmaking, 14, 126, 130–31
   autoconsumo and, 139–40
   background of, 118, 123
   Canalseisdejulio and, 112, 119
   Défossé and, 122–24, 130–31, 140, 148
   Frente and, 139–40
   Palma Novoa and, 121–22, 126, 130
   See also *Romper el cerco/Breaking the Siege* (Canalseisdejulio and Promedios, 2006)

Weather Underground, The (Green and Siegel, 2002), 159–60
Will, Brad, 61, 77
Wolf, Eric, 96–97
Wollstonecraft, Mary, 106
World Social Forum, 8
World Trade Organization (WTO), 16
Wortham, Erica Cusi, 15

Yashar, Deborah J., 101
#YoSoy132 movement, 19, 91, 92–93, 111, 177n5
YouTube, 14, 169

Zapata, Emiliano, 32, 173n4
Zapatismo
   compañerismo and, 92, 96, 98–100, 102
   Frente and, 34, 58, 98–100, 99
   impact of, 16
   liberation theology and, 100
   Promedios and, 123–24
   protagonismo and, 95, 96, 98–100, 102, 109–10
   La Sexta and, 116–18
   urban supporters of, 111
   use of camera and video by, 70, 71
   Zapata and, 173n4
   See also Otra Campaña, La (social movement)
Zapatistas: Crónica de una rebelión (La Jornada and Canalseisdejulio, 2003), 71, 118, 176n7
Zedillo, Ernesto, 19–20
Žižek, Slavoj, 158

www.ingramcontent.com/pod-product-compliance
Lightning Source LLC
Chambersburg PA
CBHW030111010526
44116CB00005B/196